DATE DUE

Maurice Chevalier

Books by Michael Freedland

MAURICE CHEVALIER

GREGORY PECK

THE TWO LIVES OF ERROL FLYNN

JEROME KERN

SOPHIE: THE STORY OF SOPHIE TUCKER

FRED ASTAIRE

JAMES CAGNEY

IRVING BERLIN

AL JOLSON

Maurice Chevalier

Michael Freedland

WILLIAM MORROW AND COMPANY, INC.

New York   1981

Copyright © 1981 by Michael Freedland

Library of Congress Cataloging in Publication Data

Freedland, Michael, 1934–
     Maurice Chevalier.

     1. Chevalier, Maurice, 1888–1972.   2. Singers—
France—Biography.   I. Title.
ML420.C473F7   784.5′0092′4 [B]   81-38423
ISBN 0-688-00652-3   AACR2

Printed in the United States of America

First Edition

1   2   3   4   5   6   7   8   9   10

BOOK DESIGN BY MICHAEL MAUCERI

FOR

MAUREEN AND VIVIAN

HELEN AND MAURICE

RACHEL AND HAROLD

Thank Heaven for Wonderful Friends

Acknowledgments

Writing a biography is like doing a jigsaw puzzle. You start with the picture on the box (the one in your mind) and you proceed to shuffle the pieces that make up that picture. Occasionally, however, something surprising and rather strange happens—the pieces don't all fit together in the way you thought they would. Straight edges unexpectedly become complicated designs that lead to the heart of the puzzle, and the whole picture is framed differently from the way you imagined it would be.

The Maurice Chevalier story was that sort of puzzle. The finished book is not the one I expected to write, because new stories constantly superimposed themselves on the old ones. Tales people imagined were part of show-business history turned out to be legends beneath which were buried stories no one had previously unearthed—for the simple reason no one knew they were there.

To get that far involved meeting a great many people, starting with Maurice Chevalier himself.

It is to his memory that my first thanks go—as well as to so many others who provided background information. At the top of the list are three people who were of immeasurable help: Janie Michels, the Comtesse de la Chapelle, Mme. Ginette Spanier, and Mme. Thérèse de Saint-Phalle. In addition to sharing memories, these ladies allowed me to borrow letters and photographs from their personal collections. Very special thanks, too, go to M. François Vals, who was Chevalier's right-hand man for more than twenty years. He was of tremendous assistance to me and always with great kindness and patience. It is impossible to single out as more important than anyone else other people who gave me their time and their consideration—sometimes by telling a great many stories and on occasions generously providing leads which drove me into unexpected but thrillingly important avenues.

So, sincerest thanks to:

Charles Aznavour, Henri Amouroux, George Burns, Rouben Mamoulian, the Duchess of Bedford, the late Joan Blondell, the late Bing Crosby, the late Merle Oberon, Jacqueline Cartier, Frédérique Hébrard, Louis Velle, Annette de Bretagne, Leo Robin, Ted Shapiro, Angela Lansbury, Hermione Gingold, Alan Jay Lerner, Sam White, Fifi D'Orsay, Princess Beris Kandaouroff, Denise Grey, George Jessel, the late Morris Stoloff, Jack Cummings, Olivier Todd, Tim of *L'Express*, "Miss Bluebell" of the Paris Lido, Eric Morecambe, Ernie Wise, Judith Dagworthy of the Savoy Hotel, London, and the proprietors of A. E. Olney & Co. Ltd., Luton.

Nor can I forget Ann Kaye who with my daughter, Fiona, translated letters, press cuttings, and other documents.

My thanks, too, to the librarians of the Academy of Motion Picture Arts and Sciences in Los Angeles, the British Film Institute, the Museum of the Performing Arts at Lincoln Center, New York, and the British Library, London. To Jack Dabbs of the BBC, who was especially helpful in the earliest days of my research, my gratitude.

It would all have been much more difficult without the kind consideration of my editors, Marcia Fenwick in London and Howard Cady in New York, whom I trust and admire greatly.

And none of it would have been put together at all without the devotion of my secretary, Hilda Alberg, who typed the manuscript and smoothed so many rough edges for me.

Finally to my wife, Sara, for whom the gestation period of this book has not been the easiest of times, lovingly warm thanks.

MICHAEL FREEDLAND

London, March 1981

Contents

I Remember It Well

If he had been born in England, where the great comedians are honoured with titles, he would have become "Sir Maurice." Here, he could lay claim to a title, a particular one worth much more than all the others. Here, he was and remains in the memory of all who knew him, "Maurice de Paris."

—René Clair

When I last met Maurice Chevalier at the Savoy Hotel in London, he told me he was in the midst of his eighty-third winter. I had the feeling then that he knew there wouldn't be another one. And because I believe I was the last journalist to speak to him, the time we spent together gave me something of a proprietary interest in a man of whom President Pompidou said: "Chevalier's success far outstrips the simple talent of a singer and a comedian. The French saw themselves in him and foreigners found a gay and warm image of France."

There were, perhaps not surprisingly, others who saw in him more of a caricature of the French. Well, that was to be expected. Sometimes legends become clichés. But he was unique, even though the Chevalier straw hat and the jutting lower lip were as symbolic of his country as the Tricolor or a bottle of Chablis.

His songs, like "Louise," "Mimi," and "Valentine," presented a picture of curvaceous girls in slinky black dresses split to the thigh. His Hollywood films only confirmed the image. He was the great lover personified—from, of course, the land of the great lovers. That, too, was a cliché, even if it was one carefully constructed by an army of press agents. He repeated for me one of his favourite lines: "I don't think the French really make the best lovers. It's just that they like to talk about it more."

The eminent Hollywood director Rouben Mamoulian told me: "There were few entertainers for whom the people of the world opened their hearts as they did for Maurice Chevalier." And yet, Mamoulian went on, "As a singer, an actor, and a dancer, he was not much, but put them together and the result was much bigger than the sum total of those parts." Ginette Spanier, the Paris *couturière*, expressed it even more simply: "He had star quality, but I can't tell you what that is. I once asked Noël Coward to define it and he couldn't either—except to say that Chevalier had it."

When we talked about his rapport with an audience, Chevalier claimed to be equally baffled, although he used what was for him a favourite phrase to say so. "There is," he told me, "something mysterious in the way people suddenly feel that the artist is bringing them something that makes them rejoice. Those people are bringing him strength also. It is a kind of meeting and that mysterious harmony either happens or does not happen."

He was never a modest man, even though he maintained that those inexplicable qualities still fascinated him. "I think it is the most mysterious thing that nobody can explain—but if it could be explained, almost every entertainer would have that sort of response. . . ."

"Thank God," Chevalier said as he reflected on a career that spanned seventy years, "it was my good luck not to have had any voice. If I had, I would have tried to be a singer who sings ballads. But since I am barely able to half-talk and half-sing a song, it made me different from a hundred other crooners who are neither good nor bad. If I had had any voice, I would have been content to rest on my voice and learn nothing else. Since I had no voice, I had to find something that would hold the interest of the public. Any third-rate *chanteur de charme* has a better voice than I. But they sing from the throat, whereas I sing from the heart."

Perhaps that was it. Perhaps, too, it was more easily summed up in a single word—style. The gamin may have turned into the boulevardier, yet he remained unique.

Jean Cocteau, a man who came to symbolize another kind of France and because he was an intellectual, one with whom Maurice could never feel totally comfortable, described him as *"le grand sympathique."*

Chevalier was a man for whom real happiness only seemed to come when there was a camera or a spotlight focussed on him. It was, after all, the only way he knew he could prove how good he was. Everything else, he told me, was governed by another "mysterious" factor—"the complex of inferiority." Neither riches nor women—commodities he had in abundance—ever removed that complex from his shoulders. I hope the following pages, which began to assemble themselves that day at the Savoy, will explain why.

Maurice Chevalier

1.
The Night They
Invented Champagne

There was a great deal of the child in him. He was in great need of friendship. Friendship was greater for him than love.

—Rouben Mamoulian

Ménilmontant, on the right bank of the Seine, northeast of Notre-Dame, wasn't anyone's idea of paradise. It was Delancey Street and Whitechapel Road shaken up in a bottle of *vin ordinaire*. It was the smell of cats and of horse droppings mingling with the odours from the horsemeat *boucherie* and the more pleasant warm and homely aromas from the *boulangerie*. From some places in Ménilmontant it was possible to see M. Eiffel's new tower that was already dominating the city. In time the world would recognize the dominance of that other Parisian symbol born in the same year, to Mme. Joséphine Chevalier.

Joséphine, as her neighbours along the rue du Retrait knew

her, had had eight babies—all sons—before Maurice Auguste Chevalier was born at number 31 on September 12, 1888. Of the eight, only two had survived—Charles, who was born in 1880, and Paul, born five years later.

Whether or not the responsibility of having three sons was too much for their father, Victor Charles Chevalier, no one will ever know, but it is certain that he tried to escape those responsibilities whenever possible. He told people he was a house painter. Those who saw his work in the better streets of Ménilmontant, and sometimes as far afield as Montmartre, said he was a good one, too. But he was more frequently seen propping up a bar than painting a house, more often observed draining a glass of *eau-de-vie*, that peculiarly French means of internal combustion, than stirring a pot of paint.

It all put an intense strain on Joséphine, who at forty took to wearing an old woman's bonnet, perhaps as a sign that she had given up hope of things ever getting any better. With her worn, strained face, she looked at least sixty-five. Joséphine not only had to feed, clean and clothe her family, and try against all odds to keep her verminous, two-room flat clean, she also had to be the breadwinner—usually, a day-old loaf set aside for her by the owner of the local *boulangerie*, who let her have it for a couple of sous (a tenth of a franc). If work was as important to her as breathing, it was an ethic she transmitted to Maurice from the time he was first able to reason such things for himself.

Joséphine was Flemish and had come to Paris in the wake of the war with Prussia. It seemed to offer the hope of a better living than any of the Belgian provinces could give a young girl. She brought to France the skills she had learned as a lacemaker's apprentice. Her lacemaking was an art, and now she practiced it in the light of the only window in the flat, the one on pavement level.

While she embroidered the intricate lace patterns on a society girl's wedding dress, her boys would sit by the coal-burning stove, munching a piece of dry bread as they watched the feet parading outside the window above. They couldn't see higher than the ankles, so it was something of a game to try to guess the makeup of the rest of the pedestrians' bodies.

But there wasn't much time for games of any kind. At eleven

Charles went to work assisting his father, and when Paul reached the same age, he became an engraver's apprentice.

The Chevalier family didn't take much of a part in the activities of Ménilmontant. There wasn't time for socializing, and most things cost money that they didn't have. When he was six years old, Maurice sat on the doorstep of his home, weeping while the other boys and girls of the neighbourhood marched in a church parade. His mother couldn't afford the price of the black suit he would have had to wear. They didn't see very much of what the newspapers were calling *La Belle Époque.*

If the greatness of so recently defeated France was being taught at the Frères School to which Maurice went dutifully each morning, it was a fact that had to be accepted on trust. Ménilmontant certainly didn't have much greatness about it, and the Chevalier family had little to boast about.

The fact that their father was rarely at home didn't help the boys feel as though they belonged to a family at all. With the two older Chevalier sons at work six days a week, the only time they did get together was on a Sunday. Then, the most frequently heard sound was that of Chevalier *père* bawling out some obscenity or other as he demanded a bottle which Joséphine had, against all odds, managed to hide from him. When he was not drunk, Victor was a lot gentler than the man the family and their neighbours thought they knew. But those occasions were rare. Joséphine was abused and the boys were made to feel usurpers in their own home.

When Maurice was eight, however, everything changed radically. Victor left Ménilmontant and vanished from the Chevalier scene. If Joséphine knew where he went, or in fact if she saw him again, they were secrets she kept to herself.

Charles, however, found that at the age of eighteen he was the family wage earner, bringing in seven francs a day. It was not a role he relished. Within a matter of months, he met a girl, and immediately decided that life with her would be preferable to trying to support his dowdy mother and two ungainly brothers—the tall, gawky Paul and the short, tubby Maurice. Without a word he left home and, like his father, totally vanished from the scene.

Now it was Paul's turn to become head of the family. A much

more caring boy than Charles, Paul, like Maurice, was devoted to his mother. Indeed, Victor Chevalier had frequently complained about what he considered to be the almost unnatural relationship between his two younger sons and their mother. One might wonder about the ultimate effects of such strong ties, particularly on Maurice who, even more than Paul, appeared to crave only his mother's affection and approval, but it was clear that Joséphine represented warmth, comfort, and stability to both boys.

Paul certainly took his job as an engraver seriously, and when he completed his apprenticeship, there were another seven francs a day coming into the household. It was enough to allow the three Chevaliers to move into a slightly better apartment, at number 15, rue Julien Lacroix—one flight up, first door on the right.

Life was, however, still exceedingly hard for Joséphine, and she worked at her lace from dawn until late into the night, when she could barely stay awake. She suffered from severe anemia, a fact not helped by eyes so strained that the lids actually bled.

Maurice was barely nine when she collapsed and was taken to the hospital, where she was convinced she would die. He was sent to what everyone called "the poor boys' school," the Hospice des Enfants Assistés, a long bus ride away on the rue Denfert-Rochereau.

Paul stayed alone in the apartment, while Maurice began what he saw, despite his anxiety over his mother, as an exciting adventure. He actually didn't mind the rough blue cotton shirt and trousers which were so uncomfortable and smelled of carbolic. The priests who ran the school were stern but kind, and the boys with whom he worked and played seemed as happy to welcome a new friend as he was to be with them. There were other times when he was morose, desperately homesick, and missed his mother intensely, and before long the fun of the school turned into intense loneliness. But the cloud was to lift. Three months after his arrival, his teacher rapped him on the shoulder and gave him the news: "You can go home today." His mother had recovered.

Joséphine was no sooner back home with her two sons than she was once more at work, her fingers negotiating the intricate lace patterns for which she had earned a reputation as a crafts-woman. Her work and Paul's income made a great deal of difference at a time when a couple of francs could buy a wholesome meal. For the first time that she could remember, there was just a little left over for what previously would have been regarded as luxuries.

With a clear conscience she could take the boys to a Sunday evening café-concert. It seemed a friendly and undemanding way to relax, and she had always liked to laugh at the red-nosed comedians in their baggy checked trousers, or to stare open-mouthed at the feats of acrobats who seemed to defy both gravity and the normal limitations of the human frame. And if the people on both sides of the smoke-laden platform were a little vulgar, well, she was not sophisticated enough to realize it.

She and the boys drank cordials while all around them other patrons were going through bottles of rough red wine or glass upon glass of *eau-de-vie*—a beverage that was especially popular in those establishments, since the stones of the red cherries floating in the colourless liquid made perfect missiles to fire at less than satisfactory acts on the stage.

Paul was occasionally more interested in the activities of his fellow audience members, watching—till Joséphine suggested he do otherwise—the men in black berets and stained jerseys pawing the breasts of the girls sitting with them. Maurice was perhaps too young to bother. For him, the songs coming from the stage, the coarse jokes, and, above all, the acrobatics were diversions that were spellbinding enough.

From the time Maurice was nine and a half, his week at school was no more than an unavoidable break between the Sunday visits to the Belleville, the Concert de l'Univers, and any one of the 150 or so other cafés-concerts in Paris. "I only thought about the Sunday evening past and the Sunday evening to come," he wrote years later. "To me these were no little cheap music halls, but the most beautiful places in the world."

It was only at the cafés-concerts that he felt, to use his expression, "in my shoes," and he would work hard running errands for neighbours to find the money to pay for these expeditions, if his mother didn't have it. He usually also picked up enough samples of the shopkeepers' wares to keep the hunger away. The errands were not Maurice's only expedition into the world of finance. For ten sous he had a nice sideline watching out for unsuspecting wives or husbands who were likely to interfere with their spouses' extramarital relations. While the citizenry of Ménilmontant occupied themselves in their bedrooms, Maurice would stand outside their windows ready to whistle loudly if a husband or wife came home too early.

He wasn't above playing truant from school if there was money to be made, and not just for himself. In the bitterly cold winter of 1897, nine-year-old Maurice allowed the Frères to do without his company so that he could help the municipality sweep the snow and clear the sewers. When it was all done, he had enough money to buy his mother a Christmas present—a piping hot, newly baked loaf of bread. Years later he recalled the day he delivered his present and said he could still taste the bread and smell its aroma. "Surely, it was the most delicious I have ever tasted," he said. As for his mother, "How I remember her smile as I handed it to her!"

It was just another demonstration of the relationship between mother and son. They talked to each other not as parent and child but almost as contemporaries, and as other children gave each other nicknames, so Paul and Maurice gave one to Joséphine. They called her La Louque. It remained with her until she died, and Maurice referred to her by that name all his life. But he never revealed what it meant.

After a visit to the Sunday café-concert, the family would sometimes go to the umbrella-shaded terrace of the Café Les Tamaris, not far from the place Gambetta. There they sat for an hour or more, going over the acts they had just seen. While they talked they munched crisp, salty fried potatoes and sipped glasses of weak beer. Afterwards, to save the bus fare, they walked back home to Ménilmontant, usually through the Cimetière Père-Lachaise, where the very tombstones told more about the history of Paris than Maurice could ever have learned at school, an establishment with which he soon parted company.

Maurice had just turned ten when his mother decided that he had to follow Paul into the engraving shop as an apprentice. In his hand was the certificate which showed he had achieved the minimum accepted standard of education, and he was happy

enough—for the time being, at least—to leave the classroom behind. It would not be very long before he developed what he
told me was his "complex of inferiority," due to the fact that
"I had no instruction." But in 1898 there seemed no reason to
waste any more time in front of a *professeur* in a shabby chalk-
covered overall, and in the company of boys, some of whom
didn't even know what a café-concert was. Maurice had by now
already made up his mind that it was in one of these places that
his future had to lie. La Louque was not convinced. There had
never been any theatrical people in the family, and she wanted
Maurice Chevalier to be a respected, hardworking man.

Maurice had no choice but to accept her decision to send him
to work with Paul. The family needed another breadwinner.
La Louque was not just making lace during the day, she was
also going out at night to clean.

But Maurice and the engraving industry did not get on well
together. As soon as the apprentice master disappeared from
sight, Maurice took off for the nearest lavatory, locked himself
in a cubicle, and imagined he was on the stage. Sometimes he
sneaked a couple of tennis balls into his overalls pocket. In the
relative security of the toilet, he was sure he had the makings of
the best juggler that Paris had yet seen. On other days he knew
that he had full command of the art of the ribald songster. Unfortunately, his employer did not share his enthusiasm. One morning he followed Maurice to the lavatory, discovered he was not
using the room for its intended purpose, and told him bluntly
that he had no future as an engraver.

La Louque once more had to take a hand. She sounded out
one of the neighbours and heard there was a job her son could
take making nails and tacks. That, too, he used as a sounding
board for what he believed were his remarkable talents. Once,
so overcome by his own hypnotic ability at telling rude stories,
he mesmerized himself into placing his right thumb into the press
instead of a piece of iron. The result was with him for the
rest of his life. He was once asked if the disfigurement of the
thumb caused him any problems. "Only when I have tried to
unbutton a lady in a hurry," he replied.

He had to agree that he was not cut out to make nails. Would
a paint shop be more promising? He gave it a try and it did seem

to work, though he still lived only from one Sunday to the next.

The Chevaliers had by now become regular patrons of the Cirque d'Hiver, the winter circus, where for ten sous they could stand in the gallery. There Maurice was to write, ". . . we held hands with paradise itself and we pledged never to let go. The show unfolded by us like a magic spell . . . the equestrian acts, the clowns and jugglers, all the acrobats with Monsieur Loyal, the master of ceremonies. One number called Francisco, the death-defying bareback rider, left me paralyzed with admiration."

But it was the star tumblers who thrilled Maurice more than all the other acts in the ring put together. He could easily imagine himself among their number. In his mind the boy in the ring, who looked exactly his own age, was Maurice himself. He watched enthralled as the young star standing on his father's feet was catapulted high into the air only to be caught, sitting, as it appeared, in midair. A crash of cymbals and then once more another somersault. Again the miracle of being caught in space.

The vision of the acrobats swam in young Maurice's mind. Could anything be as wonderful as this? After the circus performance, their mother took them to the stage door, from which they followed the artists to a nearby café, eavesdropping as the circus folk relived their night's work. To Maurice this was perhaps even more stimulating than the performance itself.

It was after one of these heady sessions that he persuaded his elder brother that the time had come to form an act of their own. Paul, though older, had always found it difficult to argue with Maurice's logic; he agreed.

Their first "performance" was in the neighbourhood gymnasium, with Paul as the man at the bottom and Maurice as the one who did all the tricks. Even though his elder brother was exceedingly spindly, Maurice convinced himself that his shoulders were sufficiently broad to sustain the supporting role. As for himself, he knew he had both the coordination and all the natural attributes of the boy acrobat he had seen so often. It was the sort of self-assurance, lying to himself when necessary, that a future star needed. It would be years before he would admit: "I was without the strength of a kitten."

The boys even had a name for their act, dictated more by circumstance than intuition. In the window of a printers' shop

they had seen a bundle of posters portraying a couple of mus-
cular acrobats under the name of "The Martinon Brothers." The
fact that these particular brothers hadn't succeeded well enough
to collect their posters wasn't allowed to dampen the Chevaliers'
enthusiasm. Maurice knew they were the key to his own success
and somehow managed to persuade the printer to part with the
coloured sheets. With the help of a friend who had been able to
stay the course in the printing industry, he pasted over the name
Martinon with a sticker bearing the word CHEVALIER in block
capitals. How could they go wrong with a name like "The Chevalier Brothers"? The word brothers—so very English and so
stylish—was a virtual guarantee of luck in the circus ring.

Of course, it was all *too* easy. The day that the posters were
ready for distribution—the younger Chevalier had convinced the
neighbourhood merchants to exhibit them—Maurice climbed onto
his brother's shoulders, began his somersault, and prepared to
land on Paul's forearms. Instead he slid down his back and his
face collided with Paul's head. That night Paul brought Maurice
back to La Louque with blood pouring out of his swollen nose
and with tears welling in his eyes.

"Just a little accident, *maman*," he said.

That was the moment when La Louque extracted a promise
from her sons—particularly from the more forceful Maurice—that
their acrobatic days were over. Now he just had to get back to
the paint shop. His job there was to paint dolls' faces. But at
eleven Maurice discovered he was more interested in the un-
painted face of a live doll called Georgette. One day he took
the girl, who had the most beautiful golden curls he had ever
seen, to the back of the paint shop and sang one of the love
songs he had heard at a café-concert to the giggling ten-year-old.
The shop owner heard the performance and told Maurice not
to bother to come back the next day.

It happened again and again. He tried to be a carpenter and
attempted to train as an electrician. He went through twelve
jobs in six months, and every time La Louque would be there
to reassure him, bolster his ego, and fortify an ambition that was
steadily growing more and more prodigious. He thought of
nothing but the Sunday evening cafés-concerts.

Occasionally, at the Cirque d'Hiver or on very special occasions when La Louque would take them to the famous Eldorado music hall, Maurice could see the leading stars of the Paris of the 1890s. There was Dranem who, in his short checked trousers, rough-cut jacket, and cloth cap, was known as the best comic in Paris. On stage, he seemed simple and naïve. Off, he knew exactly what his public wanted of him. Another top star was Polin—fat, with the face of a peasant, who used to come on stage in the crumpled, loose-fitting uniform of a private (*poilu*) in the French army.

When newcomers came along at the cheaper cafés-concerts, they attempted no more than to imitate these stars. A young artist trying to be original, singing his comic songs, telling jokes or doing pratfalls on the rough floorboards of the café-concert stage, did so by adding a false nose, a shaggy wig, or a pair of big shoes. Sophistication was rare, but it came in the form of Félix Mayol. He wore evening clothes and sang love songs about shopgirls and millinery apprentices, and had his own unique style of dancing. He was a homosexual and his approach on stage was distinctly effeminate. Yet even the labourers who were the staple audience of the cafés-concerts loved his performances. Mayol later owned one of the most famous cafés-theaters in Paris, but in 1900 he was still the toast of the Eldorado and the Cirque d'Hiver.

Chevalier wrote of Félix Mayol: "If the word 'charming' or 'charmer' must be used to described a man, then quickly pin it on him. . . . His songs, his face, his voice followed you all the way home. You dreamed of it. And then you saw him again, singing. You looked, your eyes puckered. And then his beautiful mug, his voice, you relaxed." Maurice determined that before long he himself would hear the kind of applause Mayol received. Paul laughed at his presumptuousness, but La Louque didn't. "You'll eventually find the work you most like to do," she told him, and then with a smile added a small detail about the Café Les Trois Lions, one of the cafés-concerts to which they occasionally went on Sunday nights. She said she had heard that on Saturdays, they had amateur nights.

She really didn't need to say anything else. With that smile and that piece of casually dropped information, she had given her blessing to Maurice Chevalier going into show business.

2.
Innocents of Paris

There are some things that get into people's blood and never get away.

—CLAIRE CHEVALIER

Paris may not have known it, but Maurice Auguste Chevalier felt he was about to take the town by storm. After all, he reasoned, he had seen all the top acts, his mother had made him a pair of baggy checkered trousers, his muffler was precisely the kind he had seen every Saturday on the stage, and the big red putty nose La Louque had fashioned would have the men and women out front rolling in their seats.

Paul may have been more apprehensive as he sat with his mother and brother through a succession of acts at Les Trois Lions on the boulevard de Ménilmontant, but Maurice was sure he was going to show the rest of the amateurs on its stage that he would outdistance them all. He was just twelve years old, but the year was 1900 and he felt he had the verve that was going to symbolize the new century. It did not matter to him that the comic before him had been pelted by cherry stones and that the woman with the huge bosom who sang country songs had been forcibly dragged off by the manager. They were amateurs. The manager had promised Maurice a cup of coffee at the end of the evening, and that meant he was a pro—a pro who had never performed in public in his life. Another woman had been shouted off the stage, weeping into an off-white lace handkerchief, when the manager walked into the center of the smoke-filled auditorium and, with his hands in a damping gesture, tried to get his patrons to lower their conversations.

"*Messieurs et dames,*" he shouted. "*Et maintenant . . . Le Petit Chevalier.*"

Maurice hadn't discussed the billing with the manager—he had never given it a moment's consideration—but he liked the way it sounded, and the applause, initiated from the table where La Louque and Paul sat nervously, spurred him on.

He looked in the direction of the heavily moustachioed piano player and began to sing a song called "V'là les Croquants." The audience's response was all that he could possibly have imagined. He had barely opened his mouth when he was greeted with uproarious laughter from the customers. The more he sang, the louder they laughed. To be heard above their laughter—few old-timers would have dared to expect such a marvellous response—he sang louder and as he did so, the audience laughed louder, too.

At the end of his first number, Maurice was overwhelmed—until the pianist sidled up to him, not altogether pleasantly, and said: "If you want to sing with me, at least use the same key. You were singing three keys higher than I was playing." Maurice didn't really understand what the piano player meant, but instinctively recognized the sound of a responsive audience.

The people drinking at their tables called for another song and he delightedly obliged—still singing in the wrong key and making them laugh and shout all the more. When he finished that number, they demanded another—and another. As he sang, he moved his hands faster and twisted his mouth into what he believed were still funnier shapes. The crowd was delighted. What he didn't know was that they were laughing at him and not with him, but kindly.

As he recalled years later: "I was so full of thankfulness and joy that I needed in some way to return to them what they had done for me. They had been kind to me, they had welcomed me. They had opened to me the world of my dreams."

The whole thing was summed up later as *"un grand succès d'hilarité."* He didn't know he had been laughed off the stage. And if he had, it wouldn't have mattered. When the manager handed him his cup of coffee, he felt as though he had really made it.

Mme. Chevalier tried to persuade Maurice to find another form of employment, but he insisted that the cafés-concerts were not merely places to visit on a Sunday night, they were also establishments for working in the rest of the week. And with his experience as a pro at Les Trois Lions, how could he go wrong?

At first going wrong seemed all too easy. No one wanted him. Maurice continued to spend time haunting the cafés-concerts stage doors, and near one, he heard a couple of performers talking about an audition they were attending next day at the Casino des Tourelles. He went along himself with his red nose and his baggy pants and sang the same number he had performed at Les Trois Lions, this time making sure he followed the piano player a bit more closely.

The only person who looked at all interested was the manager's wife, who was known to succumb readily to the charms of an attractive child, and she convinced her husband that Maurice had a great deal to offer.

He was promised twelve francs for a week's work. Le Petit Chevalier was in business.

Neighbours and the shopkeepers who had kept him supplied with tidbits heard about his triumph and went to the Casino for his first night at the bottom of the bill. Again Maurice sang songs that were outrageously inappropriate for a twelve-year-old and again the audience seemed delighted. After all, the double entendre was a staple part of French show business and it was no more than they expected.

The audience responded warmly enough for Maurice to be

certain his career was assured, but at the end of the first week's performances the manager shook Maurice's hand, gave him the envelope containing his twelve francs, and told him that he wasn't quite right. The pro had learned another lesson.

His mother, who had sat enthralled and admiring through every performance, cried with him that night. On the long walk back to Ménilmontant, La Louque was stopped by another performer from the Casino, Jean Gilbert.

"Madame," said M. Gilbert politely, "may I suggest that your son take some singing lessons? It will do him good for his chosen profession."

La Louque took the advice to heart. She found a teacher and rashly agreed to pay him twenty francs for two lessons. It was twenty francs more than she had, but the man had a daughter about to get married and modified the fee to a complete lace trousseau.

Maurice took the lessons and showed up for a series of auditions, but he found little work. He did a night at one café-concert and was told not to return. It was the same story at a dozen others. He expected his mother to try to persuade him to find other work, but now she didn't. When he cried despondently, she simply told him to be a man and face up to his difficulties.

But there was one job that was more encouraging. A photographer asked Maurice to pose for a series of postcards—not, of course, the kind that were furtively handed around in the bistros of Paris and in the red-light districts of a dozen other capital cities. For a series of half a dozen or so prints the boy who had recently been trying to make a living wearing baggy pants and a red nose donned a smart business-type suit, adopted a carefully parted hairstyle, and wore a well-scrubbed mischievous look on his face. In one picture he looked lovingly into the eyes of a curvaceous young girl in a white dress, with hair down to her narrow waist. In another, Maurice scratched his head as he pointed to a calendar.

This, too, was a kind of show business. The extroverted Maurice enjoyed posing before a camera in the days when the very first movies were being displayed in the occasional Paris arcade. It was a means of escaping from reality. When eventually he did land another job, it was for a mere five francs a week at the Concert du Commerce, another of the establishments to which La Louque would take Paul and him on Sundays. Things looked up, however, when the Ville Japonaise, a slightly higher-class café on the boulevard Strasbourg, offered him twenty-one francs a week.

So far, when he did work he received a fairly warm, sympathetic hearing. But things were to change. At the Casino de Montmartre on the boulevard Clichy, Maurice was blooded. He had an audition before a crowded audience that he said was made up of "savages." The acts were performed on stage before rows of pimps and prostitutes, as well as other characters who looked as though they had stepped straight out of an Apache dance routine. They heckled the show people, shouted obscenities at each other, and turned their backs on the performances—which, after all, was the best way to play cards without being distracted.

But Maurice had an act that was tailormade for them. It was brimful of sex and as coarse as the cloth from which most of the customers' clothes were made. He sang of girls whose breasts were too big for their dresses, of milkmaids who were up to no good in the hay, and of elegantly dressed ladies seducing innocent farm boys. The people out front loved every vulgar line of it. The fact that it came from the mouth of a thirteen-year-old made it all the more enjoyable.

Maurice was learning about growing up, and in a hurry; thrust headfirst into a world where razors were brought out as quickly and as frequently as the waiters delivered the *eau-de-vie*, and where women plied their trade in café doorways or were picked up on the streets outside.

The girls in the Casino de Montmartre were a different breed from any he had known before. They, too, found the youngster with the outrageous repertoire attractive, and he was fascinated by the sight of so many of them walking about behind the scenes virtually naked. There were two girls in particular to whom he would have devoted his life, given half a chance. One was a brunette named Fernande Deprat and the other, Maria Spinelli, was a sixteen-year-old blonde with a magnificent figure. But they wouldn't keep him away from what he considered to be his inevitable advancement, which seemed likely after a seven-day booking at the Concert de l'Univers on the avenue Wagram.

There he dared to sing "Volonté d'Fer," which one English scholar had translated as "Display Determination."

> *Display determination.*
> *It's the main thing that I know*
> *The male part of a nation*
> *Had better let it show.*

At which point, Maurice stuffed his hand in his pocket and pushed himself forward as though demonstrating his own manhood. He later described it as "a gesture of lamentable vulgarity," but at the time he thought he was magnificent.

The Univers was such a rough place that most acts refused to play there for more than a week. Some even refused to do encores. Maurice, however, was intoxicated by the response he got and stayed for three months. Word about him had by now spread to other parts of Paris and, more important, to other branches of French show business. Mayol himself heard about Maurice and asked Georgel, a friend working on the same bill as Le Petit Chevalier, to bring him over for supper. Maurice, as admiring of Mayol's talent as ever, was delighted and very flattered.

Well enough groomed to be photographed for another series of postcards, he arrived with Georgel for a supper that was better than most meals he had had in his life. His host was charm personified, asking kind questions about the boy's progress on stage, and, as a finishing touch, signing a photograph of himself: "To Le Petit Chevalier, with all that I think good, Félix Mayol."

Maurice was overwhelmed. However, when the older performer started to get emotional, he began to wonder what sort of man Mayol was. The gentle squeeze on the nape of the neck was a little too kind for Maurice's taste. When Georgel left the room, Mayol started to tell the youngster how much he wanted to get to know him better. "I'm really quite lonely," said the most famous star on the Paris variety stage, tears welling in his eyes. "I have no real friends at all."

It achieved the desired result. "I'm your friend, Monsieur Mayol," said Maurice.

Mayol then hugged him so tight that the gold watch chain he wore about his waistcoat impressed itself onto Maurice's chest. The hug was disconcerting. Mayol's hand moved higher up on

Maurice's trouser leg, which was now visibly shaking.

Maurice jumped from Mayol's grip.

"I want to be more intimate," said the star. Maurice felt his face go red as he inched his way back to the door. "Please, monsieur," he cried, "you've made a mistake."

Mayol was slightly bewildered. After all, why else should he want to entertain a thirteen-year-old boy whom he had no wish to see perform in public?

Nothing that took place that evening could, however, remove from Chevalier his admiration for Mayol the performer. "It never stopped me esteeming, admiring, loving him," he was to write years after Mayol was dead and forgotten by all but a few aficionados of the Paris music hall.

As for Maurice's own career, it proceeded at a painfully slow pace for more than a year. Finally, he was given what he realized only too well was his biggest break to date, a chance to appear at the sophisticated Petit Casino on the boulevard Montmartre, a place that catered to audiences as different from those at the Casino des Tourelles as its plush red drapes were from the stained backdrops in use on the boulevard Clichy.

He went on stage and began his opening number: "Display determination. . . ."

He didn't get further than the first verse when the audience was in an uproar. "Shame," shouted a man in the front row. "Disgraceful," called another. "Send him back to school," came a chorus from the gallery. Vulgarity was an essential part of the French music-hall tradition, but there were areas where the line between taste and coarseness was more finely drawn.

Until now Maurice had imagined that one group of people was much like any other and that if he could satisfy one, he could please all. It wasn't true. It was a vitally important lesson that he learned in a hard, tough way. For the first time, he perceived that an act had to be tailored to the audience watching it. What he had done at the Petit Casino was plainly not a good fit. Fortunately, an innate sense of showmanship inspired him to switch immediately to a more genteel popular song of the day.

For most of the week, Maurice was received in polite silence. But performance after performance, he worked as he had never done before. Each show was a rehearsal for the one that came next, and his act improved daily. With a hat that looked like a pimple on his head, Maurice impersonated Dranem and Polin. He was good enough for the manager to suggest that he might like a second week there and perhaps a third. . . . In the end Maurice stayed four months, enjoying every moment. What he enjoyed almost as much as entertaining, it appeared, was being able to stay in bed late. La Louque was so proud of her youngest son that when he decided it was eventually time to get up and enjoy a leisurely *café au lait,* she was only too delighted to supply it for him.

It was success indeed, and one that lasted until July when everything began to close down in Paris. The break couldn't really have come at a worse time, for Paul was now married, and with Maurice and La Louque alone in their flat, the only income they had was from her lacemaking. It could buy them little more than the barest necessities of life, and for weeks it seemed that they lived solely on herb tea and baked potatoes. Maurice managed to get an occasional one-night stand, but it didn't buy more than another small bag of potatoes.

Yet Maurice had by now learned a few tricks of his trade, the most important of which was to spend even the unemployed moments of the day with other show people—hugging an empty glass in the cafés they patronized and lolling with them on street corners. With no sexual interest in Le Petit Chevalier, they saw Maurice as a youngster in whom they could confide, someone to take under their wings. He heard snippets of information about shows waiting to be cast. Frequently there would be pieces of genuine advice: Who were the managers he could really trust, which were the shows where he would do best.

It was in this way that he got a small part in the revue *Le Tirebouchon* ("The Corkscrew") at La Parisiana, the most fashionable of the boulevard music halls, the sort of place to which men in starched white shirts and elegantly cut tailcoats would come with ladies wearing long dresses. It made a pleasant contrast to the restaurants where they had probably dined an hour or so before.

The show was unlike any Maurice had played in before. He was a solo act in the midst of a totally orchestrated revue. Maurice still wore his outlandish costume—he now pasted his face with chalk-white makeup—and impersonated the stars of the day, but now he was being recognized as a performer in his own right.

His first-night reception at La Parisiana was so warm he basked in its glow all the way back to Ménilmontant.

"*Maman*," he cried as he hugged his mother, "I'm a success."

There wasn't anyone in the audience that night who could deny it. It was an experience that was repeated every time he went on. The name Maurice Chevalier was not yet known outside the café-concert and music-hall circuits, but at fifteen he was already the center of attraction in his own environment. He felt sure, with the optimism which then characterized his whole being, that it was only a matter of time before the whole of Paris knew of him.

To the music-hall patrons, he had the sort of attractive fascination which people in other circles found in a juvenile prodigy who played the violin or piano with the skill and confidence of a maestro. To the girls on the bill with him he seemed to awaken one of two distinct reactions. Either he inspired all their latent maternal instincts, or else they felt an insatiable urge to take him to bed. They all had their favourite tricks. They would either pull out still further the protruding lower lip which was already a Chevalier trademark, or they would playfully pinch his cheeks. The more daring among them would catch him unawares and kiss him on the mouth. It had also become a dressing-room game to speculate on which one would before long deprive him of his virginity.

The opportunity came when—whether by prior arrangement or simply by fortuitous circumstances we will never know—Marguerite, a superbly built blonde, buttonholed Maurice in the corridor outside the girls' dressing room. It was an awakening which even in old age he never failed to recount with a sense of the excitement he felt at the time. Marguerite knew that when she eased herself gently into her dressing room, he would follow. And he did, looking around the stale-scented room, idly kicking the discarded makeup tins and soiled costumes lying on the floor as he self-consciously took her lead.

His first sexual experience changed his whole outlook on the business of growing up. What did not change was his attitude towards his mother. At the end of every show, she was the one to whom he would run with precise details of what had gone on that night—at least on stage. As his salary increased, he moved with her to better apartments. Other boys of his age were busy contemplating leaving home. Youngsters in Paris show business who had experienced the delights of boudoir encounters only wanted more of the same and better opportunities in which to enjoy them. But Maurice couldn't contemplate living anywhere but with his mother.

As he impersonated contemporary stars, he added little touches that set him apart from his fellow performers. What came across was an effervescent charm that was in no way spoiled by his loud appearance. He already knew that if he were really to succeed he had to be different from any performer who had gone before him. No one else had pouted his lower lip as he was doing with increasing success. And he was merging more and more different characters into his own.

Fragson, an English variety entertainer enjoying a greater success in Paris than he ever experienced in London, had brought the song-and-dance routine to France. The idea of tap-dancing *comiques* was totally strange to the French, but Fragson did it at the Eldorado. After seeing his show, Maurice went back to La Parisiana and on its empty stage practiced a similar routine for himself. It was very impromptu, and very rough, but the Parisiana audience who first saw him perform in public for the late show that night had never seen anything quite like it before and told Maurice so in no uncertain terms. They clapped so much that he had to reprise the routine again and again. By the time he had danced and joked his last encore, he had mastered another Chevalier trademark.

English acts were enticing to Maurice. He saw the Tiller Girls in Paris and said afterwards that he "went mad" watching them present an act called "Yankee Doodle Dandy." He told friends he was convinced about the British superiority on the variety stage. Every performer from England whom he saw only served to make him more certain that they had something no French artist could provide—or at least had yet provided. The grass was a whole lot greener on the other side of the English Channel.

At the back of his mind was the idea of making a trip to see for himself how these marvellous performers operated in their home territory. But he was too committed to La Parisiana to make definite plans about going away; La Parisiana, for its part, was very much committed to him.

By 1904 Maurice was no longer alone in thinking his talent was something special. The shouts for more and still more from this boy in his new outfit of a sailor's jersey and a bowler hat—and the inevitable red nose—were testimony enough. If further proof were needed, it came from the people who continued to throng his dressing room after a show. Fragson himself came. Even Mayol, despite his previous rebuff, turned up to show that his interest was now strictly professional. Mistinguett, then the queen of the sophisticated revues that were just beginning to thrill the smart set and to establish a reputation that would last for the best part of a century, came, too, and told Maurice how she had been "electrified" by him.

Maurice soon returned the compliment by going to the Eldorado and telling Mistinguett how much he enjoyed her performance. That was when, as he told me, he first decided he had "fallen a little bit in love" with Mistinguett.

3.
On Top of the World

*I love things like beautiful thick materials. It must be
my Flemish blood.*

—MAURICE CHEVALIER

Success for Maurice was being never without a job, and being
able to rent a better apartment for La Louque. If it had been
difficult to get out-of-season work before, now when the Parisiana
revue closed for the summer, managers seemed to be vying with
each other to find Maurice spots on variety bills. He was not yet
a number one act, but his name on a poster was already sufficiently good reason for people to buy tickets.

Sometimes he wasn't entirely sure what that name should be.
At the Eden-Concert in the Paris suburb of Asnières, he was
billed as "Chevalier M. of La Parisiana." Another poster called
him "Le Petit Jésus," wholly inappropriate considering some of
his antics at the time. *"Une représentation extraordinaire,"* declared the bills, and that indeed was exactly what Maurice's

dancing-singing-monologues appeared to be. His most popular numbers were "Les P'tit Pois" and "Les Foies Gras," but he was already at the stage when he could have knocked patrons out of their hardbacked seats reciting "Frère Jacques." Had he just been a singer or a dancer or a monologist he might never have had a job at all. But now, compared with his life just a few months before, he was rich—enough for La Louque and him to move at last out of Ménilmontant to an apartment on the rue du Faubourg Saint-Martin. They were now in the heart of the café district, where all young show people who considered themselves worthy of the name would gather. Their favourite haunt was the café-restaurant run by the amply proportioned Mme. Pages, who seemed to have taken a proprietary interest in all her customers. As Maurice once wrote:

"She seemed to feel that she was the mother of all us fledgling professionals, girls as well as men, who met at her place every night after our shows. She bossed us, pushed us around like a dictator—and always with love."

She also smiled at their nocturnal expeditions into Montmartre. After all, that was where everything happened; where prostitutes, male and female, prowled constantly like soldiers on guard and protected their own territory just as determinedly. It was where one bar nestled close by another; where artists set up easels by day and their models by night, where priests from the nearby church of the Sacré-Coeur would try to reform pimps and thieves and murderers who were protected by the confessional booth. Montmartre was also Paris at its bawdiest.

Maurice and his friends, after their own shows had finished or on an occasional evening off, found in Montmartre a lasting education, though not the kind they would ever have had at school. Under the windmill at the Moulin Rouge, they shared the thrills of the cancan between visits by the *gendarmerie*. It was still the time when a high-kicking girl would show glimpses of pubic hair along with her white thighs and black garters. Wearing frilly underpants as part of the ensemble was just a tease for the other times when they wore nothing at all underneath all those dancing petticoats.

But the young showmen were not to be satisfied with the voyeurism available to tourists. After being aroused with the hors

d'oeuvres at the Moulin, the entrée was in the street outside
where there was one object in mind: for each to pick up a girl—
without paying the usual fee. Somehow that was not quite as difficult as might at first be imagined. In his book *Maurice Chevalier's
Paris*, Maurice recalled that the ladies of the night had a prearranged signal for the boys, who at a wave would fall out of
doorways and into their arms.

Business wasn't always on an even keel, and rather than spend
hours marching up and down the street, swinging a handbag
with no discernibe result, the prospect of hopping into a warm
bed with an attractive young man was preferable by far. The
girls' regular customers were frequently elderly, flabby, and reek-
ing of sweat and spirits. Maurice and his friends were young and
slim and provided even these women, who sold their bodies three
or four times a day for a couple of francs, with sexual satisfaction
they seldom experienced. They represented a useful barrier between the girls and their rougher paying guests. This was a time
when a number of young men from the Argentine had descended
on Paris in search of a fortune that nearly always remained elusive. Their favourite resting places were the El Garron and Le
Capitol nightclubs. Their idea of sport was to try to steal one of
the young prostitutes just as she was walking away, arm in arm,
with Maurice or his friends. There was always a fight and the
victor would walk off with the girl. When Maurice found himself
too often on the ground, he decided it was time to take boxing
lessons.

Maurice's first theatrical experience outside France was close
to his mother's home territory, in Brussels, and it seemed that the
Belgians took to him as warmly as the French. But it was in
France where he had to build up his reputation. At Lyons he met
Colette, who was to remember him when she wrote *Le Vagabond*, which was based on the young *comique*. He topped the
bill at the Lyons Kursaal. But it was not as important to him at
the time as the fact that he was working with an English company there who called their show *An Evening At the Music Hall*.
Being so close to British artists was intoxicating to Maurice. He
soaked up every detail of their act, and any nuances he could
adapt to his own performance, he took and made his own property. He had never before seen the polish that an English com-

pany could provide. Watching a comedian pretend—or perhaps he was not really pretending—to be tipsy was a revelation.

But what he found most irresistible of all was the young daughter of the head of the troupe, an English rose with whom he fell hopelessly in love. Hopelessly because her father employed the stage manager and virtually everyone else in his pay to keep her away from Maurice.

"How I loved her!" Chevalier recalled years afterwards. "My heart behaved like a battering ram if our glances crossed, and had she actually tried to talk to me, I think I should have passed out. My love was real, honest, respectful, passionate, and it was making me quite ill."

The love was apparently reciprocated. When they lunched together on his seventieth birthday, as Maurice revealed in one of his books (she had summoned up enough courage to write to him after more than half a century apart), she told him that she had had a loveless marriage, partly because no one had ever been able to replace in her heart the French teenager she loved at Lyons.

In 1906 Maurice saw his first American entertainers, probably the first Americans to play the Paris music halls. They had on him an even greater impact than that of the British entertainers. They seemed even more polished and from them, too, he took ingredients which, mixed in the casserole of his act, became essential parts of the Chevalier performance.

He sang a new song which roughly translated went:

> *I'm a good-looking American guy*
> *I'm most precocious with a roving eye.*

When Maurice sang it in Marseilles, Sarah Bernhardt went backstage to offer her congratulations. She was not, however, a typical member of the audience. Playing the Café Alcazar was the hardest period he experienced since entertaining the "savages" on the boulevard Clichy.

For one thing, it was virtually impossible to follow a comedian, who had been having his audience in stitches with stories about the recent Russian-Japanese War. For another, Maurice's Parisian accent wasn't easily understood. Later that night, he admitted he had panicked when he saw he wasn't getting across to them the way he had been doing almost everywhere else.

Then he sang "Le Rondeau Populaire," a medley of song titles strung together in a lyric. This was more familiar to the audience, and they clapped and asked for more.

In one scene he came on as "Le Bébé Maurice." Wearing a bib around his neck, he climbed into a giant basket cradle and the crowd roared. Maurice was proving a fact that he had known all along, but which most of his French stage contemporaries had ignored: Being a visual entertainer added a dimension that made him stand out from all the others.

He celebrated his success in Marseilles by buying himself an outsize cap made in London, a Scottish sweater, and a pair of thick-soled shoes. "I'm afraid," he noted years later, "that I will always have to fight my taste of the too loud and the too solid implanted in me by years of poverty."

He didn't want, however, to fight his taste for English-style entertainers. When he met J. W. Jackson, the leader of a dancing troupe which gloried under the name of "The Eight Lancashire Lads," he didn't need much persuading that London was where he had to go.

When his off-season tour of Marseilles and the south came to an end in the early spring of 1907, Maurice decided to cross the Channel. La Louque was asked her permission—for as sophisticated and experienced as he may have considered himself at eighteen, his mother's approval was still the main consideration in his life—and, with a little reluctance, she agreed.

In London Maurice checked into a cheap hotel near Victoria Station—he had promised La Louque not to waste his hard-earned money—and made immediately for the Victoria Palace, one of the best of the Edwardian music halls. He was overwhelmed by what he saw—George Robey with his deep voice, wide smile, and giant-sized eyebrows (which he used to amazing effect), heading a bill of singers, dancers, acrobats, and jugglers who were superior to any he had seen in Paris. As he told me, he found the same standard in a dozen other London music halls—watching Harry Wheldon, "Little Tich," and Wilkie Bard bringing the house down night after night. They were all from poor backgrounds similar to his own; each had a unique visual style which, back in his hotel room, Maurice could dissect and practice in front of the mirror.

On his return to France, he wasted no time in putting his London experiences to good use. On stage his act was more fluid, funnier, and much better to look at. Women seemed to think the same of him. In bed with a different girl almost every night—he told friends he preferred "the Apache type"—his now wide experience gave him a reputation as a man who knew how to excite them. Girls waited for him wherever he went. They told him they loved his singing, went overboard for his dancing, but most of all they loved his physique. Maurice was very conscious of that and went back to the same gymnasium where he and Paul had tried to become acrobats, and took up boxing again, this time more seriously than ever.

Coincidentally, Georges Carpentier, the famous boxer, was using the gym at that time, too, and before long the two young men were embarking on what was to be a lifetime friendship. It was also a period of reunions. Maurice and Mistinguett met once more. She saw him at work and told him: "You will do very well. You've got a lovely mug." In her autobiography she wrote:

"It was a revelation. He put the song over as if he were humming to himself for his own pleasure with a rhythm and a sureness of touch that took my breath away."

They met again, when Maurice visited the Variétés Theater, where Mistinguett was playing.

"We used to pass each other on the stairs," she wrote. "He smiled and I smiled back. He called me plain Mistinguett and I called him Chevalier."

Soon after this meeting, Maurice had his biggest break to date. Dranem, the *comique* whom Maurice had so assiduously studied and who was now starring at the Eldorado, was taken ill. If Chevalier could take his place, it would mean that for the first time the name Chevalier would be emblazoned in lights outside a major theater. Take the spot? He jumped at the opportunity, and the audience laughed and cheered at the spectacle of the young man in the bowler hat, skimpy jacket, and sailor's jersey singing and dancing.

Among those who also jumped was P. L. Flers, perhaps the top producer in France. He called on Maurice in his dressing room with a proposition. "Come," he said, "and join my new show at the Folies-Bergère."

4.
The Love Parade

I had the most beautiful women in the world in Holly-wood, but in fact the only thing that mattered to me was the public.

—MAURICE CHEVALIER

The Folies-Bergère represented not just another show, another step on Maurice's way to the top. It *was* the top.

Two years earlier Florenz Ziegfeld had opened his own Follies on Broadway, and if Ziegfeld could already claim that through the portals of his theater walked the loveliest girls in the world, then by rights he should have added: "Except those at the Folies-Bergère." The name was by then synonymous with the most magnificent showgirls on any stage—tall and statuesque, draped in silks and ostrich feathers, or merely in rouge and powder—girls whose figures seemed to have been sculpted precisely to M. Flers's specifications.

Any *comique* who could survive that sort of competition had to be good, and M. Flers thought Chevalier was just that. But he was only in the Folies on trial, and if he failed he alone would be the sufferer. With those girls hardly anyone would notice the absence of an indifferent male performer. It was up to Maurice to prove that he was anything but that. With the supreme confidence that was typical of him at the time, Maurice felt he could succeed where dozens of others had failed. It was not simply a case of justifying his position at the top musical theater in Paris, but more that the Folies would have to justify its association with him.

Full of that self-assurance, he went into his first number on that vast stage, "L'Enfant d'Amour." He sensed immediately that all was not well. By the time he had finished his first chorus, "From the moment I was born, child of love, that's me," the audience sat in stony silence. He followed it with a dance routine. Again only a scattering of not altogether polite applause, which was no more enthusiastic when he left the stage.

La Louque was waiting for him in his dressing room. "I feel as though I've had a slap in the face," he told her.

But he hadn't—at least not from the management. Flers knew how Maurice felt and came to offer a modicum of instant comfort. His young *comique* was assured he was not going to be fired, although the following day he would be put on earlier in the bill, which made him feel better. And one of his songs would be completely cut, which made him feel worse. But before the surgery could be implemented, the readers of the Paris newspapers would learn of the failure of the man whom everyone —not the least himself—had previously felt could never go wrong. The most prestigious paper of them all, *Le Figaro*, was biting. Their critic wrote:

"Where could they have found this clumsy booby? And who let him loose in our leading music hall? He is vulgar beyond belief. His song is nothing but filth."

Maurice bought the paper outside the theater, a shudder running through him as he read the review. He slunk back into his dressing room. There, in front of the mirror, he tried hard to stifle his sobs.

He recalled many years later—the bitterness of the experience was still vivid—that he took refuge in a bottle of Cognac, pro- vided by the management as a first-night gift. He consumed a quarter of it in two hours, but it only served to increase the enormous wave of self-pity which descended upon him like a black storm cloud.

By some miracle he managed to go on stage and get through his act—better than the night before, but with none of the verve with which he had previously performed. The old confidence had simply left him. At the age of twenty, he seemed bereft of all his former security. It never really returned, but in a way this crisis made him a better performer.

Night after night he was tortured by disappointment; barely able to offer a civil word to his mother, the stage-door keeper, the stagehands, or anyone else in the cast. But when the music for his numbers started, he bounced onto the stage as though propelled by a catapult and worked as if there were a fire under his feet.

In spite of Maurice's qualms, Flers was confident that the young performer was earning every sou of the 1,800 francs he was being paid. At the end of the winter season, he invited Maurice to come back to the Folies the following autumn. Maurice was delighted.

Meanwhile, there was a whole string of summer bookings awaiting him at the Alcazar d'Été, the Ambassadeurs, and the Chez Fisher nightclub. There, he thought he had fallen in love again; this time with the beautiful Fréhel, who was already a big star of the cabaret circuit.

He was overwhelmed by her and felt himself consumed by the fire that seemed to radiate from her body and face. Her influence extended beyond bed, too, but Maurice had the sense to realize it before it was too late. He knew that with her he was enjoying too much alcohol and that if he was not careful the sensations that came over him when he took drugs with her were powerful enough to be his ruin. He decided that Fréhel was indeed too dangerous a woman for comfort, and thus they parted company. His "heart was bleeding," he wrote in his autobiography, but he was sure he had made the right decision. Fréhel herself never forgave him for leaving her, and within a couple of years her career was in decline.

Before long Maurice was searching for new girls to conquer.

It wasn't difficult, although as his success increased, his taste in women changed. Now he sought out girls from a more exclusive social background. They presented him with new problems, however. They had expensive tastes, and Maurice, so recently freed from the austerity of Ménilmontant, was not very pleased at having to indulge them—as one of them, a now highly respected elderly lady, told me. But Maurice was young, and to turn his back on all the excitement they seemed to offer would only emphasize his inadequacy in the glittering world he wished to join.

He took them to nightclubs and expensive restaurants. At Maxim's, he booked a private dining room, an institution in Paris, where the food was exquisite and the service discreet. His highborn company were ladies who knew exactly how to behave in public and, most important of all, precisely how to dress. Their style of dressing caused him untold misery, as he related years later. After wining and dining the girls, came the difficult job of unbuttoning their bodices with his damaged thumb. Once the buttons were all unfastened, he had to unravel what seemed to be miles of corset lacing, unhitch suspenders, and search extensively among mountainous folds of petticoats. By the time the expedition was completed, the initial incentive had all but vanished.

The Folies, however, had not lost interest in having Chevalier back for the 1910–1911 season. He was given an additional 500 francs and what was more valuable—the chance to work with Mistinguett. The girl who had been born Jeanne Bourgeois, daughter of a fortune-teller, was then forty, nineteen years older than Chevalier. It was rumoured that her legs were insured for a million francs. She would swing them on stage, sitting on an ornate couch, and hitch her skirt well up to her thighs as she did so. She was mistress of ceremonies in the show, making her entrance at the top of a huge staircase, wearing shoes with heels so high and thin they looked lethal and a crown of ostrich feathers that seemed quite as tall as she was. Looking back on Mistinguett in that very last interview he gave me, Chevalier said of her:

"She was not terribly pretty, but she was so attractive. She was a strong artist—solid, a great mixture of show woman, attractive woman, funny woman, and chic woman. She could bring the audience from laughter to tears and then back to laughter again. She has not been replaced in France. When I was twenty-one she was forty, but it did not show at all. She was sensational."

A contemporary writer described her like this: "Elegantly, she at first lifted her long skirts just enough to reveal those famous legs, agitating them provokingly. Her bust was like an artistic vase resting on the perfect pedestal of her hips. The bodice, of quite the latest cut, revealed softly rounded breasts like ripe fruit ready to burst. Her throat was nothing short of ravishing. Magnetic fires scintillated from her velvety pupils, but occasionally her expression registered disdain, contempt, even indifference."

The language may have been flowery, but it said a great deal about the experience of seeing Mistinguett on stage.

From the beginning she had an intense, almost maternal desire to see that Chevalier succeeded where he had almost failed the year before.

"I don't think I've ever been so paralyzed with first-night nerves as I was that first night at the Folies," she wrote in her memoirs. "I was not only nervous for myself, but also for Maurice. Stage fright is the nearest thing to a nightmare that I know. Nothing helps. All help drains away and you are left clutching at a few straws of hope. Gamblers know this feeling. The real ones, those who lose. I am not a gambler. I like to win."

When she heard Maurice sing she sensed that he was captivating the audience by his own personal magnetism. "He's got 'em," she murmured to the electrician standing next to her in the wings. "He's made it."

Paris had never known a hero like Chevalier. A city with a music-hall tradition which some regarded as sacred as *le Quatorze juilliet* [Bastille Day] had found an artist with a new style.

"*Si j'avais su . . .*" he cried. "If I'd have known . . ."

And his audience applauded the innuendo in this song about a young man who wished he had been more careful making love to his now-pregnant sweetheart.

It meant he was a star, but a star had to have a peculiarly individual stamp, something about him that no other entertainer had ever had. Maurice perfected his mélange approach, incorporating into what he had been doing all the time various touches picked up from the Anglo-Saxon artists he admired so much.

"Now," said Mistinguett, "I can start teaching him his job, how to work properly."

And she did, although her interest was not simply confined to helping a young, comparatively inexperienced Folies performer to develop his career. At first they were merely partners on the same bill. In one memorable scene, in which the traditional violence of the male Apache was reversed, Mistinguett had to slap Chevalier's face twenty times.

"I was a boxer." He laughed, recalling that number. "So I could take it."

After the slaps the pair began an eccentric dance routine, "La Valse Renversante," in which almost every stick of furniture on the crowded stage was seemingly smashed in front of the audience and then thrown into the wings. It looked like violent passion. Soon that was precisely what it would become.

From being wreckers of furniture, they became acrobats with a roll of coconut matting. Using the most meticulous timing, the two would dance their way into a horizontal position and then roll together inside the carpeting. The combined aroma of the mat and Mistinguett's perfume was a heady mixture, Chevalier told me. "In the dark, inside that mat, our two eyes met and night after night, we took longer and longer to unroll, while the orchestra played the same piece of music again and again."

In the privacy of that carpet, with two thousand people only yards away, they kissed. The second time it happened, they embraced each other tightly. The third time they embraced still tighter, with Maurice caressing Mistinguett's breasts as she pressed herself against his legs, simulating the lovemaking they were so anxious to perform. That third night, before they allowed the rug to unroll, they told each other just how strong they felt that love to be. When they finally leaped out of the carpet together, the audience roared its admiration—almost as if every person in the stalls and balcony had heard each word and was giving wholehearted approval.

From their standing position, center stage, Maurice and Mistinguett jumped out of a prop window. Away from everyone but the stage hands, they kissed again. At 3 A.M. they left the theater and spent the rest of the night and most of the next day in bed in her apartment.

Mistinguett was known to her admirers simply as "Miss." Next to her Maurice was at all times a novice. Before a vast audience and in private she was a woman who oozed sexuality. On stage she used it to dazzling effect. It was almost as if from the moment she entered on the heels of the kicking chorus, every man sitting out front was overcome by a kind of nerve gas. It remained that way until she took her last bow, following it with a final display of those enticing legs. Then, as she bent low to acknowledge the roar of the crowd, the display of cleavage brought an orchestrated sigh from the men in the front rows. In the privacy of her apartment, she introduced Maurice to techniques that made the women of Montmartre seem like girls newly liberated from the convent. In both definitions of the word, she became Maurice's mistress.

With Maurice's comical outfits on stage, there was very little about him to which an audience could immediately respond without some additional chemical reaction. And he could initiate that just by opening his mouth. But it was Miss who taught him how to exploit it. She instructed him in the way a sophisticated audience like the one at the Folies needed to be at first teased and then pampered; to be made to feel that it was taking part in something of a love feast. "Do you want to hear that again?" Maurice would call now. He knew they would shout, "Yes—we do!" The fact that the audience was actually asked made it feel important, vital to his success.

Miss taught him good manners. She provided him with a fashionable dress sense, although his taste for "solid," expensive clothes was inspired less by her advice than by the fact that he could never have afforded it in Ménilmontant. She also made him lose what some women had admired most of all—his gaucheness.

Looking back many years later on those early days together, a slightly jaundiced Mistinguett described in her book how he "swaggered down the boulevard" in his first dinner jacket. "He was so swollen with his new importance," she wrote, "you could not have slipped a cigarette between his bottom and the seat of his pants." Maurice himself recalled that his first meeting with Miss was like a peasant visiting a château. But it wasn't long before he was very comfortable indeed crossing the drawbridge. And on her part, Miss felt great pride when she saw his progress.

"I'm making you a star," she told him one night.

He didn't like that at all. "I was already a star of the new generation when I first came here," he answered, as though to give away any of the credit was in some way demeaning his own abilities. It would be a recurring factor in their relationship, although at that time he was still only too delighted to accept her life-style.

The second Folies season was followed by a third, in 1911–1912, with another 500-franc-a-year increase in Maurice's salary. Miss once more shared his act, his bed, and his excitement with each new success. She knew, too, how nervous he was before each show. As he stood in the wings waiting to go on, stagehands could see him frantically wiping the perspiration, first from the palm of his hands, then from his forehead, and once more from his hands before dancing onto the stage as if it were the easiest and most natural thing in the world for him. But if he were unsure of himself at that point in the evening, he was quite the opposite at Miss's apartment after the show.

Maurice asked Miss to marry him—several times. She constantly refused. "Why spoil such a lovely thing we have together?" she asked.

Together they experimented with drugs. The purer derivatives of the opium poppy represented another brand of forbidden fruit to be sampled at the society parties to which Miss took him—but at which he never felt quite comfortable. He could not be sure that his fellow guests weren't secretly laughing at his humble origins. He only really felt himself when he was alone with her after a hefty dose of the most vital drug of all—the solid worship that came from an audience at the Folies on a night when he knew that both he and his admirers in the stalls and gallery had done well.

He and Miss did not live together. Sophisticated he might now consider himself to be, his place was still with his mother. He felt he had to keep returning the devotion she had shown him when he was very young and which she constantly demonstrated even now. And no one was more thrilled by his success than La Louque. She knew about his friendship with Miss, but it is doubtful if she knew the extent to which they were involved. Mistinguett was the essence of tact whenever she met La Louque. If she had not been, or if La Louque had objected to the relationship, Maurice would probably have broken off their affair. Years later he said that one of the things he liked most about her was the fact that "she loved my mother."

Doubtless Mistinguett had decided that marriage with Maurice would be virtual bigamy. Since almost every conversation between them was peppered with his words of admiration for La Louque, she knew that her role would always be a subordinate one. But in the confines of the existing setup, she was willing to accept it and was amazingly affable to Mme. Chevalier.

Frequently the three of them would go out together, dine at fashionable restaurants as guests of the proprietors (Maurice was not keen to foot the bills himself), or sometimes even "slum" it in the audience at one of the cafés-concerts which had been Maurice's nursery, and which his mother still preferred to the Folies.

It was in 1912 when a different area of his past caught up with Maurice, and in a totally unexpected and quite painful way. He was at La Cigale with a bunch of friends—Miss had decided not to accompany him that evening—when he heard a voice that he instantly recognized. *"Bonsoir, Maurice,"* it called, and he could see, standing over him, a poorly dressed man with dishevelled hair. He looked about sixty.

Maurice invited the man to step outside the café with him and there in the street, underneath a lamp, came face to face for the first time in seventeen years with his father.

The two embraced. The older man was delighted by his son's reactions. He told him how proud he had been to learn of his success, and asked about his brothers. Victor Chevalier said that for him things had been hard, that he had been misjudged in the past, and that really the only thing he had ever cared about was his family. Then, haltingly, as though he had been trying all the time to summon up the courage to do so, he looked straight into Maurice's eyes and asked: "Is your mother well?"

"She is well," Maurice replied, "but I'm not going to tell her I've seen you. Your name has not even been mentioned since you left. Don't come to see me again. We've forgotten you." The way Maurice said it proved just how the old man had been anything but forgotten. But the memory was bitter.

They never saw each other again. As if to ease his conscience, Maurice tried to forget the meeting ever happened. Indeed, in one magazine article Maurice wrote in the 1930s, he claimed his father had died when he was a child. He later changed that attitude, and in a number of books wrote that one of his greatest regrets was that he made no provision for his father's old age. This could simply have been for public consumption. When, old himself, he told the story of the meeting with his father to a friend, he added—probably far more truthfully—"I couldn't possibly help him after all the suffering he had caused my mother." Doing so would have meant spending some of the money he had now set aside for La Louque and his own amusements.

Miss had no one to dilute her affection for Maurice, and he wanted to keep it that way. More vital even than that, both were at a stage in their joint careers when they wanted to think of becoming even more successful. The Folies was still the top of the tree, but Miss said there were branches that could be explored to their mutual benefit, and Maurice agreed enthusiastically.

Their reputation spread far outside Paris. When the Queen of Romania arrived in the city, she said that the first thing she wanted to do was to go to see the "two M's—Mistinguett and Maurice Chevalier." She liked the show so much she went around to both stars' dressing rooms after the performance to tell them so. There were even rumours—fostered in no small way by the Folies' management—that the Queen had fallen in love with Maurice.

He was fast becoming the king of Parisian night life, and to prove it, was invited to make guest appearances at other shows. When his contractual obligations to the Folies didn't interfere, he was always delighted to accept. He grabbed every opportunity to extend his audience. As early as 1908 he appeared in a one-reel film called *Trop Crédule*, and three years later made three others with the man known as "the French Charlie Chaplin," Max Linder: *Un Marié Qui se Fait Attendre*, *La Mariée Recalcitrante*, and *Par Habitude*. All served to take his name beyond the Paris music-hall circuit.

Yet at the back of his mind was still the feeling that even the whole of France represented only part of his potential. He thought of it when he took Miss to London, this time not merely doing the rounds of the music halls, but also to see as much as possible of the musical-comedy scene.

Most startling of all the shows they saw was a production that summed up the new age of which all young people liked to think themselves a part, *Hello Ragtime*, starring Ethel Levey. But what really struck home was a number called "The Wedding Glide," in which the male star, Gerald Kirby, appeared dressed entirely in white.

It was perfection and Maurice wanted it for himself in the Folies. As soon as he returned, he suggested it to M. Flers, who was not amused. Change an act—and, worse, a leading performer's style—when everything was going so well? Maurice was brilliant as a low comedian. How could he now contemplate ruining it all? The answer was, he must not be allowed to.

So Maurice had to store the idea for the future, just as he had to with a plan to make a new movie—this time with Miss. Late in 1913 Pathé came to them with the notion of filming their "Valse Renversante" routine. It was a marvellous idea at the time, but there was one problem: Maurice had just been ordered to join the Army.

5.
Panic button

Maurice was always sad—except when he was on the stage.

—DENISE GREY

Maurice should have joined up in 1908. But a sympathetic draft board—all of whose members apparently thoroughly enjoyed a good café-concert—took pity on the sole supporter of a deserted mother and allowed him to defer his call-up.

It couldn't last indefinitely, however, in a country which had looked at its German neighbours with considerable anxiety ever since the Franco-Prussian débâcle of 1870–1871. Anyone in the least bit interested in the Paris theater knew that Maurice was a great success, and his file showed that more than adequate provision was being made for La Louque. The draft board reckoned, not unreasonably, that he should have put enough by to be spared for a couple of years.

There were, of course, always indications of trouble ahead with Germany, but war was still a fairly distant proposition. Maurice worried about the prospect of two years away from his mother, two years away from Mistinguett, and, perhaps most important of all, two years away from the stage at a time when he felt he was consolidating his position. It was one thing being a big success with everyone able to see it, but he was anxious about the possibility of a fickle public forgetting him completely by the time his service ended.

Maurice was drafted into the 31st Infantry Regiment for training at Belfort, and, in his ill-fitting *poilu's* uniform, he was subjected to all the discipline for which one of the hardest military regimes in the world was justly famous—nighttime marches with full gear; polishing boots till they shone like mirrors, only to have them deliberately thrown in the mud by sadistic sergeant majors; work schedules tough enough to make strong men cry for their mothers. On the other hand, however, the military were not unaware of the public-relations value of a major star serving in their midst. When Maurice had his first leave early in 1914, they allowed him to film "La Valse Renversante," the one-reeler he had planned to do with Mistinguett. When the second leave came, they did not object to his stage appearances with Miss.

All that, of course, was to change in August of that year. War hit Maurice like a personally incribed shell. After that second leave, Miss went to see him off at the station, and she later described seeing a thousand men move away with tears in their eyes. Maurice had made her promise that she would look after his mother for him. She could have reacted by flinging the idea back in his face. While she was in Maurice's company, it might have been politic to tolerate La Louque, but now there was no need to feign affection. Nonetheless she promised to act as a dutiful daughter-in-law, even though she continued to refuse to play wife. Those refusals to provide him with a certain comfort to take away to the trenches were a bitter disappointment to Maurice. In fact, all his hopes and his ambitions, to say nothing of his love affair, appeared to collapse as Germany thundered through Belgium.

He was positive now he was going to be killed—or worse still, so maimed that neither his public nor Mistinguett would want to take him to their hearts again. It was a shattering, depressing thought that wouldn't leave him. He thought of La Louque pining for him in their Paris apartment, and he was totally overcome. He dreamed of Mistinguett in bed with someone else and woke up in a cold sweat. At the age of twenty-six, he had had a life crowded with triumph, but now he told himself it was all over.

Maurice, a fully trained soldier, was sent into action almost as soon as the fighting started. On his first day under fire at the Battle of Cutry, the sound of shells exploding all around him brought sheer terror with every volley. His division had been ordered to advance, but it was one of those humanly impossible orders given all too freely by staff officers who know nothing of conditions around the barbed wire.

Everyone was frightened, but it wasn't cowardice that drove men, incongruously dressed in blue tunics and red trousers, to fall like sacks into ditches, clutching their soft pillbox caps—steel helmets were not introduced until the following year. It was sheer necessity, the instinct for self-preservation and survival.

As Maurice jumped into one of these holes in the earth, a burning sensation ripped through his body. It was the last thing he knew before he blacked out.

Maurice woke up in a shabby hall-like room. A blond nurse was peering down into the iron bedstead on which he was lying. Next to her stood a man wearing a white coat over what was obviously a grey uniform. The uniform was not French, nor was the conversation that Maurice could dimly hear going on around him. As he gradually came to, he realized he was being tended by Germans. In halting French the nurse told him he was in Magdeburg, inside a German military hospital, a prisoner in a war that had just begun.

The pain in his chest was unbearable, but the wound, he was assured, wasn't going to be fatal. His left lung had been punctured by a piece of shrapnel, which the doctors had decided to leave alone—the lung would be damaged far more by attempting to remove the metal than by letting it remain where it had a good chance of healing.

Maurice had little idea of how the war was going for everyone else, but for him it seemed to be over. It was a feeling that increased the day he was loaded unceremoniously onto a cattle truck and equally perfunctorily ordered to jump from the tailgate of a truck inside the compound of the Alten Grabow prisoner-of-war camp. If any of the guards or the officers in the camp knew he was a famous star of the Folies-Bergère, it was a secret they kept to themselves; a secret that had repercussions in Paris, where the conversation along the boulevards, in Montmartre, and inside the Folies itself was that Chevalier had become the latest victim of German atrocities. Each tale was worse than the one before—he had been sexually mutilated; his limbs had been amputated for sport; his right eye had been gouged out; his ears had been cut off.

Naturally, La Louque heard the stories and collapsed. Miss heard them, too, and was escorted from the Folies in tears. There seemed no option other than to believe the tales. Maurice, it appeared, hadn't written to either of his two loves.

In fact he had, and to both women—letters in which he poured out his heart and his misery, but the censors wouldn't allow them to be delivered. Then after three months, a note from a more cheerful and healthier Maurice did manage to get through. It was a joyous day for both La Louque and Miss, to say nothing of the Folies patrons who loved the unique Chevalier performance. Miss gave the news from the stage of the theater and the audience went wild.

For the time being, however, there seemed no chance of any more of those performances from Maurice. There were thousands of prisoners in Alten Grabow—one story published in a contemporary report had it that there were twenty thousand men in the camp at any one time, but that seems to be a healthy exaggeration. Certainly, there were enough to heighten Maurice's belief that the Army he had joined was finished. In the camp with him were English and Russian prisoners, too. As enlisted men they could be made to work, but despite labouring jobs inside the camp perimeter, time went by slowly. The order of the day, each day, was sheer boredom.

It was boredom that made Maurice volunteer as a medical orderly. It was a job normally reserved for Red Cross men who had been engaged in similar tasks before their capture, but Maurice's suggestion to the chief French doctor was accepted, and before long *Infirmier* Chevalier had learned how to give injections, administer medicines, and apply bandages in the camp hospital. The work was reasonably satisfying, but it didn't exactly make him happy. He was asked to take part in a camp concert, but he didn't want to. Some of the men thought this was mere snobbery on his part, as the shows couldn't be guaranteed to resemble the Folies and would obviously demean him. It wasn't that at all; he just couldn't put his mind to it. Nothing could make him smile if he didn't feel like it. Months of inactivity, however, did give him time to think, mostly about La Louque and Miss. Every time he wrote to them or whenever a letter from them finally reached him, he would be engulfed in depression.

It was on one of his better days, seeing a new detachment of English prisoners arrive at Alten Grabow, that he formulated an idea that probably would have as much effect on his life as that first visit to a café-concert. Somewhat gingerly he approached the British sergeant major and, with the help of a fellow orderly, asked him: "Can you find someone who could teach me English?"

If he could learn English, he thought, perhaps he could experience from the other side of the auditorium the brilliance of the British musical stage, he himself thrill audiences in London.

The sergeant major shouted an order. "Kennedy," he thundered, "teach this man 'ere to speak English."

Sergeant Ronald Kennedy was an inspired choice. He was a schoolmaster from the north of England and having a pupil once more at his elbow represented a return to a semblance of dignity. He struck a bargain with Chevalier. "I'll teach you English," he said, "if you teach me French."

It turned out to be a pretty one-sided affair, as Kennedy remembered some fifty years later in a BBC radio broadcast. He didn't learn very much French, but in Maurice Chevalier he had a pupil who was not only willing to learn but extremely able. It is clear that Maurice, for his part, was more than helped by Kennedy's own natural gifts. The Englishman knew how words needed to be moulded to situations before they had any meaning —while all Maurice was able to do was to point to things and provide the French for: "This is a table. This is a chair. This is a music-hall singer!" As Maurice said many years afterwards: "Those words, he could have found them all just as easily in a book without my help."

Night after night, in the dimly lit barrack room, they went through simple books, which Maurice devoured with the avidity of a starving man suddenly faced with a tray of piping-hot food. What Kennedy was not able to do was to teach Maurice to speak English the way he spoke it himself, but in any case, Chevalier's subsequent unique approach to the language was to be the ticket to a fortune.

Kennedy didn't restrict himself to teaching Chevalier from books. When a sheet of music found its way into the camp in a prisoner's kit bag, he shifted his lessons from the books to the song. Maurice's eyes lit up. If the books had been a meal, the song was a feast. So much so that he now asked the organizer of the camp's next Sunday concert if he could after all join in. And it was in that dark, dank, lice-ridden hall that Maurice Chevalier sang a number in English for the first time. Using all the old mannerisms which had proved the sensation of the Paris café scene, he positively electrified Alten Grabow that night. The applause was beyond belief. British prisoners who had never heard one of their own songs put over in that way, were over-whelmed.

From then on there was no stopping him. Maurice asked Kennedy to teach him more songs, and before long a cottage industry had grown up in the camp, supplying first the English sergeant and then Maurice with new numbers which they knew he would be only too willing to sing to them the following week. In a way, Maurice was happier singing in Alten Grabow than he had been at the Folies. There wasn't the same pressure before every performance, his hands didn't get clammy at the thought of entertaining an audience, which, until he had had an opportunity of overwhelming it, was always an unknown quantity. The prisoners knew they were going to be spellbound, and it helped Maurice to be assured of the fact.

Meanwhile, Miss was trying to find a way of getting her lover out of what she still believed to be an unmitigated hell. For months, honouring her promise to Maurice, she had lived with La Louque in a village outside Paris, hoping that the serenity of the atmosphere somehow would make life more bearable for them both. Instead, they felt even worse, guilty at being free while Maurice was a captive. When Miss heard that a scheme was afoot to repatriate French prisoners in exchange for a similar number of Germans held in France, she decided the time had come to act. One requirement of the scheme was that the negotiations should be conducted in complete secrecy. What was more, if any approach were made on behalf of a particular prisoner—or if anyone were suspected of trying to organize the release of any individual—the deal would be called off. The arrangements were negotiated in Switzerland.

Miss was too impatient to allow such an important matter to be left to chance. In a long, black, shapeless dress that hid both her legs and her curves, and with no makeup on her face, she journeyed to the Swiss frontier, where, as she reported in her autobiography, she was promptly arrested while still in her nightgown. She was charged with an unlawful attempt at leaving the country. But she was lucky. She was instantly recognized by a policeman who had previously lived in her old hometown. "Why," he said, "if it isn't little Jeanne!" Her cover was blown, but she was released and managed to find her way to Geneva and the International Red Cross office where the repatriation was being organized.

There she learned that King Alfonso of Spain was in Geneva, acting as an intermediary in a new exchange of Red Cross personnel. The King had been an admirer of Mistinguett for years —rumour had it that they had more than once been lovers. She threw off any pretense at travelling incognito. She bought herself a new dress, made up her face, and asked for an audience. The King readily agreed. Once more it was rumoured that they slept together. Certainly their meeting, whether in bed or simply in the office put at the King's disposal, had its effect.

Two weeks later, twenty-six months after first being wounded, Chevalier and a group of other Red Cross personnel at Alten Grabow were called into the commandant's office. Standing next to the German colonel was the senior French doctor who was helping to arrange the repatriation scheme at the camp. The commandant looked at Chevalier and instantly recognized him.

"You are not a Red Cross man," he said. "Your name is on the list I have here from Geneva, but your records show you to be in the infantry." And then he looked closer at the now very bewildered prisoner, Chevalier. "I know you. You are a singer. I have seen you at our Sunday concerts."

"No," said the doctor. "I know this man well. He helps at the hospital." The commandant picked up a Red Cross book. It was full of first-aid hints and details about inoculations.

"Right," he said to Chevalier. "I'll now ask you some questions."

Maurice could only hope that the details he had picked up as an orderly would hold him in good stead. The German studied him, looked at the book, and then closed it again.

"Application passed!" he shouted. "Next!"

Maurice never knew what made the German colonel unbend at that moment. The fact that he did meant that he was about to be freed.

Soon after his release, reports appeared in the Paris newspapers of his incredible bravery and how he had dressed up as a Red Cross attendant specifically so that he and another *infirmier* could escape from the prisoner-of-war camp—which they did. For years the story of his displaying that courage and breaking out of the camp enclosure at risk of his life constantly resurfaced. It was picked up by *The New York Times* when Maurice first went to work in America in the late 1920s and was used as part of an interview feature about him. He never denied the tale, which showed him in such a good light.

In truth, of course, the whole experience at Alten Grabow was a nightmare, and when he was released in 1916, his instant reaction was one of intense relief, joy, and excitement. What he was not prepared for was the sense of anticlimax when the train drew up at the Gare du Nord in Paris.

Miss was waiting with La Louque on the platform. All through Maurice's imprisonment, she had watched over Mme. Chevalier as though the old lady were her own mother. Now tears were streaming down both women's faces as they saw an ashen-faced, emaciated Maurice descend from the train and walk slowly into their outstretched arms.

It was La Louque with whom Maurice went home that night. For days he shut himself away in his mother's apartment. When he did see Miss again, briefly, he told her he was still troubled by his wound—and he was; the pain would never leave him completely. He wanted to get back to work, but he was plainly not well enough to do so yet. He wanted to make love to Miss, but somehow he couldn't bring himself to do that either. When eventually they did spend a night together, it was as though their great love had never happened. For him the magic they had once experienced so perfectly together had gone, and the depression its absence caused hung heavily over him.

6.
Paris, Stay the Same

I don't sing for the old or for the young. I sing with the philosophy of my age, sing like I walk, breathe, pray. I sing to live and live to sing.

—Maurice Chevalier

Mistinguett wrote that Maurice came back from the war "without energy, means, or spirit." And she added: "What else could he do but bow to my wishes?" When she suggested he seek work in a Paris that seemed to have forgotten him all too quickly, he did so almost blindly and without bothering to care about the consequences. When she took the initiative in their lovemaking, he accepted it without questioning his own role in their lives.

It was a topsy-turvy world in which Miss seemed to be perfectly happy, hoping all the time that he was equally satisfied. She knew that he wasn't, but she said, "because he was unhappy I believed we were close to each other and that he was mine.

He had lost himself and was not prepared to do anything to get on his feet again." He was, she recognized, "limp and broken inside." Every time he tried to find work, he was told to come back again when he felt better. He knew that these were just polite words from people who had found new entertainers and who had no use for yet another war veteran. The French government showed a better sense of gratitude and timing. Early in 1917 they presented Maurice with the Croix de guerre both for his bravery under fire and for his subsequent fortitude at Alten Grabow.

A friend suggested that Maurice try to get back to work gradually, not at the Folies or at one of the top Paris cafés, but to try something smaller, in a hall that would lead him back gradually to his professional life.

So, in a tiny music hall in Montparnasse, a place which he remembered well as a popular "number two" booking before the war, he made his first appearance before an audience since Alten Grabow. While he waited in the wings, he wrote many times afterwards, he was eaten up with the kind of nervous reaction that hadn't bothered him since his first night at the Folies.

Had it not been for the orchestra striking up his initial number as he waited behind the curtain, he would have run off, never to appear in public again. But as he got through the verse and then the opening chorus, he felt better. By the time the last line of the song was on his lips, he knew he was back. Or was he? The song was greeted with only moderate applause. He told a couple of jokes. They both fell flat. Through the floodlight concentrating on his increasingly sweating forehead, he could see people moving out of their seats and walking towards the door.

It wasn't like the Folies; worse still, it wasn't like Alten Grabow either. The love of the Folies' audiences was missing; the sheer excitement that the prisoners of war had shown so emphatically was totally absent. In their place was not hostility but complete indifference. He felt rusty and sounded it. His voice was so feeble, he couldn't even reach the balcony. By the time the show was over, he felt not merely unsure of himself but totally exhausted. Had Miss and La Louque not been with him, he probably would have run away.

The pressures, it appeared, were growing insurmountable. If

a performer doesn't have an ego to sell, little else counts. The ability to work hard is terribly important, talent is absolutely vital. But without the drive and energy that only a belief in one-self can generate, an essential element is missing. The greatest talents in the world will lie dormant if their owners can't present themselves as well as a businessman selling his product. Maurice was so eaten up with depression that he could no more sell him-self than he could go back to Alten Grabow. Miss, however, worked as hard at putting him on the market as she had always sold herself.

It was Léon Volterra, who had begun his working life selling programs at the Olympia, who brought Maurice and Miss back on stage together. He had bought the Casino de Paris during the war, for what can only be described as a song, and now he was signing the pair for a show that he felt would make his theater the most exciting in Paris.

The show wasn't brilliant, but it broke the rut. When the two-week run was over, Miss and Maurice did a musical play together. For *Gobette de Paris* they had scenes specially written for them. But at first these didn't work too brilliantly.

In one scene Maurice was supposed to turn on an electric light. The trouble was that he couldn't find the switch, and in looking for it—as he described it years later—"I appeared to be scratching my bottom." He thought it would be the end of his career as a dramatic actor, but the audience liked it. They bought more tickets for future performances. At last, he had had a response that could be made to look positive. If he could make it funny one night, he told himself, he could do it again. That was when Maurice Chevalier knew he was back in business.

The Folies obviously thought so, too. They invited him back with Miss, and between them they were once more a sensation. It was news that quickly flew from one end of Paris to another. The old partnership was in full swing again.

From the Folies the couple moved on to La Cigale, where it seemed that a new Maurice took to the boards. He did at last what M. Flers had been so determined he should not do. His eccentric costume was left behind for one number, and instead, dressed completely in white, reminiscent of what he had seen in London, he and Miss danced to the new English ragtime hit, "A

Broken Doll." It was so good that people in the audience responded by dancing in the aisles. Once more, Maurice and Mistinguett looked made for each other. They were magnetic on
stage, gathering the support of their audiences as a child draws
a soft drink through a straw.

Maurice again suggested that they marry, but Miss still said
she didn't want a formal piece of paper to spoil what they
already had. Better to be tied to each other through natural
devotion than via a legal document. Yet, before long there were
new tensions between them, stresses that could be summed up
in one word—jealousy. At the Casino de Paris the "two M's" were
invited to take over the leads in the revue *Laissez le Tomber*
("Let Him Fall") from Gaby Deslys and Harry Pilcer.

It seemed like a marvellous idea; one step beyond what had
previously seemed to be the top—except that Miss was going to
have lead billing. Maurice demanded equal status on the posters
and other advertising matter. Miss dug in her heels, refused, and,
as she added in her memoirs, "the trouble started . . . our success had no doubt gone to Maurice's head a bit and he probably
thought I was trying to sabotage his performance. He stopped
calling for me at the end of the performance as he had done
every night without fail for ten years."

As to equal billing: "I couldn't grant him this. If I had done
it, the other actors would have reacted as only actors can."

For the moment he accepted the situation, if reluctantly. On
stage he and Miss dressed up as American sailors, which elicited
a marvellous reaction from the large number of U.S. troops in
the audience. It was a historic moment. For the soldiers' and
sailors' benefit, he sang in English for the first time on the professional stage. He had learned the vital lesson of matching his
material to his audience. And to this crowd of foreign service-
men in Paris he had exactly the right number: "How You Gonna
Keep 'Em Down on the Farm After They've Seen Paree?"

When years later he was as popular in America as in his homeland, he joked: "It must have been funny to hear me sing that
song because I had then a very strong French accent. Now, I
hope you have observed, I speak almost as if I am born here!"

A note appeared in the program of the Casino show aimed specifically at the men in uniform who had bought tickets: "M. Chevalier himself has served as a soldier and has been honourably discharged. If he is now playing while you are fighting, it is simply because he has already done his job."

The success of "How You Gonna Keep 'Em . . ." prompted him to decide to learn other English lyrics. He found it all engrossing, but there were limits as to how far he was prepared to go. When Elsie Janis, the American star who had established "Give Me the Moonlight, Give Me the Girl" as her own theme song, asked him to star in a London show with her, he hastily said, "No. My English is just not good enough."

But if his fighting the Germans had ended, his war with Mistinguett, a love war in the truest sense, was just beginning. Chevalier said of her: "She just thought of me as a foil for her talent. She never thought of me as an equal on the stage or as a rival. This saddened me because we could never see a solution to the problem. I loved Miss but I adored my profession, my independence."

Even now they talked of marriage, and again the talk turned to nothing. "He could never understand why I refused to marry him," Miss said in her book.

Maurice told a friend: "If you get involved with her, she will offer you pity, but it will be *la pitié dangereuse* [dangerous pity]. You will have no life of your own. She is so possessive." To attempt to marry her, he conceded years afterwards, "would be to limit her loyalties, and to bind them in matrimony would have been as unnatural as trying to wed the wind."

There were jealousies that were not confined to the stage, although it was very plain that Miss felt eaten up inside at his success. In 1918 every triumph for thirty-year-old Maurice seemed to spell disaster for forty-nine-year-old Mistinguett. She was still fantastically popular; her body and face still looked as fresh and young as ever. Yet she worried that her day was over. In her show she sang "Mon Homme" ("My Man"), a doleful ballad that would before long be taken over by Fanny Brice. Miss sang it as though she were already mourning Maurice's fast and inevitable disappearance from her life. "I feel no resentment against Maurice," she wrote later. "I wish him no harm. But I think he harmed me. Because I loved him as and when I did, he forced me to look for love in the eyes of the public, to seek my own truth in the music hall."

By this time, although officially still living with his mother, Maurice had taken a small flat in the center of Paris, which was—or so his story went for La Louque's consumption—more convenient at the end of a long night at the theater. It was also a perfect love nest to enjoy with Miss in their better moments. Miss decided—without letting Maurice in on the fact—to redecorate the apartment. So that she could plan precisely the colour and fabric schemes she was going to use, she took an afternoon off to go down there to study the layout. What she discovered was a pink chemise, a pair of lace-trimmed knickers, and a couple of silk stockings casually littering the floor. They were not hers.

She didn't tell Maurice about her discovery. She simply opened the door and walked out. That night she was ice cold to him, but still she said nothing. As they parted at the stage door that night, she added: "In future, only come to my apartment if you see a red handkerchief out on the balcony!"

Maurice took it as a joke, but Miss was deadly serious. If she didn't want to see him, she simply failed to exhibit the handkerchief and refused to allow him in. She never told him why.

Maurice claimed, of course, that a lot of the girls whom he found hard to resist forced themselves on him totally against his will. Sometimes they even made public spectacles of themselves.

While he was playing at the Casino, a seventeen-year-old redhead grabbed hold of Maurice one night as he left the theater and pressed herself against him so awkwardly that he tripped. In a newspaper article published many years later, he said she was "unfortunately not very pretty."

Perhaps that was why he didn't react more favourably. She was holding on to his hand so tightly that a group of friends nearby had to drag her away. "None of you can do anything," she called as Maurice got into his car. "I love him and I know he loves me. It's fate."

The next Sunday—"she must have been busy during the week," Maurice said, laughing as he told the story—the same girl, now distinctly dishevelled, stood in front of the stage while Maurice was performing a song-and-dance number, and sang the song with him. The audience thought it was terribly funny. Maurice was less than amused. At the end of the song—for some reason or other, no one had thought of doing it earlier—four men hauled the girl out through the auditorium and across the promenade section while she cried: "You can't keep me away from him. You can try, but you won't succeed. He is mine."

And she continued to press her suit. She found her way to Maurice's dressing room. He ordered her out. Again she waited for him as he got into his car. This time Maurice thought he would be friendly. There were too many people watching out for him to risk causing a scene. So he held his hand out towards her. She grabbed it so strongly that it felt as though his fingers were being crushed by a pair of pincers.

"You're completely twisted," Maurice shouted. She threw him a kiss and called him *tu*, which made it seem as though they really were lovers and that he was merely trying to avoid the public scandal of revealing their affair.

"This is absurd, *chéri*," she cried. "We're not children. Stop playing hide-and-seek."

After that she disappeared. Then a few weeks later she was waiting for him by the elevator outside his apartment. That was when Maurice lost his temper. He shouted at her, he said, "like an Austrian yodeller," and chased her as she raced down the stairs, four at a time. Down the street to the next corner they ran, Maurice shouting abuse at her as he pursued the chase.

Suddenly, he realized that he was making an idiot of himself and providing free entertainment for the people staring out of their windows. Any minute he would probably be taken to the neighbourhood *gendarmerie*. He stopped in his tracks. A few meters down the road, the girl laughed.

"My poor friend," she called. "You're completely mad and you've forced me never to see you again."

Maurice now was not the least reluctant to try to make a show-business stand without Miss. If only there were an opportunity to do so. It was while pondering this point that he decided to get in touch with Elsie Janis.

"Is your offer still open?" he asked in a letter sent after yet another fight with Miss.

It was; Miss Janis had checked with Sir Alfred Butt, the

proprietor of the Palace Theater in London, and he was offering a hundred pounds a week—a huge sum in postwar England—for Maurice to take over the lead from Owen Nares in his show *Hello America*. Elsie thought Maurice could add a special sparkle to her show and provide what she called "Gallic charm," something no Englishman could possibly have.

He accepted the invitation like a child grabbing a new teddy bear. It was what he wanted and it offered him a chance he would take close to his heart. At the back of his mind was an important consideration—Miss had always been the bigger star, but her success had never really travelled farther than the borders of Paris. *He* was going to be international. Simply to be told he was wanted—and being in a foreign country—did much to restore his ego, which was once more fully inflated. Arriving at Victoria Station, however, was a different story entirely. People talk about having butterflies; Chevalier had pigeons pounding their wings in his stomach. At the theater he felt even worse. As he stood in the wings ready to go on that first night, sweat beaded every exposed part of his body. But as the orchestra struck up his number, Cole Porter's "On the Level, You're a Little Devil," he bounced into life as even he had never done before.

His style was unique—a song linked with a monologue in which he appeared to be arguing with himself, but always with the chuckle which was already being established as an identification point. It provided an intimacy and a charm that were infectious. One British critic commented: "Monsieur Chevalier is well worth watching."

Maurice succeeded because he thought of the audience as a single person: someone sitting two or three rows from the front on whom he could "home in." Everybody in the audience saw what he was doing, but each of them was sure it was to him or her he was showing his affection.

"I enjoy rather to feel that I am in a room with friends whom I like and who like me," he later wrote.

To take up the British critic's words, it wasn't difficult to keep watching him.

Miss was convinced Elsie Janis was at the center of a new love affair with Maurice. Miss spoke of her rival with a bitter cattiness: "She is a tall, chilly-looking blonde. He must have had a sort of refrigerated passion for her."—and also for the English. But Chevalier didn't really feel comfortable on the English stage. He said baldly: "I am not in my shoes." Even so, the show ran for three months and after that, Miss reported sourly: "He came back with English manners, English chic, and two trunks full of Savile Row suits."

He also brought back *Hello America*—a French version of the show, which opened and closed almost before the paste fixing the show's posters to the wall had dried. Nobody blamed Maurice for the failure. When the show ended for the last time, he was immediately invited back to the Casino for a new production with Miss. But they only did one number as a double act.

The "two M's" quarreled and haggled. Maurice once more demanded equal billing, and this time the management agreed. When Miss heard that she stormed out and announced that she wouldn't come back until the theater dropped this stupid arrangement. The management stood firm. Maurice would get his star status.

Miss walked out of the Casino.

For the first time Maurice Chevalier's name would be in lights outside a theater—alone.

7.
Beloved Vagabond

He has a unique magnetism. A trivial song with him can become a gem.

—Charles Boyer

There was nothing now to stop Maurice from being a solo hit —except that he took Miss's departure badly. He was headlining an entirely new show at the Casino, but he couldn't put his mind to it. He felt ill at ease, insecure, almost as though the management were making sport with him. There had to be a new ingredient, he decided. People had been telling him for a long time to make better use of his finest asset—his appearance. Now nothing was going to stop him taking their advice. Gaby Deslys, for one, had never been able to understand why he took shelter beneath all that makeup. "Maurice," she said to him once, "you're not ugly. Why do you make yourself up to be so ugly to sing? Why don't you dress properly?"

So for his second show at the Casino, he all but abandoned the low comedian's baggy trousers and the red nose. He deliberately kept them for only a couple of routines and then just because people expected it of him. In one number he wore a smart brown tailcoat. In another, he put on the garb that was soon to become the trademark of Fred Astaire—a top hat, a white tie, a pair of gloves the colour of butter, and a suit of tails.

The people out front loved it and so did the management. His success meant that Paris was talking not only about Chevalier, but also about their theater. Seeing how the wind was blowing after the second night's performance, the manager called to see his star.

"You have your contract, monsieur?" he asked formally.

Chevalier handed over the document that was still in his dressing-room drawer. The manager looked at the paper, took it firmly in his hand, tore it up, and threw it into the wastepaper basket. Maurice was aghast. But before he could say anything, a new paper was handed to him.

"Look at the bottom line," the manager instructed. That was the part of the document which stated Maurice's fee. The old, torn-up contract had stated that he would earn 600 francs a night. The new one read "1,000 francs." It also pointed out that the following year he would be paid 1,500 francs for a third Casino show.

Maurice now had an all-consuming ambition, not just to maintain the consistent standard he was showing in the second Casino show, but to be absolutely positive that he would do still better in the third. When he retired to his dressing room after an exhausting evening on stage, it was to plan what the next show would be like. He was happy to accept that his days as a low comedian were over, but he wasn't sure that he liked the starched formality of the top hat and tails. Somehow it didn't really suit the lad from Ménilmontant. He didn't feel entirely at home in that outfit; it almost made him feel a fraud.

One night at the end of the show, he pondered the point in his dressing room as he changed from his stage clothes into the dinner jacket he was going to wear at a party. Wouldn't that look better on stage? It hadn't been done in France before, but the manager agreed it might be worth an experiment in the last few nights of the 1921 season.

"But you'll need a hat," he said.

Maurice knew that. No performer worth his makeup tube would ever consider being seen on stage without a hat to go with his suit. A topper perhaps? No, it just didn't go with the dinner jacket.

The manager suggested a bowler. Maurice tried one. It was all wrong. Much too funereal. "I was something so terrible," he wrote in his autobiography, "that I closed my eyes quickly to forget what I saw there in the mirror."

"A felt hat?" he asked himself, or a flat cloth cap. But the latter was "too bold, too rough. There was no entente between that cap and the dress suit."

The hat was a problem he took with him on his next trip to London. There he met a couple of girls he had dated in Paris, saw all the big musical shows and the top variety turns, and paid the now customary visit to Hawes and Curtis in Savile Row. He asked everybody for advice, but nobody came up with an idea that matched his needs. And need was precisely what he felt. His hat would be the prop on which he would hang his next show, and in his mind its importance was escalating to the point where it was becoming an obsession.

No ideas came to him. But then outside a theater on his last evening, he saw a young blade—leaning against a wall, talking to a girl. He wore a dinner jacket. And a straw hat—a boater, as the shallow, narrow-brimmed headgear with the colorful ribbon was called.

"I saw that fellow," Chevalier told me, "and I thought he looked so smart. I said to myself, 'That's it. That's it.' Once more, it all goes back to London."

Back in Paris the straw hat was not quite the instant success he had expected it to be. He was faced, as he wrote in a *Saturday Evening Post* article, with "a silence which freezes my bones. I look for that smiling face to which I may talk and in all the world there is no smiling face. There are only puzzled faces, impatient faces, cold faces. Thinking to soften their hearts, I take off my straw hat. How I blame myself! How I wish for that fine old costume in which to hide. But to wish is no use. I am here. I must sing."

And that was when it happened. "They are puzzled still, but they are no longer impatient and, best of all, they are no longer bored . . . I see that the faces grow brighter, and presently someone calls my name. That is like a signal."

Maurice then took his straw hat into an operetta called *Dédé* at the Bouffes Parisiens Theater. It quickly became such an integral part of his personality that it had to be written into a book show, which was itself important. For the first time, Maurice was required to act as well as sing and dance throughout a show. The operetta had a running story about a shoe shop, and Chevalier found himself learning lines that were part of a continuing story instead of for a couple of sketches.

Most important of all, after the huge success of the Casino ventures, the fact that Maurice was billed in his own show meant that he was without doubt a performer of the first magnitude. The Paris newspapers were constantly referring to him as the top star in the country.

It wasn't easy to settle into the routine at the Bouffes Parisiens. For the first four or five days, he once more felt himself floundering before packed houses. He hit out with his acting in the same way he always had with his songs, and it plainly wasn't right for what was a play with music. But after a few days it all seemed to fit in beautifully. Maurice Chevalier had learned a new lesson.

Dédé became the show that Paris theatergoers talked about more than any others in the capital. It was the one production that newly arriving British and American tourists just had to see. Listening to Maurice singing the very naughty "Je m'Donne" ("I Give My All") spiced any evening on the town. He was playing opposite Alice Cocéa, who stood on Maurice's toes as he danced.

His affair with Mistinguett had cooled significantly, to the point where contact seemed to be confined to arguments between them as to who was the bigger star. Matters were not helped by his continuing dalliance with other women, each of whom, he claimed, made his stage performances even better. But if they spent more than one or two nights with him, they had to contend with two additional facets of his character—his preoccupation with his mother and his growing reputation for stinginess.

Stories appeared in newspapers and magazines which took the latter to ridiculous extremes. One widely published account alleged that Maurice had an agreement with a beautiful young girl that he would go up to her apartment only by a prearranged signal—when she dropped a five-franc piece out of her window. On one occasion he took an hour to respond to the call. "Where were you?" she asked. "I lost the coin and was on my hands and knees looking for it," he was supposed to have answered.

Few girls were immune to his charms—particularly those in his shows. Years later one of them chuckled as she told me how she and a friend considered themselves rivals for his affections. Each thought she had found the way to get him on her own. On one celebrated occasion, Mlle. A. slid through the inner door of his dressing room at the precise moment that Mlle. B. tiptoed into the outer doorway. Both were then confronted with the spectacle of a third girl helping him out of his trousers.

There were other women in the show who at first hid their feelings. One was a leading dancer and singer called Yvonne Vallée, who later said she fell in love with him the moment he first sang to her in the show. But Yvonne and Maurice spent very little time with each other off stage, and there was no way he could have known the sentiments she felt towards him. Besides, Maurice was more interested in his career.

He enjoyed his status as a celebrity. When a murderer called Dédé was sentenced to death by guillotine, Maurice sat in the press enclosure to watch. A journalist friend had suggested it might make good—if macabre—publicity for the show, *Dédé*. It was an experience that shook Chevalier considerably—for, as he later wrote, he knew the about-to-be-decapitated prisoner. He was a man who had gone to the café-concerts where the juvenile Maurice played. Dédé had told him how good he thought his performance had been at a time when others weren't so considerate.

While *Dédé* ran and ran, the Paris film studios were courting Maurice, anxious to have his name on their roster of stars. In his first eighteen months in *Dédé*, from the end of 1921 until 1923, he made three more comedy shorts for French studios: *Le Mauvais Garçon, Le Match Criqui-Ledoux* (in which Chevalier was able to put his boxing experience to good use), and

Gonzague. Douglas Fairbanks, Senior, and Mary Pickford came to the Bouffes Parisiens and were thrilled by the Chevalier they saw on stage, although they had probably not watched his films. Both of them spent hours trying to persuade Maurice to come to Hollywood to make "real" feature pictures for their three-year-old United Artists studio.

"I can't," he said again and again. "I'm not right for you yet." They tried to explain the fact that the still-silent cinema was the main international icebreaker—stars from a dozen countries had made America a neutral base from which their talents could explode around the world. But he couldn't be persuaded. Maurice was frightened stiff of landing flat on his face.

If Douglas Fairbanks didn't convince him to make a movie, he did manage to persuade Maurice to go to America. A few days after returning to the States, Fairbanks cabled to say that he had the offer of a deal with the top American impresario, Charles Dillingham, to bring *Dédé* over to the States.

That idea was more than tempting to Maurice; he accepted the offer. He was relieved to hear he wasn't going to have to perform in New York until after the Paris show finished. Since everyone knew that *Dédé* was booked so solid at the Bouffes Parisiens it could run there for another year, it was easy enough to put off the moment of departure and all the risks of a new venture.

When the Paris theaters closed down for their summer break in 1922, Maurice took off for New York to spy out the land. He took Miss with him in an effort to patch things up with her. The only trouble was that Miss brought along the person of Mr. Earl Leslie for the ride, in addition to a dozen cabin trunks. She let it be known that Leslie was the important new love in her life. Whether she really loved him as passionately as she had loved Chevalier is open to doubt, but at the time she paraded him in front of Maurice's nose at every opportunity. Maurice was not in the least bit pleased to see the way they behaved together, slinking off arm-in-arm to Miss's cabin on board ship and then, once installed in New York, into her hotel room.

In a way, though, he was even more shocked by what he witnessed on the stages of Broadway. It convinced him he wasn't yet ready for America. Stars like Al Jolson—at the peak of his career electrifying audiences in *Bombo* with new hits like "April

Showers" and "California Here I Come"—totally frightened him. Chevalier left Jolson's 59th Street Theater, at the corner of Seventh Avenue, shaking. "I think I ought to get right back on the boat," he said only half-jokingly to the man the show-business community knew as Jolie. But Maurice told me that he liked to think that he got from Jolson some of the punch that he tried to introduce in his own French way. "And from Sophie Tucker . . . Sophie, a little fat, yes, but so attractive."

The American songs were catchier than any he heard in Paris. The American voices were better. Even American jokes, he decided, were brighter and livelier than anything on the French stage—although he couldn't always understand what the comics were saying.

His mind was made up again. There could be no question of his starring in *Dédé* on Broadway. He met Dillingham—who with Ziegfeld and the Shubert Brothers was one of the top three Broadway producers—and told him that the deal was off. But instead of being relieved at knowing that he wouldn't have to do *Dédé* in New York, Chevalier was only more depressed. It gave him new cause to fight with Miss and Earl Leslie. Before very long, every member of the party seemed to be fighting, too, and when it came time to catch the boat back to France, no one was talking to anyone else. On the voyage back Maurice spent most of the time in the bar, drinking Cognac.

When the ship reached Southampton, Miss, with Leslie at her heels, walked down the gangplank and finally out of Maurice's life; he sailed on to Cherbourg.

8.
Love in the Afternoon

I've always dodged tragedies and my good sense has been a shade stronger than my passion.

—Maurice Chevalier

Miss wasn't surprised at the death of what Maurice later described as "not only a partnership, but a long love affair that was one of the most beautiful moments of my life." The lovers had become competitors and this proved to be a more important factor in their relationship than their lovemaking ever could have been. As Chevalier told me: "We were both serving the same kind of drinks. You understand? She was jealous of me because I was younger. She could not bear to grow old. So we had to part." To succeed they each had to marry their audiences. To Maurice his relationship with Miss always had the taste of an extramarital affair, exciting but inconvenient.

Miss was not reluctant to put her feelings on record. "Everything was black for me," she said soon afterwards. "Even the sun." She later wrote: "In our oasis of happiness, the grass was artificial, the palm trees were mounted on a ramp. The summer skies were made of canvas and the sea of painted cardboard. But there's nothing like painted canvas and cardboard to see if one has loved or not . . . But Chevalier, I loved him too much to want to understand him."

What really bothered Chevalier was the nagging question of whether he really understood himself. At thirty-four, he was consumed by the fear that he would never remember his lines for the next performance of *Dédé*. He even hired a man to act as a prompter. The fear was totally irrational but quite real. As the show neared the end of its second year—the time when he might have been thinking about opening in the Broadway edition of *Dédé*—he was more demoralized than before.

La Louque once again tried to offer him support. But he didn't think she could possibly understand. He tried other women, but was dissatisfied with what they offered and what he accepted. He drank heavily. Once more he turned to drugs. He reached the stage when he couldn't walk straight, his head swam, and nothing made him feel better.

He didn't realize that perhaps he had been merely overworking. He starred in *Dédé* by night and in a new three-reel version of his own early film short, *Par Habitude*, by day. It was all too much. By the time the picture was finished and *Dédé* had completed its two-year run, he was displaying alarming tendencies. It wasn't just the drink, the drugs, and the women; he was saying strange things to La Louque and to people whom he would befriend in maudlin moments.

"*Maman*," he told a very frightened Mme. Chevalier, "I'm going away." To Yvonne Vallée, who had by then become a very firm shoulder on which Maurice could cry huge tears, he said, "I'm going to move my mother out of the city and into the country. Then I will go out and shoot myself."

It was no idle threat—he had bought a pistol with which he could accomplish the deed. But his friends were closer to him than he imagined. A couple of them arranged for a doctor to meet Maurice at the theater, and it was to him that he poured out all his anxieties. He broke down completely as he unburdened himself. He was a failure as a performer. He knew that his success was going to turn into a flop. He was useless as a lover. He had nothing to offer as a human being.

He plainly needed instant attention. The doctor arranged for Maurice to be admitted immediately to the clinic run by a Dr. Dubois at Saujon. He was driven there by Yvonne.

At the clinic Maurice rested, but he grew even more morose. When Yvonne went to visit him, he talked frequently of somehow getting hold of another gun and this time succeeding in shooting himself.

Gradually, however, Yvonne managed to talk him out of it. She wasn't the sophisticated girl-about-town that Miss had always been. She would never be a great star, but she could provide exactly the kind of comfort Maurice needed. When she told him: "Maurice, you have to get to work again," there could be no suggestion that she was also offering professional rivalry.

She finally talked him into the idea of entertaining again. Not in the center of Paris, but in a tiny obscure hall somewhere; a place where he could relax and not worry about losing his self-confidence or forgetting his lines. No critics would be there. No one would ever hear about it. But of course it could never be as simple as that.

Dr. Dubois found a hall near the clinic that matched Maurice's needs perfectly. It was tiny and rundown, with green paint peeling off the walls. The regulars who went there for weekly concerts were totally unschooled in the arts of theatrical entertainment. Most of them had never seen a Paris show in their lives.

It all seemed totally removed from reality. The week before the show Maurice rehearsed in front of the long mirror in his private room. As the day of the concert drew near, he became consumed by panic. He couldn't possibly succeed. People would hear about him. He would become a public laughingstock.

But at Yvonne's bidding he agreed to press on. Finally, the night of the show arrived. A dour-looking Maurice walked arm-in-arm with Yvonne through the clinic. As they approached the *concierge*'s desk, the man on duty called over to him. "Monsieur Chevalier," he said, pleasantly, "I have a letter for you."

It was the sort of note that people with a particularly twisted frame of mind sign "A well-wisher," which, of course, says precisely the opposite of what they actually do wish. This missive enclosed the latest of the thousand or so press notices which were by now regularly charting the Chevalier career. It read: "The favourite topic of backstage conversation remains the sad story behind Maurice Chevalier's absence from the Paris stage this season. According to sources that should know, it comes down to this: One of the capital's greatest stars, apparently destroyed by too much wine, women, and the worst indulgence of them all, drugs, is now locked away—a wretched, finished hulk, whose mind is as lost as his memory. The talk is that many friends who have made the long journey to visit him found it was a waste of effort, for he neither recognized nor remembered them. The sad conclusion is that the audiences that loved him will have to live on memories. Chevalier is finished. He will never return."

The ferocity of the newspaper story made him as determined to succeed as he had been when making his debut at the café-concert amateur night. Except that he had felt excited that time in 1900 when he took those first faltering steps. Now he was frightened, more so than he had been in the ditch at the Battle of Cutry. No theater anywhere had ever meant more to him. No show had ever been more vital to his future life.

He got through to his audience that night without making a fool of himself, but without any of his old verve either.

The more nervous he was, the more determined he became to triumph over those nerves, and to know his limitations. He was certain he was going to get better, but he was equally sure he was not going back to the Paris stage. Not yet.

He next found himself a little movie house which he knew also offered live entertainment. "Would you let me perform here?" he asked the manager, like a keen amateur waiting for another break that would project him towards the big time. The manager couldn't believe the question he was asked. When he was sure that it really was Maurice Chevalier standing in front of his desk—and moderately sane, too—the manager fell over himself to accept. That night of the show, Maurice was a great deal better than he had been the week before.

He went on to Marseilles. He wanted to see how much punishment he could take. He took and he gave. After only a few minutes on stage at the music hall, he had taken over. For the first time since going to Saujon, he felt in charge.

Now he was ready for Paris again. The Empire music hall on the avenue Wagram had once nagged him for months to do a season there, and he was glad to accept. On the Empire stage he sang and he danced and he let them see his impression of a man taking a dog for a walk. Chevalier was back.

Yvonne was at the Empire, too. Together they sang "La Petite Bête Qui Monte." The audience greeted them ecstatically. Now he was ready to move on to other, bigger, and better things. If he could survive a new opening at the Casino, his comeback would be an accomplished fact. They were only too delighted to have him. Indeed, people came from all over France to be there when he opened; some, no doubt, in the hope of a vicarious thrill as he crumpled in the spotlight. American impresarios and their representatives in stiff white shirtfronts were sitting in the orchestra stalls.

Maurice knew all that, and knowing it only made the minutes waiting for his cue seem interminable. Finally the moment came for his opening music. After the band had played the first chords, Maurice should have thundered onto the stage to announce firmly and definitely that he had returned. But there was nothing from his corner of the stage.

The band struck up again. Still nothing. The audience was becoming restive. The manager of the theater was panic-stricken as Maurice gave a perfect impression of Lot's wife about to become a pillar of salt. Maurice was completely rigid.

A third time, the orchestra struck the chord. At last, there was movement by the closed curtain. The spotlight played on the drapes and in the center could now be seen—a straw hat. The audience roared.

He went through his old numbers with all the former excitement. As he stomped on stage, the floorboards reverberated to the rhythm of the audience's applause. Maurice's duets with Yvonne were as instantly recognizable a part of his stage act as were the old routines with Mistinguett. Except that now there was no doubt who was the big star. Yvonne was never more than an appendage to Maurice. The most popular routine was a variation on the classic "Mr. Gallagher and Mr. Shean" number which had had such a huge success on the American vaudeville circuit:

Et c'est vrai, M'sieur Chevalier?
Absolument, Mam'selle Vallée.

Yvonne was now by his side most evenings when he left the theater, but she wouldn't let it be known publicly that they were having an affair. Whenever Maurice proposed to her, she turned him down. Perhaps she didn't want to get involved in the kind of competitive event his romance with Mistinguett had been. And, even if she could brace herself to sharing him with other women—nothing he ever said could give her the idea that he would now be monogamous—La Louque would be a different matter. Yvonne worried that Maurice was only happy when he was working: Every moment away from the spotlight—whether while walking in the street, dining in a restaurant, or making love—seemed no more than an interlude in time, and wasted time at that. It wasn't terribly pleasant to feel merely part of an intermission. What *was* exciting was the sure knowledge that after virtually every performance, wherever it might be, Maurice was more important than he had been before it began. When King Alfonso of Spain—the very person responsible for his repatriation from Alten Grabow—issued a command for Maurice to sing before him, it seemed no more than another step forward. For the King and his English Queen, Maurice sang a song that soon had the French Ambassador to Madrid in a tizzy.

"*Elle avait . . . de tous petits petons, Valentine, Valentine,*" Maurice began. So far so good; then, as he later recalled in *Maurice Chevalier's Paris*, the Ambassador's face reddened and he shuffled in an agony of embarrassment as Maurice continued:

Elle avait de tous petits tétons . . .
Que je tâtais à tâtons . . .

Maurice later translated the lyric for the benefit of an American film producer:

She had tiny little tootsies
Did Valentine, my Valentine.

And she had tiny little titties
Which I tickled with my mitties,
Valentine, Valentine . . .

The Ambassador anticipated the breaking of diplomatic relations, at least. He approached the King in trepidation, but Alfonso laughed. "Ask Monsieur Chevalier to come to me," he told the still apoplectic Ambassador.

Maurice moved reluctantly towards the royal presence.

"We enjoyed your performance enormously," said the King. And to prove it, he handed Maurice a solid-silver cigarette case.

"Valentine" would henceforth always be associated with the name Maurice Chevalier, and would be the tune the band struck up whenever he went on stage. It was the song every imitator of Chevalier would use as an instant identification symbol—especially if he could manage to make "Valentine" sound more like "Val*een*-teenah."

Maurice's English translation, incidentally, continued:

She had a tiny little chin
Did Valentine,
Ah Valentine.
And besides her little feet
Her little tits,
Her little chin,
She was curly as a lamb.

The American film industry, for whom he translated it, decided to leave the song in its more innocent-sounding French original.

It seemed that Chevalier could do no wrong. After three different shows at the Casino, he at last succumbed to an approach from London. In May 1927 he opened in *Whitebirds* at His Majesty's Theater. The show cost £28,000 to put on, including Maurice's salary of £500 a week, which the management proceeded to use to its own advantage. He was billed as "The world's highest-paid star," which even at that time probably would not have withstood too close an examination.

Maurice was shrewd about money and was equally perceptive about the sort of show *Whitebirds* was going to be. Lou Leslie, the producer, insisted that in the second half he return to his theatrical roots and take part in an acrobatic routine. Of course, it would prove that Maurice was a very wide-ranging, versatile entertainer. But he worried it might also ruin the debonair image his tuxedo and straw hat had helped create for him.

His feelings of foreboding were not unusual for him. This time, however, he had good reason. He decided to take out an insurance policy: He insisted that his first three-month's salary check be paid straight into his own French bank account—before opening night.

It was a wise move indeed. *Whitebirds* opened without the second half being properly rehearsed. To a perfectionist like Chevalier this was tantamount to making a public announcement that it was all pretty lousy. To make things worse, the first half didn't finish before 10:45 P.M., and by the time the show was finally over, it was 2:30 the following morning. During the long drawn-out proceedings, the theater emptied noticeably. The few people who remained to the end grew at first restless and then ever increasingly hostile. Not even a master of audience manipulation like Chevalier could control the situation.

But there were lighter moments during the show's run. It was on this trip that Maurice met George Bernard Shaw. The playwright had previously sent word to Paris that he would love to see him on his next visit to London.

Shaw was in a cantankerous, awkward mood. "What do you do, Chevalier?" he asked.

"I sing," Maurice answered, not concealing his chagrin at the Irishman's audacity.

"Sing, eh?" said Shaw, allowing his brogue to play with the word. "What da ya sing? Opera . . . ? I don't know what kind of singing you do."

Maurice's lower lip was pouting angrily now. But, as though calming an audience in an old-fashioned café-concert, he rallied. "Now you have put me at your ease," he said in reply. "I've never read any of your books either. So we can talk even."

The rest of the chat went swimmingly, although neither of them offered the other anything that might resemble praise, or even the merest suggestion that he was a great fan (except of himself). *Whitebirds* could possibly have done with a few kind words from Mr. Shaw. Within a couple of weeks, the show had taken a nose dive, and Maurice and Yvonne, still refusing his offers of marriage, returned to Paris.

Maurice now had a new home. He had bought a house on the Riviera, a large château-like structure at La Bocca near Cannes, which he thought was just the sort of place where he and his mother could relax—a fitting holiday residence for the old lady from Ménilmontant. Maurice called the house La Louque.

Then, on October 10, 1927, in a little church at Vaucresson, near Saint-Cloud, Maurice and Yvonne were at last married. That night they moved into a villa at Saint-Cloud, which the couple called "Quand On Est Deux" ("When One Is Two") after one of their most popular duets. It sounded like a good omen.

But if either Maurice or Yvonne ever thought that the legalization of their relationship would make any difference to their lives, both soon realized it was merely an illusion.

The most important woman in Maurice's life remained La Louque. Yvonne simply could not live up to the standards Maurice believed the older Mme. Chevalier had set. Consciously or subconsciously, openly or unspoken, he compared Yvonne with La Louque and found her lacking. The marriage never stood a chance—even if the only problem had been that he continued to go to bed with other girls. Hardest of all for Yvonne, however, was the fact that show business always took precedence over her and her feelings.

In the summer of 1927 the Keith-Albee offices announced that Maurice would make a tour of their U.S. theater circuit the following spring. But when it finally came to signing the contract, the old uncertainty returned. He couldn't bring himself to go through with it and bowed out. It was a hard decision, but Yvonne, despite her husband's usual attitude toward her, always tried to give him comfort. She told him he was right and that he should "never regret saying no." It seemed good advice.

For a time Maurice played in a revue with Dranem, the comedian who had been such an influence on his early years. Yvonne had a part in the show, too. But before long the two men fell out and Maurice left the cast, taking his wife with him.

Despite all the problems, there were moments in those early

days when the couple believed they were very much in love. As a complement to Chevalier's own style, Yvonne was probably very good for him. Certainly there were times when she brought him great happiness, and never more so than when she announced she was pregnant. The Chevaliers planned their nursery down to the finest detail, and looked forward confidently to the future of their son and heir.

Their joy was to be short-lived. Their baby—the son for whom they had hoped—was stillborn.

Maurice was inconsolable. However, he had his work to pull him through, and now it was more important to him than ever before. Yvonne didn't want to go back to the stage. Her convalescence was lengthy and painful. Before long their friends saw her drifting ever more into the background of her restless husband's life. He was much more interested in the people who came to see him at the theater. If they were from the world of show business, so much the better. Chevalier was always ready to talk shop, to discuss the prospect of a new deal.

One night Irving Thalberg, the whiz-kid head of production at MGM, came around to the dressing room with his wife, Norma Shearer. Maurice had heard of Miss Shearer, of course. You couldn't be involved in the world of entertainment without knowing the name of the most glamorous actress in movies. But Thalberg?

"I can't really see these people," he told his manager when he heard that they wanted more than just a polite chat after the show.

He admired Norma Shearer, but that was no reason to be bored by her unknown husband. But the manager prevailed, and after the other guests who always flocked into his dressing room had left, Maurice allowed the American couple to stay and talk.

"I would like you to make a test for me and, if we're both happy with it, come to Hollywood to make pictures," said Thalberg.

"For you?" Maurice asked, straining to be polite. His manager took Chevalier aside and pointed out precisely how important Thalberg was. But, as he recalled in a *Photoplay* interview five years later, Thalberg's suggestion hardly endeared the producer to him.

"I do not make tests," he said. "I have made my reputation. I have made many films in France."

But times were changing, as Thalberg pointed out. Al Jolson had consigned the silent movie to the scrap heap with a single line of dialogue in *The Jazz Singer*. Nobody had expected him to do more than just sing a few songs in an otherwise silent film. But Jolson couldn't be confined to a set of rules drawn up by anyone else, and while the sound equipment was switched on, he had adlibbed a line before singing "Toot, Toot, Tootsie." The result was a revolution. Everybody wanted talking films and all the studios needed to recruit top-flight entertainers to make them.

How would Chevalier fare before the camera and microphone combination? Not even MGM was prepared to take the risk without being sure of the answer. Maurice finally agreed to take a test, on condition that he could keep the negative.

9.
I'd Rather Be Rich

Outside of Lafayette, you're the best thing to come out of France.

—Al Jolson

Within a day of seeing the printed test, Thalberg was once more in Chevalier's dressing room—this time with an offer of $5,000 a week to make a film for the studio that was going to specialize in musicals. If the slogan hadn't yet been coined, Thalberg and Louis B. Mayer were already contemplating good reasons to make the company's initials stand for Makers of Good Musicals.

Maurice was not as forthcoming with his acceptance as Thalberg had been with his offer. After all, Hollywood had been chasing him for a long time, and he was used to resisting the eloquent promises of Hollywood producers. He had to see the test for himself. And having seen it, he wanted a second opinion.

Douglas Fairbanks was back in Paris, and Maurice could think of no one better to ask, "without keeding," as Maurice said—or so Fairbanks later reported—while he pleaded for an honest judgment.

"I think it's great," Fairbanks said after studying the print. "Great. Without 'keeding.' " Then, speaking from some experience both of the movie world and of his French friend, he added: "Stop thinking you're not good enough. You're good. You're fine. Sign your contract and get over there. They'll eat you up." Which was precisely what had frightened Chevalier so much when he was approached before. He still feared the American critics would not recognize his talent.

When Thalberg called Maurice from Baden-Baden the following day, he hoped for a "yes" and expected a "no." What he got was a "maybe." And a firm refusal of the financial reward offered for his services. The mogul's offer, quickly translated into francs, worked out at precisely half of what Maurice was now getting for his Paris show. "You can't expect me, monsieur," he said, "to leave Paris, keep my house running here, look after my wife and my mother, and go to California for half of what I am getting here in France." Thalberg was off by $5,000 a week, but he was used to dealing with such matters. He had faced them since he first stepped into one of the oak-panelled studio boardrooms.

"I can't pay you what you earn in Paris," he replied, pleading in the way that his boss, Louis B. Mayer, had taught him. He did not, however, attempt to shed any of the tears which used to drip down Mayer's face like rain at the merest suggestion of disappointment. "I know you're great. You know you're great. All of France knows that you are great . . ." Then, after the big buildup, the less-than-gentle letdown, "But America doesn't yet know *how* great you are. No Hollywood star ever received the sort of salary you are demanding without . . ." Thalberg struggled to find a way of sidestepping the situation with dignity and without Chevalier hanging up on him, "without first . . . er . . . proving yourself." He didn't know enough of Chevalier's personality to realize that that was precisely what worried Maurice most.

"Then, monsieur," Maurice said, "I must decline your offer." He felt beautifully composed. "I thank you for your kindness, but I will stay where I am. I do not bargain with you. I do not try to get you to lift your price. But I tell you simply that I cannot afford to take less money from you than I now earn. If you cannot afford to give it to me, then we part friends."

Thalberg simply couldn't conceive of anyone turning down a chance to star at MGM. He made another offer. Chevalier turned it down. He couldn't put into words the real reason for his rejection: If he were going to risk his whole reputation in a medium he didn't wholly trust, in a strange country that frightened him to death every time he thought about it, then he needed sufficient compensation to consider such a proposition. He had never felt comfortable with powerful people—whose "instruction" would inevitably have been better than his—and the college-educated Americans scared him stiff.

Thalberg said he was going back to Hollywood the next day and would ask Louis B. Mayer himself if the offer could be further improved. He would cable Maurice with the result. Chevalier felt that Thalberg would increase the bid. His status as an international star would be established, and he could worry about the nerves he would feel facing those cameras another time. Maurice expected a result in a couple of weeks. Thalberg had to cross the Atlantic, settle back in his office, and then consult with Mayer.

But two weeks went by, then three and even four without the expected cable. Maurice, who had kidded himself that he was happy merely to part as friends with Thalberg, was now sweating anxiously from his morning cup of *cafe au lait* to the final bedtime glass of Cognac. "I lost my faith," he admitted to friends soon afterwards. "It was apparent that I was not worth as much as I had believed I was." Or rather, as much as he had, over and over again, told himself he was worth.

Then Maurice did precisely the thing that no salesman with a worthwhile product should ever do. He cabled Thalberg: HAVE STILL HEARD NOTHING STOP PLEASE CABLE YES OR NO IMMEDIATELY STOP MUST MAKE PLANS FOR NEXT SEASON STOP.

If Maurice himself were weakening, why should the studio chase him any more? The result was, they didn't. It seemed to be the end of his Hollywood career before it had even begun. Once more he returned to drugs, although still managing to keep himself on the right side of addiction, and once more he found opportunities to take chorus girls into his dressing room. It didn't make him feel any better afterwards, certainly it didn't strengthen his tottering marriage, but it helped pass the hours when he wasn't actually on stage.

When newspapers printed photographs and described him as the handsome star of the musical stage, he suspected that they wanted something in return.

But other things would happen.

There were always top personalities in the audience and he wasn't surprised when he was told that sitting out front was Jesse L. Lasky (head of Paramount Pictures and the man with whom Cecil B. De Mille had virtually founded Hollywood when they made *The Squaw Man* there). Lasky was still part of the Establishment of the film town. There could be no doubt in Chevalier's mind who *he* was.

Even so, once bitten, twice eaten up with insecurity. The theater manager told Maurice that Lasky was there with a view to offering him a Hollywood contract. Maurice decided not to give either Lasky himself or his idea any time for thought. On stage he sang the regulation "Valentine" and a dozen other numbers with the sort of verve Lasky had only rarely seen before. It was uncanny, even for a tough show-business veteran such as he, to watch a man so totally in command of his audience. Chevalier did not merely sing his song, he attacked it, cherished it, laughed it. You didn't have to understand French to know that he was singing about a beautiful, if sometimes naughty, girl. That night, as always, Maurice danced with the showgirls, mimed another number, and brought the house down with a comedy sketch.

When Lasky later called around to his dressing room Maurice simply offered him a glass of Cognac and allowed the Paramount head to flatter him on his performance. The subject of a possible Hollywood contract was broached and Chevalier came straight to the point: "I am getting ten thousand dollars a week. I will not work for less. And if you want a screen test, I shall refuse to make one."

The mogul was willing to concede all points but the last. Just as Thalberg had said, times were changing. And Lasky emphasized his point by taking Maurice's hand in a gesture of confidentiality. Every studio had to have a guaranteed way of getting the very best out of its leading stars.

"I shall not make a test, Monsieur Lasky," said Chevalier, "because I already have made one for Monsieur Thalberg. But I have it here and if you would wish to see it you are welcome."

The next day Lasky hired a projection room at the Pathé studios in Paris, saw the Thalberg test, and within minutes telephoned Maurice to confirm his $10,000-a-week offer. Two hours later they were both signing a contract at Lasky's hotel.

The news seemed to help Maurice's relationship with Yvonne. When things were going well with his career, he was happy enough to share his good fortune with her, and the world was now looking very sweet indeed. Of course, the idea of a lengthy separation from his mother was another matter, but she had a companion and he knew she would be well looked after. And he would come back to her just as soon as the films were finished. La Louque may not have been overjoyed at the idea of being parted from her son, but she was nevertheless as excited as he at the prospects this new development offered to his career.

Maurice and Yvonne got ready to sail for New York amid tremendous excitement in Paris but with no great fanfare in the States. Americans had read a great deal about European stars coming to their country only to disappoint almost everyone who saw them as soon as they opened their mouths. Why should this Chevalier be any different? In truth, Lasky didn't know. But he had a hunch, and from such hunches fortunes had been made in Hollywood before.

The night prior to the Chevaliers' departure on the *Île de France*, Paris show business feted them in much the same way as their city had greeted Charles A. Lindbergh after his solo transatlantic flight the previous year. And it was understandable. In his way Chevalier was making an equally epoch-making crossing. He was going to show that even in this new age of the talkies, France could rule the entertainment waves.

Part of Lasky's genius was that he knew how to exploit the people who made pictures for him, and not just by tying them up in seven-year contracts. Once he had an actor's name at the bottom of a piece of paper, Lasky had work for him to do.

Maurice and Yvonne found a camera following them everywhere they went in New York, whether in Central Park or on top of a bus. It was only on the second day that he asked Lasky what it was all about.

"Oh, just a little movie I'm doing," he replied. After three days Maurice was told he had just starred in a three-reel short called *Bonjour New York*, which Paramount was going to put out just before his main feature was released.

Even then, Maurice didn't think he could make it. What pulled him through was a series of walks with George M. Cohan. "Maurice, my boy," said Cohan, sounding like a stage Irishman, "I feel the way you do every time I face an audience. And look at me. There'll never be an entertainer to beat me."

Chevalier, of course, was less than willing to accept that and decided to show Cohan who really could be the better performer. He was forever grateful for those walks.

Before long the critics were persuaded that Maurice was not the run-of-the-mill European performer they had been fed for so long, and they started to take notice. *The New York Times* rejoiced in greeting the arrival of "The French Jolson." Maurice read that and agreed that there couldn't be any finer compliment. To prove the point, he bought tickets for Jolson's *The Singing Fool*, which was the first talkie he had ever seen, and decided that perhaps he could make a go of Hollywood after all.

"I have a sort of large family in France," he told the *Times*. "They will expect a lot from me on the screen. It is no use making such a long journey without doing something that is really appealing, something really good. I think the story chosen for me by Mr. Lasky is really charming."

The story was called *Innocents of Paris*. Maurice was to play a junk dealer who saves a boy from drowning in the Seine and then falls in love with the child's aunt.

Maurice was plainly ill at ease in the studios. Everything the director asked him to do he questioned, as if afraid that the slightest wrong move on his part would be seen all over the world and so ruin his career forever. Eventually the director, Richard Wallace, found a way to calm him down. Together they talked about their love of boxing, and before long Maurice seemed reasonably comfortable.

The first rushes proved it. Unlike his mentor, Al Jolson, whom he so wanted to emulate, a Chevalier performance on screen was turning out to be very much like Chevalier on stage. Although the script of *Innocents of Paris* had been Americanized, it soon became clear that Maurice himself didn't vary from one kind of performance to another. And with the same performance there was the same accent. Maurice was almost totally fluent in English now. He learned quickly. But Jesse Lasky told him not to get carried away by his newfound linguistic prowess. "And," he added for good measure, "don't lose that accent of yours."

It was advice Maurice took to heart. For years people suspected that Maurice could speak English a lot better than he actually did, although he usually protested otherwise.

"I speak it," he told me, "the same way that I learned it. I do it the best that I can."

Early days at the Paramount studios were not easy for Maurice. In a *Saturday Evening Post* article he wrote:

> When I left the studio after my first day, I told myself: "Maurice, this is a game you will never learn." I was accustomed to play to an audience, and that audience was really part of my act. It was my barometer. Watching their faces, hearing or not hearing them laugh . . . I could catch the mood and try to answer it . . . But here? I am in an emptiness, in the bottom of a well. I talk and there is no answer, good or bad. I sing and there is a great silence. I put into a scene all my heart and strength and wait for something to happen. What happens? The voice of the director, crying "Cut."
>
> How, I ask myself, how shall I know without my audience if it goes well or badly? The director will tell me? Yes, but how if the director likes me and the public thinks I am all wet? . . . I must imagine that there is [an audience]. I must play to the cameras and to the microphones and imagine they are playing back to me.

He really didn't believe they could play back to him and have any success. He would forget the great successes of his life—he was still only thirty-nine—and think only of failures. This film was quite clearly going to be another.

The studio didn't see it that way. Within a week of seeing

those first rushes, Paramount offered him a year's extension of his contract and a guarantee of half-a-million dollars. Maurice was so convinced after seeing the completed movie that they would never want him to make a picture again, he enthusiastically signed the new Paramount contract and planned immediately to bring La Louque over to Hollywood to join him. The thought of being away from her for over a year was more than he could stand. Richard Wallace later told *The New York Times*: "He is one of the most painstaking men I ever have met. He ran each of the tests on the screen twenty times."

People who met Maurice socially were equally aware of his "painstaking" capabilities. When he went to the obligatory Hollywood parties, he made sure that his fellow guests knew exactly what he would be singing or dancing on the set next day. They were the perfect foil for his experiments and told him precisely what those microphones never could.

He was also lucky to meet the songwriting team of Leo Robin and Dick Whiting, who had previously worked on Broadway and were now making their first Hollywood film. Chevalier and Robin seemed all set for a collision course when they first met. As Robin told me, Maurice was handed his song, looked through it, and then decided to perform it his own way.

The song was called "Louise."

The sound film, of course, was in its infancy in 1929, and none of the studios really knew how to handle the medium. Tempers frayed at the slightest problem, whether an overheated arc lamp or a dropped safety pin. Microphones had to be hidden in bowls of flowers, or in the sides of chairs. Cameramen hid in oven-hot booths so that their whirring machinery wouldn't interfere with the dialogue being recorded, they hoped, for posterity. Musical films presented additional difficulties. Filming in the cavernous sound stages, which looked more like aircraft hangars, was done at night—to make sure that a song wasn't interrupted by passing airplanes or even a delivery truck. Huge rugs hung from the ceiling to help muffle outside sounds. When performers had to sing, they did so "live" to the accompaniment of an orchestra hidden behind the scenery; there was no question of dubbing a previously recorded number.

It was in that charged atmosphere that Maurice had to sing

to his leading lady, Sylvia Beecher: "Every little breeze seems to whisper Louise. . . ."

It was a lyric that Robin had written specially for Maurice—with simple, single-syllable words which he thought would be easy for a Frenchman to manage. It had been personally approved by the head of the studios, Adolph Zukor, as correct for Maurice's first and very prestigious musical film.

As Richard Wallace shouted, "Action," Maurice went into the number: "Every leetle breeze seems to wheesper Louise," he sang and as he did so, pointed to the tree on the set. When it came to the bit about "Each little rose . . ." he cupped his hands, indicating the frail flower. In the second chorus he did the same thing—pointed to the trees, cupped his hand for the rose. Young Leo Robin, who imagined that Broadway, in which he had had a phenomenal early success, had taught him all anyone ever needed to know about sophisticated American show business, was going crazy at what he regarded as this demonstration of the French primitive at work.

"He's ruining our song, Dick," he said to Whiting, who told him to shut up and enjoy contemplating what he was going to do with his following week's salary check. "I can't let him do this to our song," Robin repeated.

"Go tell the director," said Whiting, who knew how easy it would be to get on the next train back to New York.

Wallace wouldn't hear of correcting his big new French star who had been brought over at such expense by Mr. Lasky and Mr. Zukor. But he saw how worried Robin was and figured it would be easier to humour him than hold up production for the rest of the night. "Tell Mr. Chevalier yourself," he thundered and walked away.

Robin did just that. "Mr. Chevalier," he began, "I hope you won't mind my pointing out that we do songs a little differently in America. I love the way you're doing it. I'm crazy about your gestures, but here we wouldn't do them at the beginning when we're trying to establish the song. In the second chorus, however, it would be wonderful."

Chevalier, who never looked very happy on the set when he wasn't actually performing, glared at Robin.

"Ro-ban," he barked. "You are wrong!" And he ordered the

director to start the cameras rolling again. As "Ro-ban" slunk away, he could hear Maurice open the song: "Every leetle breeze seems to wheesper Louise" . . . and then stop.

"Ro-ban!" The sound of his name pronounced in Chevalier's French accent reverberated through the sound stage. Robin knew he was about to be fired. He stood rigid behind a prop. "Ro-ban!" Still he wouldn't move. Finally, one of the prop men found the cowering lyricist and brought him into Chevalier's presence.

"Ro-ban," Maurice announced. "You are right!"

Robin smiled. The director smiled. Adolph Zukor smiled, and the film continued in production. "Wait Till You See My Chérie," sang Maurice, and everyone seemed very pleased. He, of course, had to sing "Valentine," too—in French—with few Americans realizing he had had the temerity to mention young ladies' "titties." In fact, it was the inclusion of "Valentine" as well as "Dites-Moi Ma Mère" and "Les Ananas"—a version of the popular hit "Yes, We Have No Bananas"—that persuaded Maurice finally to make the film. At the last minute, he had complained that the script wasn't worthy of his talents.

"People want to see you and hear you sing," said Lasky. "The story really doesn't matter."

Making the film was one thing; seeing it at the premiere was another. As the film progressed, Maurice's face grew more and more green. He shuffled in his seat beside Yvonne. The sweat on his brow ran in rivulets. He took his arm away from Yvonne's shoulders and held her hand. Then he put it round her shoulders again. Halfway through the movie, he ran out to a bar and drank a Cognac—and then another, and another.

Finally, Yvonne and a group of studio executives caught up with him.

"It was wonderful," Yvonne told him.

"Nonsense," he replied. "Tomorrow we go back to Paris."

But "tomorrow," the papers said it was good, too.

Seeing Maurice on screen, both in his straw hat and in the junkman's cloth cap, audiences agreed they had found a new star. "He is the whole show," said Mordaunt Hall in *The New York Times*. It wouldn't be long before a lot of other people said that about Maurice in Hollywood.

10.
Ma Pomme

The greatest moment in my life, the thing that makes me most proud is when, thanks to Hollywood, I became an international personality.

—MAURICE CHEVALIER

Innocents of Paris was such a success at the box office that the Paramount executives couldn't get to their desks quickly enough to confirm that they wanted to take up Maurice's option for another film. In addition, would he think about the one after that?

Chevalier was happier than he had been for years. At last, his ambition to be more than just a Paris entertainer had been realized. He was very much an international star. What was more, *Innocents of Paris* helped give the talking film an enormous boost in France (it was called *Chanson de Paris* there), where the motion-picture industry was still dithering about converting to sound. The fact that Chevalier had made such a hit convinced both studios and exhibitors to go talkie.

All the newspapers showed Maurice and Yvonne enjoying the California sunshine. The protruding Chevalier lip puckered in a hundred fan-magazine covers, and whatever either of them did became big news. At one Hollywood party after the other, the Gallic Chevalier tones were being parodied by a succession of imitators of varying quality. It was an age when a number of people at the top of the entertainment pyramid felt they had to take up every offer that came their way if they were to stand a chance of not slipping. If other stars believed that, Maurice followed the rule as though it were part of the catechism.

Florenz Ziegfeld offered Maurice a contract to star in one of his *Midnight Frolic* shows on the New Amsterdam Roof. For six weeks Maurice showed packed houses what Paris had known for years.

He was accompanied on the Roof by the Paul Whiteman Orchestra and the famous Helen Morgan, but it was Chevalier about whom people didn't stop talking. *The New York Times* reported:

"His fashionable audience gave him an enthusiastic reception, pounding plates with the little wooden hammers they provided at the *Midnight Frolic* in his honour. Chevalier is blessed with a most ingratiating personality and a pantomimic gift that translates every number, no matter the language in which he elects to sing."

Of course, there was "Valentine" and, of course, there was an American song this time, "It's a Habit With Me." He also sang "Les Ananas," and a song about an elephant that went to the circus to make good. He had the stiff-shirted audience rolling in the aisles when he returned to "Valentine," this time presenting it as various types of Frenchmen would, the city sophisticate, the farm boy, the soldier, and the great lover.

Suddenly, straw hats that had been stored away in young men's wardrobes were taken out again and were as much the rage in the world of fashion as Chevalier himself was in show business.

Radio was just beginning to make an impact in American homes, and every day via the miracle of the airwaves the sound of "Every leetle breeze seems to wheesper Louise . . ." came filtering through thousands of living rooms.

The only trouble was the difficulty that the Paramount executives had in getting Maurice to show himself to his best advantage off the film set. On one occasion a publicity man was lining up a series of cameramen ready to "shoot" their important new star. Maurice was looking more morose than usual.

"Please Monsieur Chevalier," requested the publicity man, "look happy for the cameras."

"The smile," Maurice said, "will come when you need it."

He wasn't any happier when Paramount offered him his next film role—as a queen's consort in *The Love Parade*. Ernst Lubitsch would be directing, and there was nothing Maurice could object to in that. But the story? When he met Lubitsch, he told him he didn't like it one bit.

"I would be very happy to play a part in a film for you, monsieur," *Picturegoer* magazine reported he told the director, "but all this prince stuff! I cannot wear uniforms that are so stiff and I cannot make elegant gestures." The boy from Ménilmontant couldn't, even now, see himself in this guise. "Thank you very much for the compliment," he added, "but I'm afraid I must refuse." And these were not the only features of the role that worried him. "The ladies," he explained. "I think I make them smile, but I do not make them swoon. They do not say, 'Oh, that Chevalier!' When the big dramatic scene comes, I do not feel in my shoes. I try to play these parts naturally as I feel it, as I think it would happen in real life and with a little humour—although my life, to tell the truth, has not been so funny."

Lubitsch pressed the point. In his thick German accent the former comedy actor, who now had an international reputation as a director, became as serious as his reluctant star. "But you can make the role so good, so *you*. I beg you to accept."

"I like best," Maurice emphasized, "to play the part of a plain fellow that women understand, and that men understand, too."

It was a problem not easily reconciled, except Lubitsch persuaded Maurice to have a photograph taken in one of the uniforms he would have to wear if such a movie were made. Maurice posed in a high-necked collar, a fur hussar's hat, and a smile wide enough to please any photographer. Lubitsch was ecstatic when he saw it and brought the print over to Maurice to inspect himself. Chevalier's vanity was touched. He liked the way he looked, too. "Very well," he said, "I accept."

He heard that his costar would be Jeanette MacDonald, then on the threshold of her acting-singing career. When they were introduced, they seemed to get along well enough. Yvonne, however, didn't much like the way Maurice sidled so close to Jeanette both before and after the cameras were switched on. Despite all that had gone on since their marriage, she was still sensitive to his behaviour.

The Love Parade was Lubitsch's first talkie and became Paramount's biggest success to date. It ran in New York for thirteen weeks.

Mordaunt Hall in *The New York Times* was a confirmed Chevalier fan; but he knew where to lay a great deal of the credit:

"Ernst Lubitsch, the brilliant German director, has well served Maurice Chevalier, the French entertainer, in his talking and singing picture, *The Love Parade*, which was offered last night to an attentive, appreciative, and notable gathering in the Criterion. It is a production worthy of M. Chevalier's talent and something widely different from his first audible venture, *Innocents of Paris*." As for Lubitsch, the critic said, he did not seem to be "dismayed by the linking of the microphone with the camera."

He made no mention of Miss MacDonald, but her performance had a great deal to do with the film's success. When she and Maurice began making the movie, neither of them thought it would be any more than just a film in which they were each other's costar.

In the meantime, Maurice had been nominated for an Oscar as best actor of the year. The Academy Award eventually went to George Arliss for *Disraeli*, but the nomination was a welcome boost to the Chevalier ego just the same.

Soon he was back in France with Yvonne. He was able to spend time with La Louque—who had decided she was too old to go to America—and have six weeks at the Empire. There was standing room only at every performance. It seemed to be the same story in America with *The Love Parade*. Lubitsch sent Maurice a cable: YOU ARE SITTING ON TOP OF THE WORLD. He also had a new contract with Paramount, doubling his weekly salary to $20,000, and allowing two paid trips to Paris every year.

After *The Love Parade* came a series of sketches in *Paramount on Parade*, which featured most of the studio's top stars. Maurice appeared in three comedy routines: *Origin of the Apache, A Park in Paris,* and *The Rainbow Revels,* the last in Technicolor. There was also a completely revamped French edition filmed at Paramount's Joinville-le-Pont studios and called *Paramount en Parade.* Charles de Rochefort replaced Lubitsch as director of the Chevalier episodes, and later, using a mixture of the French and American versions, produced editions in dubbed German, Spanish, Italian, and Romanian.

When it came to filming his next full feature, *The Big Pond*— in which he costarred with a fellow French expatriate, Claudette Colbert—the picture was shot twice, in English and French, at Paramount's Long Island studios. Both versions again filled theaters in the United States, England, and France. They are worth remembering today chiefly for introducing his hit, "You Brought a New Kind of Love to Me." It soon became a Chevalier standard.

All the trappings of stardom were his—lavish home, big car, and servants. While Maurice continued to play the studio game, Paramount were only too delighted to keep feeding him with both his allocation of luxuries and his huge salary checks. The checks Maurice regularly deposited in bank accounts in Switzerland, the United States, England, and France. When Leo Robin asked him why he chose to spread his assets in this way, Chevalier replied: "One day there may be a revolution!"

There were times when it seemed there could be a revolution among the Paramount publicity corps, who didn't think that Maurice was pulling his weight at all; and not just in being reluctant to smile before the shutters clicked. The studio organized one of those inane essay competitions that were so beloved of the publicity outfits at the time. Women were invited to write on "Why I like Chevalier," and they asked Maurice to present the prize. He bristled at the very idea.

"How can I do that thing?" he demanded when the suggestion

was put to him. "How can I make of myself such an imbecile to stand up in front of these women and say, 'Here, madame, is a prize for liking me!'"

If other people said they wanted Chevalier for publicity work, he decided that they should pay for the privilege. The San Francisco Motor Show organizers wanted him to open their exhibition and act as a sort of M.C. through the week. It was 1930 and the country was still shaking from the Wall Street crash. Maurice said he would gladly open the show—for $25,000.

"Too much money, you think now, perhaps?" he wrote to the organizers. "I hope you will not think so later. But if you do—if you find that the motor show is not a big success, if you find that I have not earned my money when the week is over, then we will tear up my contract and make new terms."

The show was a huge success—80 percent up from the previous year despite the stock market crash—and Maurice got his money.

A New York society hostess, who had quite remarkably persuaded him to go to one of her parties, asked Maurice to sing. "Certainly," he said, "my fee is a thousand dollars." His hostess was taken aback but couldn't refuse. "The money," he told her when she handed him her check, "goes to my *dispensaire*."

Back in Paris Chevalier's agents, at his request, had set up the Dispensaire Maurice Chevalier, a clinic for which he had provided the initial capital.

But persuading Maurice to attend other people's charity functions was rather like asking Herbert Hoover to speak on behalf of the American Communist Party. Chevalier was never happy or comfortable with people who populated the pages of the New York *Social Register*.

Lady Furness, one of the most colorful social butterflies of the 1930s and once mistress of the Prince of Wales, invited Maurice to a party on one occasion and found it as difficult to get her French guest to smile as had those Paramount cameramen. After a few minutes of painful small talk, Maurice disappeared. The hostess, the *New York Herald* reported gleefully, afterwards found him alone in a small room—listening to his own records on her Victrola. It was his basic insecurity again, afraid of being laughed at by people whose social pedigrees inhibited him. When that happened he sought refuge in company with whom he knew he could cope—himself. He later told her he had had a wonderful evening.

Travelling back by train to California was even better. His fellow passengers seemed more his kind. Instead of sitting in his own private drawing room, Maurice found it more pleasant chatting to a couple of prisoners handcuffed to their guards as they were being transported to a new jail.

"You remind me of my friends in Ménilmontant in Paris," he told them. "You all have great courage. Courage to do things which other men have not. It seems wrong to me to waste that courage by fighting the law." He ended the journey, he later wrote, signing autographed photos for the prisoners. He was always willing to do that at the drop of a straw hat.

He was feted everywhere he went. In New York the Friars, the number one show-biz club, made him their first foreign-born guest of honour at the annual dinner. Among those present were New York's Mayor, Jimmy Walker, George M. Cohan, Eddie Cantor, George Jessel, and Jesse Lasky.

Jessel, said *The New York Times*, told Maurice he was being honoured because "he is the representative of the only solvent country left in the world." George M. Cohan, whose "Yankee Doodle Dandy" had been the first English-language song Maurice heard, said he believed that the reason was more that he was a "truly great artist." And, he added, "a hundred and twenty million self-appointed press agents can't be wrong." The arithmetic didn't count for much, but he was referring to Chevalier's total audience. Eddie Cantor quipped that Maurice had saved him money. "I will never have to buy my wife a fur coat or a bracelet. She has danced two nights in a row with Chevalier!"

Yvonne had been at Maurice's side whenever he worked at Paramount. She was still pretty and trim, and the studio tried to persuade her to go to the other side of the camera to take the lead in one of the French versions of her husband's films.

For Maurice's next movie, *Playboy of Paris*, she agreed. In French it was called *Le Petit Café*. Yvonne played the role which in the American edition had been performed by Frances Dee. The sets, the crowd scenes, the costumes were the same. Maurice recorded the songs and the dialogue in both languages. "These are not French films," he maintained. "The language is French, but the humour and the sense is American."

But if Yvonne could feel her status improving, she also found cause enough to be jealous. She may have been the female lead in the movie, but it was Maurice who was the superstar. And it was not just his artistic success that bothered her. She was jealous of—and angered by—the attention Maurice was paying to a celebrity visitor to the set; Marlene Dietrich was frequently seen in Chevalier's company and Yvonne hated her for it. It was an emotion which she never felt for La Louque, although Maurice did still continue to turn a conversation into a monologue on how wonderful a woman his mother was. Between pictures Maurice rushed back to Paris to be with her, tell her about his successes in Hollywood, and take her to see his latest movies. Apart from his relationship with Yvonne—which worried her a great deal more than it bothered him—Maurice's continued absence from La Louque was the one flaw in the seemingly idyllic Hollywood life-style he was now leading.

If she were ill, as she was during his third visit home in 1929, he was eaten up both with the fear of her dying and the guilt of spending so much time away. The doctors Maurice consulted on this trip—he made sure that the best and the most expensive in Paris were brought in—told him there was no apparent danger. He could go back to New York content that she would be all right. In his heart he didn't believe them, yet his contractual commitments to Paramount were putting him in an impossible situation. So every day from his ocean liner, Maurice sent La Louque a cable saying that it wouldn't be long before they were together again and how pleased he was that she was getting so much better. He continued sending cables for his first three days back in New York.

Then he received the news he had been dreading ever since the day he was sent off to the poor boys' school. La Louque was dead. In fact, she had died two days earlier, but the cable from his brother Paul had been delayed. Now—and this was the hardest part of all—there was not a chance of his being able to sail back to Paris in time for the funeral.

He just couldn't believe it had happened. He had planned to

go back to La Louque the moment he finished work on his new film with Claudette Colbert, *The Smiling Lieutenant*. He kept telling people: "If only she had waited . . ."

He was two days into the actual shooting schedule at the Astoria, New York, studios when he heard about La Louque's passing, but he refused to go back there for the whole of the following week. He spent the time alone in his hotel suite, crying. Neither Yvonne nor anyone he knew was allowed near him. "I had the feeling," he told friends who were finally admitted into his room to console him, "that I had only half my blood in me."

Eventually, he was persuaded to go back to work. Ernst Lubitsch was only too aware of the problems of directing Chevalier at a time like this. "I was busy on the set," he told *The New York Times* afterwards, "and out of the corner of my eyes I would see him sitting quietly in a corner, grave and serious. He never talked much or laughed with any of the others. Then, when I was ready to shoot a scene, before us, in a split second, is the same man. The same man? No, a very different man, a man of force and sparkle, a very dynamo of a man whose underlip sticks out, whose irresistible personality has captivated millions of men and women all over the world."

But it was nothing more than an act. Maurice felt destroyed inside. Without his mother there seemed no reason at all to carry on. There was no motivation. "I did it all for her," he said later on one of the innumerable occasions over the next forty years when he would talk about her. "I did it to make her proud. I never had any other reason to do anything." And he told me: "If I ever had to choose between my career and my mother, my mother would have come first. Everything, I did for her. She was like a saint."

He went back to France in time to see the simple tombstone bearing the name "Joséphine Chevalier" in gold inlaid letters being placed in position at the Cimetière Saint-Vincent. It was a long time before he could think of La Louque without weeping.

And yet, despite all his sorrow and his doubts, he kept acting. When he laughed for hundreds of girl fans who mobbed him and Yvonne at the railway station in Paris, he didn't reveal that he wasn't totally sincere.

The New York Times's correspondent noted: "Chevalier is

about the only personage in French public life who has a following of 'fans' comparable to the American admirers of Charlie
Chaplin, Jack Dempsey or Babe Ruth."

On this occasion, all he was interested in was his mother. He
visited her grave every day.

However, he did make a film while in France, perhaps the most
remarkable picture of his career. *El Cliente Seductor*, shot at
Paramount's Joinville studio, was made entirely in Spanish, which
Maurice learned phonetically.

He returned to America, alone and still totally consumed by
grief. This time Yvonne didn't accompany him. It was not just
that he made her feel a total outsider now that the world had
crumbled with La Louque's death, although that must have been
an impossible strain for her. She had to stay behind in France
for an urgent gynecological operation. But when she read that
Maurice was consoling himself with regular dinners in the company of Marlene Dietrich, she took the first available ship to New
York. Their reunion was not happy. Maurice was drifting farther
and farther away from Yvonne.

Despite his emotional unhappiness, Maurice was growing to
love America. There seemed no pretentiousness about the Americans whom he now met daily, and he could relax with them as he
was only rarely able to do with successful Frenchmen. They gave
him every reason to be confident. When he felt like getting back
to live audiences, there were always plenty of opportunities to
do so. The *New York World* was delighted to welcome him to
the Fulton Theater in March 1930:

"For two weeks only, Maurice Chevalier will be doing 'hees
stuff' at the Fulton Theater," wrote the paper's critic, who couldn't
understand why he had never seen him at work before. "I can
say that I wouldn't have missed him for a good deal. And if he
would sing only his French songs, omitting the American syrup
about you, me and the rainbows which nothing but his infectious
humour and charming accent make bearable, I would go and see
him again right away."

The New York Times was no less restrained, as Brooks Atkinson, the most famous of the "Butchers of Broadway," reported:
"When the curtain came down at the Fulton last evening after
an hour of Maurice Chevalier, no one had any intention of leav-

ing the theater. The asbestos curtain settled into place very firmly, the houselights came on and it was obvious that the program was concluded. But, as sometimes happens in the theater, everyone sat protestingly in his seat, determined to have more, though it take all night to raise the curtain. And the general indignation worked. Presently, M. Chevalier stepped buoyantly from the wings again, sang 'Valentine,' which all the old cronies expected as a matter of elementary justice, and then a scant hour of superb light entertainment was actually concluded . . . M. Chevalier need not box the compass to be thoroughly delightful. He is French, he is tall and engaging in appearance. His manners are excellent. His smile can turn a klieg light into a shadow."

But Maurice didn't forget the folks back home.

When a benefit was held in Paris at the Empire Theater for the victims of a vicious flood, Maurice topped the bill, even though he was three thousand miles away. At the William Morris Agency offices on Broadway, Maurice, a piano player, and three telephones performed for the two thousand people in the Empire audience. His voice was amplified and heard through the static from speakers on the theater stage. It was one more example of how the local boy had made good.

He could go wrong only with Yvonne, but for the moment he allowed her to get jealous while he enjoyed the cause of her jealousy. Marlene Dietrich appeared to be much more of a threat to his wife than the nonentities whom he met at parties or in the studio and took to bed afterwards.

Another threat was Jeanette MacDonald. She made two pictures with Maurice in 1931, *One Hour with You* and *Love Me Tonight*. Jeanette's clothes were often the laughingstock of the film town; she usually seemed to find excuses to wear dresses that resembled underwear, although always emphasizing her figure. Yvonne thought she presented too much temptation to Maurice. Certainly it appeared that Maurice was more fond of Jeanette than she was of him. "I could never say that working with him was anything more than agreeable," she recalled years afterwards. "All he cared about was his career and his mother." Not quite all. She also described him as "the fastest *derrière* pincher in Hollywood."

Maurice later said of her: "A very sweet and talented girl about twelve years younger than I was, although she always professed to be younger than that. I never felt that she had much of a sense of humour. She always objected to anyone telling a risqué story."

As Yvonne observed, he had more opportunities for practical demonstrations when they were making films together. *One Hour with You* was a trite story about a doctor's affair with his wife's best friend. Both Chevalier and MacDonald also starred in the French version of the picture, *Une Heure Près de Toi*, but the part of the flirtatious friend was shared between Genevieve Tobin in the English-language edition and, in the French version, Lili Damita—soon to be Mrs. Errol Flynn. The film is best remembered for what became one of Maurice's standards, "Oh That Mitzi."

But by the time *Une Heure Près de Toi* was released in France, his own countrymen were beginning to ask whether they liked the idea of a Hollywood Frenchman. They preferred the old one. When Maurice came home for a brief visit and appeared at the fashionable Châtelet Theater, there was only a lukewarm reception from the audience.

Americans, however, loved him more and more. He had undeniable sex appeal, as did his pictures. In *Love Me Tonight* both Jeanette and Myrna Loy wore such diaphanous gowns and negligees that Hollywood's self-censoring bureau, the Hays Office, banned a number of the scenes. It was remarkable, however, what Maurice as a tailor was able to get away with, playing opposite Jeanette MacDonald's princess. Of course, no tailor could be expected to leave behind his tape measure any more than a doctor could be shown without his stethoscope. For some reason, no objections were raised to Maurice making very careful measurements of the princess's bust. Yvonne noticed the amount of trouble to which he went to do the job properly.

Love Me Tonight was by far the best picture Chevalier made while in Hollywood. Although he was again working with Jeanette MacDonald, this was the first film they made together without Ernst Lubitsch's direction. For reasons which no one was able to explain either at the time or since (unless it was again a matter of intuition), Adolph Zukor wanted a new director for the movie. He chose Rouben Mamoulian, who had just finished making *Dr. Jekyll and Mr. Hyde*. Mamoulian told me that Zukor instructed him: "This is important, you can write your own ticket." It didn't particularly impress the young director, who complained that he was far too tired to undertake something so exhausting as a musical. Chevalier was saying much the same thing, although Zukor had already convinced him to work with his protégé. Now he had to persuade the director to work with Chevalier. "You know, young man," said Zukor, tears welling in his eyes and dripping down his nose in the best Louis B. Mayer tradition, "I've created this company and we'll be on the verge of bankruptcy if you don't do this picture. You'll have to do it as a great favour and an act of friendship." The tears were flowing ever more plentifully.

"You make it very difficult for me to say no," said Mamoulian, at which point Zukor shook his hand. It was then that he looked him squarely in the eyes and admitted: "We don't have a script and we don't have a story. But you do anything you want to do." This was rather like writing a blank check, but he was not sure which bank to draw it on. Zukor said: "What we have is Chevalier and MacDonald earning fabulous salaries, which they've been drawing for eight weeks without doing any work."

That was enough to frighten Mamoulian even more. If the film went over budget because of those escalating salary bills, it would be he who got the blame. Then Mamoulian remembered the French writer Léopold Marchand, whom he had met at a party.

"Perhaps you can help me," he suggested to him. "I'm supposed to do a film with Chevalier, but I've got no script."

At that, Marchand unravelled what he described as a "sort of fairy story," which he later put on a single sheet of yellow paper —about a tailor (Maurice) who goes off to the south of France, where he then meets and marries a princess (Jeanette).

Because it was going to be an important musical, he brought in the most important pair of songwriters then in business, Rodgers and Hart. They gave him a score before anyone provided a script. It was probably the first time that had ever happened—a score brimful with numbers which became classics: "How About You?," "Isn't It Romantic?," and another Chevalier standard, "Mimi," which contained the powerful line: "I'd like

to have a little son of Mimi by and by." And there was also another number which didn't take off at all until a generation later,
"Lover."

Now, with a script and a score, came the time to meet Chevalier and MacDonald. Jeanette was no trouble at all. She either
did what she was told or was suspended from the studio. Maurice was a different matter altogether. He just *had* to be satisfied.
The problem, as the director recalled with a smile, was that both
men were determined to be boss of the outfit. Mamoulian expected to meet an actor whose personality merged with the character he was always playing on the screen—funny, debonair,
brilliant. Instead, the Frenchman he met was dour, argumenta-
tive, and thoroughly unhappy.

"When are we going to have our main meeting?" Maurice
asked. "When we have a complete script as well as the score,"
the director replied courteously.

Chevalier was not prepared to listen any further. "I don't work
that way," he declared. "I have to take part in all the conferences
about the script."

They were on a collision course.

"Monsieur Chevalier," said Mamoulian, "that's not my way."

"It's what I always do with Monsieur Lubitsch," said Maurice.

"But, I'm afraid, not with me." Mamoulian stood firm.

"This isn't going to work at all," said Maurice, by now very
hostile.

"You could do me a great favour," Mamoulian replied. "Why
don't you go down to Mr. Zukor and say this isn't going to work
out? I'll be most grateful because I didn't want to do this picture
in the first place."

Chevalier walked out of the director's office, muttering that he
didn't like the way things were moving at all. Finally, he agreed
he had to do things the director's way. But he didn't have to *like*
doing them.

The first day of shooting arrived with Mamoulian ready to
breathe confidence into his company. Chevalier was sitting in a
corner, "sulking," Mamoulian said, "like an orphan."

"This is going to be a disaster," the director whispered to his
assistant, who shared his view entirely.

"Roll 'em! Action!" Mamoulian called. "Suddenly," he told

me some fifty years later, "like a phoenix rising from the ashes, came Chevalier—with the lip, the *joie de vivre*, the sense of humour, full of energy. Suddenly, lead became pure gold. That was the mystery of the man!" But when Mamoulian called, "Cut!" Maurice collapsed completely.

After three days, Maurice and Mamoulian decided they liked each other very much and Maurice went along with whatever the director suggested. "He was like a little boy who needed friendship badly," Mamoulian said. "Like the ancient Greeks he needed friendship more than love."

Yvonne had noted much the same thing.

Nevertheless, Maurice was asked to play a love scene as though he were living it for real. "You have to make the people believe you," Mamoulian instructed. "The character you play is in love. Not just making fun."

"They'll never believe me," he said, the sulk now a genuine appeal for sympathy, much like the cry from a baby. "I've never done it."

"They'll believe you if you do it properly," replied Mamoulian, but he detected a change in Maurice's fears. Instead of doubting his ability to cope with situations he was portraying, he was afraid now that he knew all too well what to do. He was afraid of the culpability of the love scenes. They were too real to him.

Part of the shooting of *Love Me Tonight* was done at the MGM studios. They had a street set which Mamoulian thought would look better in the film than anything that Paramount could offer. Because the lot was hired from another studio, Paramount had to provide the director, the stars, the lesser members of the cast, and the technicians with an unappetizing box lunch. The more discerning members of the company left the boxes unopened and went to the Brown Derby. Chevalier was not among them.

"Why don't you come with us?" Mamoulian asked him one day. "It only takes ten minutes to get there. You can have a nice hot lunch and you will feel better when you get back."

"Can I do that?" Chevalier asked like a little boy suddenly hearing about a tea party.

"Yes, of course," said Mamoulian. The next day when Mamoulian and his assistant went down to the Brown Derby, they found Chevalier sitting alone in a corner. They all had their lunches and, as they puffed their cigars, got ready to pay their checks. In his corner Maurice could be seen arguing with the waiter. Soon he got up angrily and marched over to the director's table.

"Isn't the studio paying for this?" he asked.

"No, Maurice," he was told. "They give you the box lunch."

"Oh, I see," he said. The next day he was out on the street set again, eating his box lunch.

There was no one, however, who could say that Chevalier was anything but generous with his talent. From their seats in motion-picture theaters throughout the world, people laughed, applauded, and sang with him.

Not even Jesse Lasky, who had thought all along that he had an unusual performer at his disposal, could have envisaged the appeal Maurice would have for international audiences. Most surprising of all, he had actually established himself as the lover figure he had always denigrated.

After seeing *Love Me Tonight*, the *Los Angeles Examiner*'s critic, Jerry Hoffman, wrote: "It is one of the best, if not the very best, of the Maurice Chevalier pictures—and not the least of the cause is the brilliant direction of Rouben Mamoulian."

Mamoulian, of course, deserves credit for the enormous strides Chevalier's career took after *Love Me Tonight*. The talking film had grown up and Mamoulian had helped Maurice grow with it.

When Maurice and Yvonne went back to Paris after making the picture, they divided their time between the obligatory laying of flowers daily on La Louque's grave and receiving the plaudits of the public. The American Club in Paris gave a special luncheon to say thank you for the enjoyment *Love Me Tonight* and the earlier films had given them. They felt that his pictures, with their synthesis of American and French show business, had done more to help relations between the two countries than a dozen diplomatic missions. Indeed, reported *The New York Times*, the club's president, Theodore Rousseau, said that Chevalier was a "kind of unofficial ambassador whose contribution to friendly understanding between our two countries is of tremendous importance."

Maurice didn't agree. "I can't think of myself as any kind of ambassador," he replied, "because an ambassador generally has something to do with politics. Politics are over my head. I don't understand politics and I never want to. I would be happiest just to be known as America's biggest French pal. To me, the most wonderful thing about America is the generous tolerant reception every foreigner gets. If he has got the stuff, he is welcomed with open arms, although before I sang my first song to them, I was terribly afraid they might ask after hearing me why that French guy was brought all the way across the Atlantic!" But, he added, after hearing the terrible English of the French consul general in New York, he felt better.

Chevalier was in superb form, demonstrating that he could use the latest American slang expressions—which, with the advent of talkies, had become *de rigueur* for every foreigner who liked to think he was totally up to date—without losing the accent which Lasky and all the others in Hollywood had told him to preserve so carefully.

His love for and from the public grew in reverse proportion to his relationship with Yvonne. When he returned to the States, she stayed behind in Paris. He didn't make anything of it. He said he had to go back to America quickly to sign a contract for a series of twenty-six weekly radio shows. They would be beamed over the NBC network. "He will receive one of the highest sums ever paid to an individual for a similar series," the organization trumpeted proudly. When the shows were on the air, Maurice sang into space as though there were a horde of young women at his feet and three thousand people sitting in front of the stage —this was the man who had complained about the unemotional microphones on the film sound stage. The movies had taught him a new way to work.

There were, however, some people who didn't think he had succeeded so well. "Maurice Chevalier," said one critic, "suffers from that ill which besets all actors who brave the microphone. His magic personality loses much of its sheen when he steps into the unsubstantial air."

But there were even more important developments ahead for him. In April 1931 he gave a one-man show at Carnegie Hall. That, too, was a huge success. *The New York Times* loved his "risqué or perhaps it would be better to say 'naughty songs' in English" and his imitations of Mayol and the other French comedians who had so influenced his youth. "While the auditor who knew about Paris got the most of Maurice Chevalier's capital turns," reported the paper's critic, "there was enough left for anybody to have a great time. His gesticulations, changes in gait and physiognomy and suggestive powers put the songs across and leaped over the language barrier."

Maurice was estimated to be getting $400,000 a year. When he went to London to appear at the Dominion Theater, he was billed again as "The highest-paid entertainer in the world." This time it may have been true. His London fee was said to be five thousand pounds a week—which no one had received before.

When he arrived at Victoria station, the usual thousand or more women were there to cheer him on. Several threw autograph books at him, but only one walked off with a signature. When he got into his car, the girls stormed the police barrier and several of them clung to the vehicle's running board. They joined in singing his songs, helped by the sound of a dozen Chevalier records played on phonographs borrowed from nearby music shops. No one could ever remember that happening before either.

The British press wanted to know his secret as a lover. "I do not look on myself as a lover," he told the *Daily Express.* "I just want to make people happy. The fellow who can make a pretty girl laugh has been blessed. She is quite apt to love him—and give him a nice kiss even if he hasn't asked for it."

He followed the Dominion Theater show with a variety tour of the English music halls. There he came across a problem he had never experienced before on the live stage: censorship. The "watch committees" of the local councils demanded to see scripts or previews of every theatrical performance in the area over which they had authority. When they "watched" Chevalier in rehearsal, they decided that the sensitive British audiences couldn't be exposed to half of what American audiences were allowed to tolerate. And it wasn't just the suggestion of "titties" that worried the august do-gooders. How dare he suggest that he wasn't married to one of the ladies about whom he sang? He cancelled a week of shows in Cardiff after the committee had ordered that some of his songs should be changed. "You may sing in English," they told him. "But we understand your French songs have double meanings." In Leicester members of the watch committee interrupted a performance and demanded changes. Maurice stormed off the stage in anger. When, however, the audience called, stamped their feet, and whistled for him to come back, he returned to complete his show. The councillors later went back to Maurice's dressing room to apologize for causing a storm in a demitasse and said how much they enjoyed *most* of his show.

"I don't understand the fuss," he told them. "I don't think any of my songs could possibly be considered vulgar." Which was very tongue in cheek indeed from an entertainer whose nursery had been the ribald café-concert.

But nobody felt that way about his shows in America. When Charles Dillingham featured Chevalier once more at the Fulton Theater in February 1932, *The New York Times* wrote enthusiastically:

> The Tricolor should be waving jauntily this morning atop the Fulton Theater for Maurice Chevalier. The engaging and eminently likable French music-hall entertainer last night began a two-week engagement at that house in, as he himself termed it, the flesh.
>
> On a holiday from the film studios, he has once again journeyed Eastwards from California in a personal appearance tour. New York is the last stop in that tour, but certainly not the least. Distributing his abundant charm over motion picture theme songs and his old French favourites alike, M. Chevalier was never in better form than he was last night and an audience reluctant to be turned out into the chilly night air of Times Square summoned him back for several encores, of which one, of course, was 'Valentine.' Since his first appearance on a Manhattan stage . . . M. Chevalier has become more at home in both the language and comedy methods of Broadway and Hollywood.
>
> For all his dalliance with the motion pictures, he has not let this language or these comedy methods dominate one bit his extraordinary personality. Rather, he has made them his slaves, and if the result is a Chevalier little different in manner from the one over whom returned European travellers used to grow positively ecstatic, it is still a Chevalier

unchanged in the fundamentals of his comic art or his technique. For which Allah be praised.

When Maurice went back to California, it was to make a new film. Yvonne still worried excessively about the attention he paid to other women. Sometimes, however, she need not have worried.

Garbo was not immune to Maurice's charms, but when he and the divine Greta came in close proximity to each other at a Hollywood party, it was Chevalier, for some inconceivable reason, who said he wanted to be alone.

"Do you know how to swim, Monsieur Chevalier?" she asked him as they danced to the music of a smart Hollywood orchestra.

"*Mais oui,*" he replied, somewhat taken aback. He had heard of the racy temperament lurking inside the allegedly cold Scandinavian exterior.

"Then let's take a dip in the ocean right now," said Garbo.

"But it's midnight," Chevalier protested. "*Le Pacifique est glacial.*"

Garbo stormed out of his presence and they never met again.

It was too much for Yvonne. Just to see him with another woman was to imagine him in bed with her. Worse than that was the knowledge that in most cases she was right. She announced she would sue for divorce.

Maurice at thirteen, and the beginning of a lifelong career.
(BBC HULTON PICTURE LIBRARY)

Maurice posing for one of the early picture postcards.
(BBC HULTON PICTURE LIBRARY)

A studio portrait of the young man-about-town. Chevalier at twenty.
(BBC HULTON PICTURE LIBRARY)

Mistinguett, and the legs that sent audiences at the Folies-Bergère crazy. (BBC HULTON PICTURE LIBRARY)

Maurice in America in the 1920s. (BBC HULTON PICTURE LIBRARY)

Maurice in his Will Rogers outfit. (BBC HULTON PICTURE LIBRARY)

With Jeanette Macdonald in The Love Parade.

Breakfast with Yvonne Vallée, his new wife, in their house in Hollywood.

(Above) *Maurice and Yvonne playing opposite each other in the French version of* The Playboy of Paris. (BBC HULTON PICTURE LIBRARY) (Left) *With Gary Cooper in 1938.* (FOX PHOTOS)

(Above) *London was Maurice's in-spiration; in 1948 he renewed his friendship with the city.* (BBC HUL-TON PICTURE LIBRARY) *(Right) Maurice and his old flame, Mistinguett, at the Folies-Bergère show commemorating his fiftieth anniversary in show business.* (RAY-MOND MANDER AND JOE MITCHEN-SON THEATRE COLLECTION)

In Paris in the 1950s with Danny Kaye and Lena Horne.
(GINETTE SPANIER COLLECTION)

The anxiety shows through—getting ready for a show in 1956.
(GINETTE SPANIER COLLECTION)

(Above) *Choosing the hats which were delivered to him by the dozen by A. E. Olney and Co., Ltd., of England.* (GINETTE SPANIER COLLECTION) (Below, left) *With his brother Paul and Janie Mitchell in the 1950s.* (GINETTE SPANIER COLLECTION) (Below, right) *Janie's portrait of Maurice at La Louque.* (GINETTE SPANIER COLLECTION)

With Jojo, the boy the press thought was Maurice's son.
(GINETTE SPANIER COLLECTION)

In the garden of La Louque with Marie-Noël, Janie's daughter, next to the carved head of Maurice's mother.
(GINETTE SPANIER COLLECTION)

On stage in London. As indestructible as the Eiffel Tower, said the critics.
(CAMERA PRESS)

Maurice on his seventieth birthday. (CAMERA PRESS)

In Fanny, one of his last films. (CAMERA PRESS)

Maurice always liked to be seen with a pretty girl or two. (EDITIONS CONDÉ NAST)

Maurice and Richard Nixon, then Vice-President. To the right is François Vals.

With Shirley Bassey, Maurice meets Queen Elizabeth, the Queen Mother. 'You must have been a beautiful baby,' he crooned to her. (FOX PHOTOS)

Every act was practiced and perfected in front of a mirror and then, when it was all over, gone through again before the most critical audience of all—himself. (CAMERA PRESS)

Maurice at home at La Louque. The painting on the left is of his brother Paul. (CAMERA PRESS)

11.
It's a Habit of Mine

I wouldn't have said he was oversexy. He was charmingly irresistible.

—GINETTE SPANIER

Yvonne, Maurice said, couldn't understand him; and for his part he couldn't begin to understand her.

"There were moments when I lived with a devoted woman in sweet harmony," he wrote in one of his autobiographical memoirs, "and in one second of suspicion that woman would disappear, leaving in her place a stranger. Suddenly, I was wondering whether in the same graceful body two completely different people could exist."

When the Chevaliers did speak to each other, it seemed that neither could control what was said. Later, they regretted the words that crossed between them, but neither of them would retract.

Yvonne said that she was getting a divorce for only one reason —"to keep our old friendship." It wasn't any more convincing then than it sounds now, although it did tend to minimize any suggestion of cruelty. Maurice went along with it.

"There is no question of another woman," he said. "I am not in love with anyone else and we always will be good friends. We simply realize now that our marriage is a failure because of incompatibility of temperament."

Yvonne had not followed him back to America, and in a Paris court she asked the judges—who had already formally agreed there were no chances of reconciliation—to put the blame on Maurice and end the marriage. She told the court that her husband was cruel and had deserted her. Maurice's lawyers contested the charges and filed a countersuit alleging that Yvonne was guilty of "unjustified jealousy and of having made family scenes."

Finally, the court ruled that both parties were at fault and refused to give judgment in favour of one side at the expense of the other. They granted the divorce but awarded no alimony to Yvonne because of her own "guilt." Maurice did make a financial settlement for her out of court.

"I can only think that Yvonne and I rushed into each other's arms without looking to see if we were matched at all, on a dark and cloudy day with a bad weather forecast. My marriage was one of my failures," he said in his book many years later. "From my own point of view it was a bad performance."

People wondered whether Mistinguett might enter his life again. She began talking about Maurice and about the women who seemed to play such an important part of his life. "I was the only one he ever loved," she wrote. "I'm not jealous but when I see him with a woman it gives me a slight shock. With Maurice I still have the eyes of a lover. I may have forgotten the tenderness a little, but I have not forgotten Maurice Chevalier. Whenever I think of him I have the same tightening of the heart strings I do when I hear a bird sing. Birds sing in tune, that's their great secret . . . he didn't make me unhappy on purpose. I bear no malice."

But when Maurice returned to Paris, he showed no interest in getting together with her again. Having disposed of one chapter from his past, there was no sense of reopening another, especially now that Miss was sixty years old, beautifully preserved, but sixty just the same. He needed new triumphs, new conquests.

His social life now was divided into two distinct halves—the one he would talk about and the one he kept for his own bedroom or that of whichever beautiful girl to whom he had taken a fancy. Everybody knew about his friendships with Fairbanks and Pickford, and the newspapers delighted in photographing Maurice and Charlie Chaplin playing bowls together at Maurice's Riviera villa. He did not make public any of his other liaisons. Rumours were rife about his having an affair with Jeanette MacDonald, but he seemed happier with the other stories, which said that the two stars actually hated each other.

His relationship with Marlene Dietrich was another cause for hints both in the Hollywood party circuit and in the press. Together they went dancing at the Coconut Grove, but every time Paramount Pictures wanted to issue pictures of them together for publicity purposes—as they did now that Yvonne was removed from the scene—Marlene's mentor, Josef von Sternberg, thought it wise to try to get them destroyed.

Maurice's reputation for stinginess grew with his success. But, as one of his great friends, Ginette Spanier, told me, although nightclub hatcheck girls knew that they wouldn't get a tip from him, the handshake and smile he did give them seemed to have greater value.

Marlene got more than that, as might be expected. Mme. Spanier said he bought Marlene a huge emerald and paid the insurance premium before presenting it to her in a velvet case. The boy who once wore cardboard in his shoes to keep the rain out found it easier to give $1,000 than a nickel. He and Dietrich were sometimes seen together in Paris. The public didn't know about the other women with whom he spent time. He may have told some that he was crazily in love with them; a few may have believed him. He simply had to have them, but not quite as much as he had to have his career.

It was announced that Chevalier earned a total of $800,000 a year, which someone calculated to work out at $533 an hour. It was said now to be the largest income ever earned by a Frenchman. He was still making the most of it in Hollywood, playing along with the system, sometimes to a surprising extent. When he made *A Bedtime Story* for Paramount in 1933 about a playboy who finds a baby abandoned inside his limousine, he announced to the press that he intended to adopt the child "starring" as the foundling.

The eight-month-old actor, Baby Le Roy, had been born to a sixteen-year-old girl in a Salvation Army home. Maurice told newspapermen and newsreel audiences that he was very serious about the adoption. "He will fill a void in my heart," he was reported as saying by the newspapers, which were amazingly gullible when it came to press agents' pitches. Others speculated quite seriously that the child would take the place of the son who had been born dead to the Chevaliers, but the stories came to an end with the predictable statement from the mother that "it would break my heart" to part with the baby.

The child, however, proved most of the dictates about established artists being wiser to steer clear of appearing with babies or pets. Baby Le Roy, who had to be coaxed to cry or laugh to order, seemed to steal most of the reviews. Maurice was not happy with that. Various leading ladies were just as unhappy with his next movie, *The Way to Love*. Again there were to be French- and English-language versions, this time with Sylvia Sidney in the lead. But Miss Sydney withdrew because, it was suggested, she thought her role was so poor. Carole Lombard was retained, but she stormed out for much the same reason. Finally, Ann Dvorak was brought in. Jacqueline Françelle starred in the French version, which was called *L'Amour Guide*.

The Way to Love was Maurice's last picture for Paramount. Now he had a contract with MGM, the studio that had once balked at paying him what he considered he deserved. Irving Thalberg had a whole string of ideas for Maurice and they agreed on terms. Thalberg wanted him for *The Chocolate Soldier*, and for a musical version of *The Last of Mrs. Cheyney* as well as for a romantic comedy called *Escapade*. But first there would be the biggest musical of all. Maurice, he announced, was to star in *The Merry Widow* with not just the Franz Lehár score but, in the best Hollywood style, additional numbers by Rodgers and Hart.

It was an exciting idea for Maurice: a role everyone knew, in an expensive film for what was fast establishing itself as the most prestigious outfit in Hollywood—and it was going to be directed by his old and trusted friend, Ernst Lubitsch. Maurice's new contract gave him script approval and the chance to make films for other studios, too, if he so desired. There would also be time for him to appear on stage. Those clauses give some idea of how important he was considered now—although, in his frequent bouts of depression, Maurice chose to believe that his career was on the wane. As if to bolster his image, he began making further demands on the studio.

MGM said they wanted Jeanette MacDonald for the title role. Maurice didn't relish more bouts with her on the studio floor. Jeanette said she could do without any more pinches on her *derrière*. Chevalier's argument seemed the more forceful. "Jeanette and I have made three good films together and I believe that is enough," he said. "Besides, I believe a new leading lady alway brings out something new in me." He had a constructive suggestion to make.

"We should get Grace Moore," he told Thalberg, who was singularly unmoved by the suggestion. Miss Moore had made two films for his studio and neither had been a hit. Thalberg used his prerogative, and Jeanette MacDonald became the Merry Widow over Maurice's vociferous objections.

Now Jeanette could describe her relationship with Maurice as strictly "correct," although he could not help but be impressed by the appearance that she and the other girls cut in the picture. Jeanette's curving shoulders were ravishing. And so, as numerous females in the cast testified, was Maurice. Fifi D'Orsay told me: "He was wonderful and charming. And he was one of those great stars who knew how to use his hands."

The Merry Widow was enthusiastically received. André Sennwald wrote in *The New York Times*: "There was an inconsiderable rumour not long ago that Mr. Chevalier was diminishing in luster. Let that be spiked at once. He has never been better in voice or charm."

Nevertheless, he was getting very anxious about his screen reputation. "I'm through with giddy, wine-bibbing, lady-killing roles," he declared in 1934.

But that wasn't why he cancelled his contract with MGM immediately after completing *The Merry Widow*. The studio had now come around to his idea of costarring with Grace Moore. While their own picture was still in production, Miss Moore had had a huge hit in *One Night of Love*, as a result of which she was again a highly marketable commodity. She would, Thalberg decided, make an excellent costar with Maurice in *The Chocolate Soldier*. The trouble was that Miss Moore thought so, too, and demanded top billing in the film. Maurice wouldn't hear of the notion and announced he was going back to France for a while.

"I have always managed my own business affairs," he said. "I've always taken the responsibility for every decision and even gone against the advice of my best friends. Perhaps I've made mistakes, but I can always look in the mirror and not be ashamed of anything I've done."

It was true that he didn't always agree with everything other people said or did. When he refused to accept a bill from the U.S. Internal Revenue Service, they sued him for $475 in income-tax arrears. He had to pay, of course, but he was much more afraid of having to pay for his success with sacrifices to his integrity. And that was why he was going back to France for an extended stay.

Thalberg told him he understood his reasons for breaking the contract. "You'll come back to Hollywood bigger than ever," he said.

"I think my acting will always have the basis of comedy," Maurice remarked on the *Île de France*. "But I want to go deeper into a character. It cost me a lot of money to break my contract with Mr. Thalberg, but I have enough money and am able to do what I want."

And all he wanted revolved around a new woman. When the ship docked at Le Havre, the American actress Kay Francis was waiting for him, and together they rode on to Paris.

"We met simply out of friendship," Maurice protested afterwards. "It doesn't mean there will be an engagement."

For a time his affair with Miss Francis was a spirited one. The newspapers were constantly linking their names and suggesting marriage was imminent. Some of them were still saying the same thing, simultaneously, about his relationship with Marlene Dietrich, whom he called "Marlinou." But Maurice, possibly playing hard to get, told friends he thought she was "beautiful but too German."

For the moment he had more concerns about his career. He went back to America to make *Folies Bergère* for Darryl Zanuck. Merle Oberon and Ann Sothern played opposite him.

Miss Oberon, whom Maurice described as a "child woman," was able to turn Maurice's usual charm into an effervescent sense of humour. It was an indication of the effect a beautiful woman could have on him; his personality could change totally. The film was one of his best vehicles to date, but his heart wasn't absorbed by it. He wanted to return to his first love, the French music hall, and he wasn't sure that he could do it.

This time, it wasn't the old Chevalier insecurity—it was much more that his films hadn't had anything like the popularity in France that they had achieved in America. The French audiences, as he often said, were the most fickle in the world, and he couldn't bear to let them forget him. He had to prove to them that he was still the greatest entertainer their country had ever produced. The fact that his mother was no longer around made him all the more determined to succeed. When she was alive he had worked to show that he was worthy of her love and admiration; with her gone, his choice seemed either to give up show business altogether or to "punch" even harder—to prove that he could still do it.

"I'm frightened," he told a friend at the time, "that people will say, 'It's finished. We've seen enough of what he can do. The same twitches, the same shadows. We want something else, something new. Not him. Someone else!' " And he added: "The music hall is my first love. I belong there and not in Hollywood. I'm glad I have finished with pictures. They do not suit my temperament."

He went back to the French stage at the Eldorado in Nice. And for the first time in twenty years of highly publicized Chevalier performances, there were rows of empty seats. He was stunned, although he didn't allow it to affect his performance. That night he sang, joked, and impersonated with all cylinders firing. But after the show he broke down. He stormed angrily into the manager's office and demanded to know what had gone wrong.

The reason was the management had increased ticket prices by a third for this comeback show by the eminent international star. The following night prices were back to normal—and so, he was relieved to see, were the audiences.

Once managements could see that Maurice was truly back in form, they scrambled to employ him. In the end Chevalier's old friend, Henri Varna, proprietor of the Casino de Paris, won the contest and signed Maurice to a contract to star in his show *Parade of the World.*

But it was a hard-fought deal that they finally struck. Old friends or not, Maurice thought he knew how much he was worth after his stay in Hollywood, and it was more than M. Varna at first wanted to pay. Maurice agreed to work for a percentage of the profits and with no guaranteed salary, although he did offer to keep the percentage down so as not to reduce the salaries of everyone else in the show.

Before going to Paris he followed the Nice show—making sure all the time that the prices were reasonable enough to keep every seat filled and the audience reacting to his performances—with productions at Toulouse, Bordeaux, and Biarritz, all of them drawing full crowds. At Cannes there was standing room only.

When he finally returned to the Casino, he was rightfully greeted as the local boy who made good. He only took part in the second half of the revue, but it was enough to confirm his status. As his straw hat made its first appearance, the house roared approval. From his fellow Hollywood star and close friend, Charles Boyer, who was sitting in a box with his girl friend, to the Paris shopgirl who had saved for weeks for a seat in the gallery, the Casino was spellbound. At first Maurice couldn't bring himself to sing. He couldn't tell a joke. He couldn't dance. The applause was so strong, so loud, so long, that all he could do was smile and wait for it to die down. As he waited for this most gratifying of sounds to subside, he had a decision to make: Should he tell them how wonderful it felt to be back? How much he had missed them? He decided not to do so but, as he later put it, "to behave as if I'd sung there the day before. No stories. No sentimentality." And he gave them what they wanted.

His fears were for once arrested. It had been an uncanny instinct which persuaded him of the need to come back just when he did. The empty seats at the Eldorado in Nice had proved that the line between failure and triumph was a dangerously thin one.

To Maurice, as to any other entertainer, the most important proof of his status in show business was the reaction of his fellow entertainers. The French theater showed its appreciation of Maurice's unique talents by making him the head of its number one charity. He was made honorary president of the Ris Orangis, the organization that looked after old performers. His appointment followed the death of the previous holder of the office—the man whom Chevalier at first emulated and later surpassed on the same stage, Dranem.

His fellow artists made up a small, intimate band of close friends. He was close again, too, to his brother Paul who had long before given up engraving and had followed Maurice into show business. Paul wasn't very good at either singing or telling jokes, and it was clear he was riding on the coattails of his younger brother, but Maurice showed no resentment.

Maurice found no difficulty in finding new women to conquer, new affairs—or "little stories" as he liked to call them—to begin, to consummate, and then, when he had had enough, to end. One of these "stories" has never been told before, and, had it been revealed at the time, would have been a *cause célèbre*. Josephine Baker, the black dancer who had been one of the stars to captivate him on his first visit to Broadway, was now having a similar effect on him in her bed. But it didn't last, and Josephine told him she would never forgive him for deserting her.

Women in show business were still the ones with whom he found the most opportunities to make love, but not all of them were established stars like Josephine Baker, Marlene Dietrich, or Kay Francis. None of them appeared to mean very much to Maurice and none were therefore expected to be paragons of virtue like La Louque, which was quite clearly the stumbling block to his establishing any new lasting relationships. They simply helped his ego and fed his libido.

Then, quite suddenly at the age of forty-six, he fell in love, with a girl of nineteen.

12.
My Ideal

So you must understand that I have come to terms
with myself. There will be no more grand passions for
me—instead I shall keep away from that kind of private
love.

—MAURICE CHEVALIER

Her name was Nita Rayer. She was Romanian and Jewish, and
Maurice met her in 1935 at just about the time he was getting
back into his stride in the French music halls. She was a tall
actress with a stunning figure, and Maurice fell for her, he admitted, from a seat in the stalls. As he watched her in a tiny
role in the Paris edition of the New York hit, *Broadway*, she
captivated him. Immediately after the show, he asked for an in-
troduction and was taken to her dressing room.

He wrote later in a magazine article that he was swept off his feet by her femininity, her grace, and a "natural kindness which embellished the sort of intelligence uncommon in such a spring chicken." The latter attribute had undoubtedly come, he thought, from the worldliness of the stage.

Nita found it impossible to resist the charms of a man who was a top international film star and who now had the kind of good looks which were more evident in maturity than they had been in youth. And, of course, he was so self-assured.

Or was he? Maurice found it very difficult to put into action all that he wanted to do. Would she want a man who was so much older than she was herself? That old "complex of inferiority" had taken on a new guise. But Nita was difficult to resist.

"She breathed youth," he said. "The atmosphere of the stage hadn't yet had time to fade her and had only taught her the ways of the world. She was a surprise, an apparition in my life. I had never, in the world of show business, met such a surprising alliance of beauty, spirit, and modesty."

When he conjured up the courage to ask her to have dinner with him, he pondered how it could possibly work out between them, but it did. After he gallantly took Nita back to the small apartment which she shared with her mother, and as he politely kissed her on both cheeks, he thought that perhaps he had the answer. It was apparent that she liked his company as much as he was overwhelmed by hers. They met again and again. He resisted his stinginess and bought her presents. She stirred every fiber in his body, and aroused in him a sexual potency he had begun to think was waning.

Women had previously fulfilled two distinct needs: They were either sexual comforters and status symbols or people with whom he liked to be seen. Nita was both these things, and her whole being told him that he was still desirable. The effect she had on his morale was immense. With her, he felt strong. He believed he wanted her infinitely more than anyone he had known before.

"She came to me as a godsend, this kid," he wrote. "Unrefusable."

But he did worry about their age difference. He thought he was doing wrong and felt he had to ease his conscience. He took the unusual step of going to church to seek the consolation of the confessional. It didn't work, so he tried to make some huge sacrifice. Because he couldn't give up sex any more than he could abandon show business, he decided to stop smoking. It was really difficult because he had been smoking heavily to relieve tension. This was before anyone had suggested any connection with lung cancer, and he had always enjoyed lighting up. But he knew it was one tangible pleasure which he would miss, and therefore hard to give up. The best way to do so, he decided, was to smoke himself sick. He sat up for a whole night, thinking about Nita but puffing one cigarette after the other until he vomited. He followed that with denying himself alcohol and cut down on his consumption of food. He felt better for the sacrifices, but they didn't help his conscience.

He finally decided that only telling Nita the affair had to end would do that. He was, as he wrote, "only forty-six, hardly Methuselah, but there was a deep-felt urge to be at peace with myself." He told her the affair had to come to an end. But as he spoke, she began to cry and he decided to think again. "I'm melting," he confessed. "I'm defenseless in the face of so much charm."

Before long he had set up house with her.

He took Nita with him wherever he went. She followed him to London, where for two months he starred at the Adelphi Theater in *Stop Press*. Totally ignoring Nita, one reporter asked: "Are you going to marry Kay Francis?"

"Ridiculous," said Maurice.

Nobody would have been surprised, though, had Maurice announced that he and Nita were to marry. There were times when they themselves expected to do so—except that whenever it came to making the big decision, Maurice held back.

Even she would not be as perfect as La Louque, which was no way to start a marriage. Nor was the fact that to succeed he would first need to have a divorce—from what he always called "my profession." And that he was not prepared to do.

In London Maurice and Nita stayed, as usual, at the Savoy. Everywhere they went they were surrounded by thousands of fans who never seemed happier than when they could watch them arrive with the French Ambassador or show-business celebrities.

The Savoy staff were somewhat perturbed that he now never

drank anything stronger than ginger ale and insisted on plain English cooking. Virlogeux, the Savoy chef, was distraught that a Frenchman could eschew his special dishes. Each morning Maurice used to stand by his suite window overlooking the Thames and do exercises. Sometimes he succumbed and smoked a couple of cigarettes before breakfast—only to fling the pack out of the window in self-disgust.

The press didn't hear about that, but they did find plenty to talk about in his show. *The Times* said:

"M. Chevalier comes on late in the evening and his performance is, in essence, a music-hall turn. It exists, that is, in space on its merits, independent of any background, prepared to stand or fall on its own. M. Chevalier's personality is an elusive one and he has an engaging air of being on the stage just for the fun of it. His gift for mimicry is emphasized in the part he plays in *Stop Press*, but his temporary appearance in the cast during the next month is an occasion in itself, and after his final performance, there is no reason to believe that the press will ever stop."

"It was half past ten," reported the *Daily Mail*, "before Chevalier, complete with smile and straw hat, walked on stage to give a thirty-minute turn which proved him to be as great an artist as ever."

Instead of doing an encore by himself at the end of the Adelphi show, Maurice brought the entire cast out on stage to reprise the finale. "What sportsmanship!" said the *Mail.*

American papers reported that he was through with motion pictures. He objected to the way every film was proclaimed to be a masterpiece, they said. "Untrue," he retorted to *The New York Times*: "I have become embittered with the cheap roles that they have given me, but the report that I have definitely given up screen work is wrong. I'm getting plenty of offers from the United States, but none of the scenarios submitted suits me."

In a rare moment of candour, he said: "In Hollywood I knew I hadn't to lose my head—because some people thought they were above everyone else. Cinema is often good looks, with talent coming second. I was made to look sophisticated and romantic. I don't think I was ever that—except that I loved beautiful women. It seemed to me that there were artists in Hollywood who took themselves a little too seriously as demigods . . . I was more a lover of love than a romantic."

But when he did go back to making films in 1936, it was in France. He did *L'Homme du Jour*, about a man who donates blood to save the life of an actress (Elvire Popesco), and *Avec le Sourire*, in which he costarred, playing a confidence man, with Marie Glory.

The third film of the year was made in English by Associated British Film Distributors. In *The Beloved Vagabond* he appeared opposite Betty Stockfeld and a newcomer called Margaret Lockwood. The picture was filmed simultaneously in French—with Helen Robert replacing Lockwood—as *Le Vagabond Bien-Aimé*. It was not a wise move on his part; Maurice's role had already been rejected by Cary Grant, after being planned originally for the American crooner Russ Columbo. He played a French architect working in London who returns home after a broken love affair. He had opportunities to sing and to use his charm on Miss Lockwood, but little else.

"It will not hasten his return to Hollywood," said *Variety*, "in case the French star is interested, and in all probability will not encourage further American releases of anything he does on the other side."

The Beloved Vagabond was Maurice's first real film flop.

At any other time he would have been totally consumed with depression at the way his career was going. But now he had Nita, and he only had to look at her to forget other matters. When things were working out between them, all had to be right with the rest of the world.

And he had a new career in the offing: The man who had had "no instruction," and who always laboured with a sense of inferiority as a result, was asked by one of his country's principal newspaper editors to write a regular column on any subject of his choice.

Jean Prouvost of *Paris-Soir* came to Maurice with the idea after reading letters Chevalier had sent to friends. Each of them was long, interesting, and proved, M. Prouvost told him, that he "possessed a particular style which would be perfectly suitable for a newspaper."

What made Maurice consider the idea seriously, he said in *Les Pensées de Momo*, was seeing Will Rogers on the American vaudeville stage. The former cowboy, who gave commentaries on political events of the day as he spun his lasso also wrote a regular column for a newspaper chain and was regarded as one of America's principal humorists. Like Chevalier, he was un- educated, and had never previously written professionally. He also took most of his jokes from the world of show biz. If Rogers could do it, why couldn't Maurice? It not only inspired him to take on the job, it also provided him with his first topic. *Paris- Soir* liked the first piece so much that they wanted a series.

Having written a single article was one thing. Writing a second was another. Now he began to see the world through a writer's eyes. Is there copy in everything? Not, he thought, when you have a deadline to meet.

But he had previously arranged a tour of North Africa, and on the ship from Marseilles to Algiers was an American journalist called Marthe Richard. When she spotted Maurice, she called out: "Good morning, Monsieur Carpentier."

Maurice assumed her mistake came from mispronunciation rather than ignorance, so he thought that mispronouncing the journalist's name in return would be the kindest way of pointing out the error. But throughout their whole chat, Miss Richard called him "Carpentier." It amused him at the time and provided a handy subject for his second *Paris-Soir* piece.

The third article was inspired by a visit to the Casbah. By that time, as he said himself, his whole life was "transformed." Sud- denly, everywhere he went, in every conversation with friends or strangers, there was a subject to write upon. Why were the pretty women he saw on the street corner—and he would always study pretty women standing on street corners—looking so sad? Posing the question and trying to imagine the answer was an- other subject for a piece. Whole new vistas were now open for him. When he felt sad, he could find ways of expressing that sadness through writing. When he was happy, it was a marvellous way of saying so and letting other people see it, too.

He didn't realize that writing would present him with a whole new career. He certainly hadn't yet considered that the journalist he had discovered inside himself would eventually become an author, too. One is now tempted to speculate how different his life would have been had he had that earlier "instruction." With-

out the drive his background gave him, he possibly might have
made nothing of himself at all—either as a writer or an entertainer.

René Clair, the eminent director and producer, thought he had
managed to get him away from the usual stereotypes when he
made *Break the News* with Chevalier in London in 1938. The
film—in which Maurice and Jack Buchanan played two music-
hall artists so down on their luck that they invented a murder
as a publicity stunt—was slightly better received than his previous effort. But the *Los Angeles Times*'s Philip K. Scheuer said
it would have been better titled *Break the News Gently*.

After he left Paris to make the picture, a near riot broke out
in the lobby of the Casino where Maurice had been appearing.
Hundreds of people fought among themselves when they discovered he wouldn't be going on stage that night. Several were
arrested. The management said they couldn't understand it. They
had taken his name off all the publicity as soon as they realized
he was going to London. It may have sounded reasonable, but
Maurice was the biggest of all the French stars and to be cheated
of a live Chevalier performance was more than any red-blooded
Frenchman could allow. He was still his country's finest ambassador. When King George VI and Queen Elizabeth paid a state
visit to Paris in 1938, Maurice was engaged to appear in the
entertainment which followed the state banquet at the Quai
d'Orsay.

And in October that year came another tribute, this time from
the Foreign Ministry. Maurice officially became a Chevalier—
of the Légion d'honneur, for "signal service for France overseas."

13.
The Sorrow and the Pity

I thought he was an epoch.

—JACQUELINE CARTIER

Maurice began 1939 as exhilarated as he had ended the previous year. He and Nita appeared to be a superb combination and certainly cut handsome figures as they walked together down the Champs-Élysées, always one of Maurice's favourite occupations.

"You know I'm not interested in any other woman," he told confidants, and it seemed true. He took no more than a normal interest in the showgirls at the Casino when he played there, and when a woman tried to get him to take advantage of her, he would usually reply politely but firmly: "Thank you very much, mademoiselle, but I have already had my lunch!" It was always a good line and sufficiently discouraging to make any further suggestions pointless. Nita's only rival was the paying public, and, unlike some women, she could take that kind of competition more easily than from any "other woman."

Needless to say, Maurice still had his moments of depression, and these, as always, came from two sources—when he told himself he was not good enough and when he thought about his mother. Ten years after her death, that wound still sometimes felt as raw as when it had been first inflicted. In both instances, Nita was usually able to offer the soothing comfort he needed.

If everything looked good in Chevalier's world, the fact was confirmed by his 1939 film, *Les Pièges*—called *Personal Column* in the United States. Maurice played a murder suspect who still had sufficient opportunity to sing his quota of songs. The *Los Angeles Times* thought it had an "unusual quality . . . [with] French dialogue fairly spicy at times; but you would never know it from the English subtitles."

With the Americans giving good reviews of his French films, he had a right to believe that the tide was rolling his way. For the moment, the events discussed at the Quai d'Orsay, the Reichschancellery in Berlin, or London's Number 10 Downing Street made little impact on Maurice Chevalier. Every Frenchman and woman knew that the Munich agreement had saved them from a horrific war, and that if the Boche attacked France, they would be swallowed up by the powerful defenses of the Maginot Line. No one considered the possibility that such a war could be lost—that the Maginot Line was a mirage, a cold, damp, miserable encampment that had gone rusty underground and was already sapping soldiers' morale to a crippling degree. No one imagined that Frenchmen would lose the will to fight, or that the Nazis would march under the Arc de Triomphe. No one dreamed that statesmen could become traitors; that simple people could be labelled or accused of being collaborators. Least of all, no one imagined that Maurice Chevalier would be among them.

Was he a collaborator? To this day, veterans of the four years which degraded the name of France argue about it. There is substantial evidence that he was not. It is also equally clear that he was no hero.

Just before the declaration of war, Maurice joined Gracie Fields and other British artists to sing "It's a Long Way to Tipperary" on the radio. The program was so successful and—to quote a contemporary report—wet so many eyes, including Chevalier's, that it was repeated and broadcast by NBC in the United States. The French broadcasting authorities had long known Maurice's power over the airwaves. When Radio Paris opened new studios just before the Nazis moved in, he was asked to "christen" them by being the first person to use their facilities. He began with a paean to the "mike," which was considered sufficiently important to be filmed for the newsreels, too.

It seemed the right time for a patriotic stand by the sort of person who would represent the ideal morale-boosting image in time of trouble. Maurice with his straw hat was a perfect symbol of France at her best, and people responsible for such things knew the value he offered the national cause.

On September 1, 1939, the day that the Nazis invaded Poland, he was having dinner with the Duke and Duchess of Windsor. But as soon as war was an actual, inescapable fact, he took up his position on behalf of his country. He replaced the straw hat with the *poilu*'s fluted steel helmet and entertained the troops, going to gun emplacements and singing in mess halls on the Maginot Line itself. Josephine Baker came along, too, with the entire cast of the Casino de Paris's current show—but even with girls looking beautiful in army-style uniforms on stage, it was Maurice who stole the show. It is this which gives us today some idea of the impact he made.

For the war Maurice had a new song in the style of the World War I hit, "Le Madelon." It was called "Victoire," and Victoire— a splendid name for a country about to give the enemy a bloody nose—was Madelon's daughter. It was marvellous stuff to sing while marching towards Germany:

> *Victoire*
> *C'est la fille à Madelon*
> *Victoire*
> *C'est l'mot d'ordre du colon*
> *C'est l'cri de toute la nation*
> *Victoire*
> *C'est la fille à Madelon.*

Stirring words from the man whom everyone believed could

stir the nation best; certainly, Maurice seemed to be making a better job of it than M. Reynaud and the other members of the French government. But it was still early days. The "phony war" had not yet given way to the real shooting match.

Just before the Nazis launched the final push that drove the British Expeditionary Force to Dunkirk, Maurice flew over for a matinée performance for the troops at the London Palladium, and was back in Paris that night for his show at the Casino.

But when the Nazis jackbooted their way down the Champs-Élysées, it became clear that French pride had been battered so severely there was little that could be done to restore it.

The huge French force, which had increased in a matter of weeks from one million to six million men, was totally overwhelmed by the much smaller but more cohesive German machine. The Maginot Line had proved useless. Suddenly, the French were divided into two camps—those who either exiled themselves to fight on with Charles de Gaulle or who carried on resistance with the Maquis; and those who settled for their new fate. Maurice Chevalier was among the latter.

He protested that he had never been political, that he could see no reason to desert his country. He didn't add then—although he would countless times in years to come—"in her hour of need." The notion that Marshal Pétain wanted to foster on behalf of his German masters was one of life returning speedily to prewar normality. Chevalier asked for no more than that. Deprived of his profession, there could be no life for him.

People who had gone to England tried to talk him out of staying behind. From neutral America Charles Boyer managed to get a telephone message to Maurice urging him to pack up and return to Hollywood. His telephone was clearly being tapped, but the call was innocuous enough: "It's a good time to pick up where you left off before because the English-language cinema has never been so busy." Early in 1940 Ernst Lubitsch cabled him with an invitation to star in a film he was planning about a team of actors caught up in Occupied Europe. Maurice politely turned down the offer, and the lead in *To Be or Not To Be* went instead to Jack Benny.

De Gaulle's party hoped that Maurice would follow the Free-French lead. The propaganda value and the boost to morale among the general's followers would not be lost on London either.

Only the northern part of France was occupied by the Germans. The rest of the country, controlled directly by the Vichy regime, did what it was told by its Nazi masters while providing a means of escape for people like Maurice who were told they could travel anywhere they liked. Feelers were put out by the Resistance that Maurice could, without any difficulty at all, take a plane from Marseilles to North Africa and from there go wherever he wished. But he had no desire to go anywhere.

Why not? It was a subject he tried to avoid whenever it came up after the war years. He said then that his duty was simply not to desert his people. Much more likely was a fear that if he left France, he would never be able to come back, and a French entertainer deprived of his French audience would, he thought, lose all.

He loved America, but his Hollywood experiences were not happy enough to want to risk repeating them. If he failed in America, where could he go? To Britain? Prospects for England didn't look very healthy in 1940, and what would happen if the Nazis captured him after once having escaped their grip? The prospect was too frightening to contemplate. And even if he managed to live out the war years securely in a foreign country, his instinct was that the French wouldn't have him back. In 1940 it seemed that the taint of desertion was a more likely and more painful allegation to fight than the suggestion of collaboration.

There was also an additional problem: If he escaped, could he take Nita with him? Flying a Jew out of France was altogether different from allowing Maurice the freedom of the skies. And without her there would be nothing to hold on to; she was his security. With her at his side, he knew he was still the greatest and strongest entertainer in France. Without her, he knew he would fall apart.

So he decided to stay, but for a time he took a holiday. His Riviera home was unmolested. His food came in regularly. Nita lived with him as before. They were actually at La Bocca at the time the armistice was signed.

The Germans didn't know how to handle Chevalier. They sent a polite word to his villa suggesting that it would be a good idea if he appeared again in Paris. He said he wasn't feeling well.

When he didn't immediately jump, the Germans arranged for the Paris press to do their dirty work for them. One paper reported: "Nearly every important entertainer who has any allegiance to his country is here in Paris helping to restore the faith of their compatriots. But the cowardly Chevalier remains on the Riviera with his Jew."

It did the trick. Maurice came back from the Riviera and Nita came with him. *The New York Times* said he planned to do either a play or a film in Paris, although neither happened. Henri Varna, manager of the Casino, persuaded him to do another season at the theater. "You must do your best to make Paris smile again," Varna told him. In the light of the press campaign it seemed good advice.

Once more Maurice sang and did his impersonations on the Casino stage. The theater was packed with men in German uniforms. Nazi cameramen found plenty of opportunity to photograph both him and his audience—the officers and their French girl friends—together.

"Would you make some jokes about Churchill?" asked a German officer in Chevalier's dressing room as he congratulated him on his performance. "I don't make political jokes because I am not a political person," was what he later said he replied. He possibly didn't realize at the time how wise a decision that was. But as Henri Amouroux, the principal historian of the war years in France, emphasized to me, he did change the sort of songs he was singing. There were no more tunes about the admirable French. Now he was helping to foster the ideals that Marshal Pétain was telling everybody were so vital—the importance of work, family, homeland. His "Chanson d'un Maçon" ("The Song of a Mason") —was typical. It had the right image for the time, he was told, and he accepted it. After all, his duty was to give his audiences what they wanted. If there were no audiences, he had no career.

As Maurice began working again, it did seem that life was getting better. He told people that he admired what Marshal Pétain was doing for the country—and most ordinary French people thought so, too. He explained years later to François Vals, his secretary, that he had liked the trim, clean, dignified figure the aged marshal cut. Maurice always liked trim, clean, dignified people.

When a German composer arrived in New York from Vichy France in December 1940, *The New York Times* reported his saying: "Maurice Chevalier is allowed the freedom of France because he is well liked by the Nazis."

It was true. He was well liked. His two months at the Casino were a sellout, and without German participation the box office couldn't have been the least bit healthy. But did that make him a collaborator? When he was begged to sign up for a new season straightaway, he asked to be allowed to take a rest. It was not good enough for the Germans, nor did it totally allay the anxieties of the Resistance. They were gradually building up a dossier on his activities, but were still not sure what it all proved.

The Germans were happiest of all when Maurice was appearing regularly on Radio Paris. He sang all his old songs and some new ones that toed the Pétain line without being treacherous, but the station was the Nazis' most blatant pro-German propaganda weapon. Maurice should have had the sense to realize that he was being used to make that propaganda palatable. His singing was the sugar on the Nazi pill. Even more important, he was giving the radio station his own "seal of approval" at a time when the Resistance would have preferred their countrymen to confine their listening to the French Service of the BBC.

Maurice was very well paid for what he did on Radio Paris, and this was among the facts that came to light in one of the collaboration trials after the Liberation. Jean Hérold Paquis, a political writer, was on trial for his life. According to the official transcript of the hearing, he told his accusers: "They reproach me, but Maurice Chevalier got a lot of money for singing." Paquis's lawyer stated, in the evidence for the case, that "for two minutes of popular songs [a man named] Claveau earned two thousand francs a broadcast while Chevalier earned sixty thousand. You must think that the music-mad Germans paid better for music than for treason."

It was Chevalier's bread and butter and he felt happier singing on the radio than on stage in front of row upon row of German officers. He was embarrassed by it, though, and there were times when he feared for the consequences. "I am torn apart by my love for my country and my profession. Have I done wrong?" he would ask.

The Nazis responsible for public morale wanted him to go back to the Casino. "It is too big a strain for me," he told them. "I am not feeling up to it." That was easier to turn down than another request with which he was constantly being bombarded: "Monsieur Chevalier," said the officer in charge of propaganda, "we should like you to go to Germany to entertain the French workers who have gallantly gone there to help the war effort."

Maurice balked at that. These men were not working in forced-labour battalions, but had been lured by the greener fields of Germany and the promise of good food, comfortable beds, and—in many cases—beautiful women to fill them. A team of French painters had already gone to Germany to demonstrate not merely their art but also their total belief in the correctness of the Nazi cause. Although billed as a cultural exchange, it was actually very much a one-way affair with a group of elderly artists who made the trip purely out of cowardice.

Others went farther still, while remaining in Paris. Meanwhile, Maurice was still sleeping with Nita Rayer, a fact that was not lost on the Nazis.

14.
A Breath of Scandal

Any third-rate chanteur de charme *has a better voice than I. But they sing from the throat, while I sing from the heart.*

—MAURICE CHEVALIER

When the Nazis again asked Maurice to entertain French prisoners of war in Germany, they added: "And afterwards, Monsieur Chevalier, we should like to make you welcome in our country. Emil Jannings, our distinguished actor, would so much like to meet you."

The same thought flashed through the minds of both the Germans and Chevalier: pictures in the newspapers of the two great stars together. Chevalier said no.

Two days later he was called again to the office of the occupying general. Once more he was asked to do the tour of the camps and again he pleaded ill health. Before Maurice left, the Nazi added a footnote to their conversation: "Your lady friend is Mademoiselle Rayer? She is Romanian, I believe." Maurice knew what he meant. Foreign-born Jews were being rounded up all over the occupied zone and, with the help of Marshal Pétain, in the south, too. He was presented with the vital issue: Should he stick by Nita or save his own skin? He decided to stay with Nita. One day, with the beautiful brunette at his side and her parents sitting in the back, Maurice drove Nita's tiny Fiat into the Dordogne. There, they took up residence with some friends at their home near Mauzac.

Was it heroism that made him decide to stay with his mistress? He wanted to protect her certainly, and to do otherwise would undoubtedly have branded him a coward. But he still needed her. Taking her parents with them was both a gesture to her—Nita wouldn't have gone without them—and the only decent thing to do. He solved the problem—or so he thought—by announcing that he had retired, and for a time the Germans accepted this. The local Commissioner for Jewish Affairs called to see Maurice but told him that since she was the protégée of such an eminent entertainer, the authorities would not enforce the law in Nita's case. The Germans had more important cards up their sleeve.

Otto Abetz, the Nazi military commander in Paris, insisted that Maurice go to Germany. For a time Chevalier stalled, and the Germans contented themselves with requests that he take part in a Red Cross gala in Paris. Either Maurice was naïve or he succumbed to the beckoning magnetism of a real-live audience. Whatever the reason, he accepted.

The day after the gala the newspapers were full of the story. On the front pages were pictures showing Maurice on stage, and handsome blond German soldiers—many with strategically placed bandages—sitting in the audience. The German-controlled French-language magazine, *Signal*, showed similar scenes the following week. Within a very few days, newsreels in movie houses all over France and Germany showed them, too. When Maurice did a three-week stint at a Paris nightclub, the audience once more consisted almost entirely of German officers and their French mistresses. The Germans wrote back home of the marvellous entertainer they saw, and the Resistance members squirmed in their cellars when they saw the pictures of Chevalier entertaining the Boche.

Every so often Maurice received telephone calls, supposedly from members of the Maquis, warning him not to continue singing for the Nazis. "If I don't complete this engagement," he told them, "other lives besides my own will be threatened."

It was a hard decision he had to make. Had he failed to appear at the club—a man whose reputation was that he never, but never, failed to honour an engagement—then it would have meant difficult explanations to the Nazis, to say nothing of the likelihood of Nita and her family being carted off to Auschwitz. But going on with the show meant placing his life in the hands of his own countrymen. Certainly, he could never ask for protection—doing so would be to tie himself to the Germans and be a virtual signature on his own execution warrant.

He went on stage shivering more than usual, but he performed as he always had and no threats were ever put into practice.

As always, there were still more cameramen. Maurice said afterwards that he was angry at the publicity, but he loved the sound of a cheering mob. When the Casino de Paris asked him to do another two months at the theater, he agreed. He went back to Vichy France at the end of the standing-room-only season.

Very courteously, Radio Paris asked him to do more broadcasts. He didn't turn them down and so helped the Germans' propaganda efforts once again.

At another concert—Maurice said years later he thought it was in aid of French war wounded—he sang before twelve hundred well-heeled Germans and French. Maurice's old boxing friend, Georges Carpentier, was also in the audience.

The Nazis were now putting on the pressure. Maurice Sampini, who was responsible for the French government department looking after the interests of prisoners of war in Germany, asked him to entertain the men. When Dr. Hans Dietrich, head of the German Propagandastaffel in Paris, mentioned the matter, it was difficult for Chevalier to say no. Veiled hints were dropped at the wisdom of Maurice living with a Jewish woman.

He presented the Nazis with a counter-suggestion: He would do a concert at Alten Grabow, where he himself had been a pris-

oner in World War I. And he demanded something in return for
the show. Had he not done so, people really would have suspected he was working for the Nazis. He didn't want money, he
told them. Instead, he asked for lives. His fee was to be allowed
to travel incognito and to obtain freedom for ten prisoners, half
from his own suburb of Ménilmontant and the other half from the
working-class Belleville district.

When the Germans agreed to his terms, Maurice went, but in
this too he displayed a certain naïveté. Did he really think that
the Nazis wouldn't exploit the trip? He had told them he didn't
want any publicity and he wouldn't make the tour of Germany
they requested. Even now, he decided against meeting Jannings.

He went to Germany by train, and to get to Alten Grabow he
had to travel through other towns, where the train would stop
and where there would be conveniently placed German cameramen. He spent a night in a luxury hotel in Berlin—cameras
snapping as he walked across the threshold, a picture of Hitler
hanging conspicuously in the background.

Despite all that Maurice had said before, he was informed that
Herr Jannings and a delegation of very important German artists
were going to come to the hotel and were now ready to meet him.
Maurice said that he intended the visit to be strictly incognito.

"We hope you will perform at the Scala in Berlin," one officer
suggested.

"I don't think so," said Maurice. "I have now retired."

The manager of the Scala was not to be put off. He handed
Maurice a blank contract. "Please, Herr Chevalier," he said,
"write in your own price." Maurice put the document in his
pocket and, as he wrote later, threw it away. When suggestions
were made that he ought to toe the occupying power's line, he
would always protest that he knew nothing of what the Germans
had in mind, but by going to Alten Grabow he had climbed onto
a Nazi caravan from which he could not jump. It was more in-
criminating that he was travelling first class; the Allies later made
a great deal of the well-dressed, obviously well-fed Frenchman
travelling in luxury at a time when the King of England announced to the world that he never allowed himself more than
four inches of bath water. Maurice just said he saw the trip as a
way to help the prisoners.

Before he left Germany, he was promised that the ten prisoners of war would follow, and they did; among them, two named Chevalier—René and Paul. Neither was any relation to Maurice, but the Allies saw it as further good publicity for the Germans.

Three days after Maurice returned to France, Germany's propaganda minister, Joseph Goebbels, went on the air and "revealed" details of the Chevalier tour of Germany. A journalist from a neutral country asked Maurice about the conditions under which the French prisoners were living: "That is a very delicate question, my friend," he replied—suddenly aware of what could result from one of his statements. "My mission is to make France laugh."

One section of France was not laughing when it read of his activities at Alten Grabow. Recordings of the concert were now broadcast on Radio Berlin—intended, it was said, to give comfort to other French prisoners in Germany. The news spread throughout the Allied countries. The Free French were furious. They weren't much happier several weeks later when the first pictures appeared in the French newspapers showing Maurice shaking hands with the camp commandant, meeting German high brass, standing on station platforms with German place names in the background, and on stage surrounded by a band of happy *poilus*. In these, Maurice wore a smart, heavy overcoat and highly polished shoes, and, despite their camera smiles, his audience looked considerably more down-at-heel.

Would a real French patriot have even set foot on German soil? There were a million Frenchmen in prisoner-of-war camps and the fact that Chevalier had gone to entertain some of them had two distinct reactions. Some shuddered at the thought of what he had done; others treated his performance simply as a means of giving comfort to his countrymen. The dichotomy would remain for the rest of Chevalier's life.

In April 1943, after the Allies had landed in Sicily and the Italians who had been stationed in the south of France had left, Maurice and Nita were back in their villa at La Bocca. The downfall of Germany now seemed a distinct possibility, and after his experiences in Germany Maurice decided not to go back to Paris to work, except when it was impossible to resist the offers to broadcast on Radio Paris. He made doubly sure that none of the songs or any other part of his repertoire could be construed as being the least bit political.

Maurice, Nita, and Nita's parents took off for an extended holiday in the country, at Saint Meyme, a quiet place where Germans were rarely seen. For the first time in almost a year he felt able to relax. He decided to spend time taking the advice of his friend, Louis Chauvet of *Paris-Soir*, to start penning his memoirs.

It was, he discovered, "a marvellous escape" from what was happening to France. He wrote about seventeen chapters, "making a pilgrimage to the past," and then put the work aside. It seemed all too personal, too much baring of the soul.

Maurice and Nita appeared to lead a normal social life at times. They played cards for clothing coupons with Maurice doing his best to try to persuade people like Princess Beris Kandaouroff to dispose of a few for his benefit. The coupons changed hands like gold dust on the black market, and Maurice liked to pay above the going price for these no more than he ever enjoyed overpaying for anything.

When a group of Maquis called "Le Soleil" started operating in the forests nearby, Maurice wondered if he would be picked up, either by the Germans as a suspected Resistance worker or by a misguided patriot who considered him a collaborator. But he was left alone.

Maurice made things more difficult for himself subsequently by giving an interview to the Pétainist paper, *Petit Parisien*, in which he said: "If Pétain wants better understanding between all countries, that is good." The newspaper stressed in the opening paragraph of the piece that this indicated Maurice Chevalier "approved of collaboration." He later denied that he meant any such thing, but nonetheless it was another bit of procollaboration mud, and it seemed to stick. In New York *Variety* said that Maurice had urged collaboration in a series of broadcasts on Radio Paris, but no evidence was ever produced that such broadcasts were made. Nevertheless, he was now branded all over the world as a Nazi-lover. The London *Daily Mail* reported he had "gone pure Boche." The BBC, very much the voice of the Underground, took up the theme enthusiastically. In one broadcast a French songwriter—whom Maurice had previously considered a friend—

listed the Chevalier name among a collection of show people he described as collaborators. When Maurice heard the news on the radio he felt bathed in a cold sweat; the shock held him rigid in his chair.

In 1943 a group of Belgian patriots blew up an electrical installation at Charleroi, where Maurice was to make one of his increasingly rare appearances. He cancelled the show immediately. Press reports both in Nazi Europe and in the Allied countries described him as "now a member of the New Order."

This didn't help his image with the Free French, nor did the fact that Belgium, still under German control, awarded Maurice the Order of Leopold. He didn't reject it.

The BBC, in particular, warmed to the notion of Chevalier being the collaborator *par excellence*. As a nicely aimed insult, they broadcast parodies of his songs.

Maurice began to worry again about Nita. Her parents were living on false papers just outside Nice—but with a promise from the head of police for the Préfecture des Alpes Maritimes that he would not harm them. The head of police had, needless to say, made a similar promise concerning Nita herself, but now the Commissioner for Jewish Affairs for the area was himself asking questions. He ordered an inquiry about her, but Maurice's influence was strong enough to dissuade him from taking it very far. The Gestapo were much more interested in why they hadn't seen the name Maurice Chevalier on any billboards recently.

Maurice said he had been ill.

"Then I think you ought to be examined by one of our doctors," said the official—only to have the suggestion thrown back in his face by headquarters in Paris. There they still felt the velvet-glove approach was best. As much as ever, they needed Maurice Chevalier on their side. The BBC reports had been the strongest weapon in their hands since the photographs at Alten Grabow and Berlin.

At last, Maurice had a stroke of luck. An actor called René Lefèvre somehow got a message to London: MISTAKE FOR MAURICE. STOP CAMPAIGN. ILL-TIMED. STOP. CHEVALIER GIVEN US PROOF AND WILL GIVE MORE.

Almost immediately the message took effect.

He was no longer spoken of on the BBC as a collaborator. The song parodies were suddenly dropped. But no apologies were broadcast, no withdrawals made. The Resistance was not going all the way in clearing his name. For most of the people in the Maquis, Maurice Chevalier was still a name to be spat on and one which left a bad taste afterwards. And now that the Allies were marching through France, the Maquis were the government in much of the country.

As France was liberated there were daily reports of vengeance being wrought on collaborators. Before long there was news that Maurice had been arrested by a Maquis "hit" team. This was followed by a further announcement—he had been shot by a firing squad. Everyone wanted to be free of the slightest taint of collaboration. Those who weren't were put on trial or simply shot. For a while it seemed that Maurice Chevalier had been among them.

The first to claim this were the Germans—who liked to show that they had had such a splendid entertainer on their side. He was shot, they said, by the Maquis in the street and—appropriately enough—died in the arms of two girls. The American press joined in the obituary game, saying what a pity such a marvellous talent should have so degraded himself. The *Washington Post* editorial was perhaps the most poignant of all:

"The report, not yet fully confirmed, that music-hall actor Maurice Chevalier has been executed as a traitor by the French patriots induces a note of sadness into the universal rejoicing over the Liberation of France. . . . Perhaps the tragedy of it is that to every American and Englishman, Chevalier, a child of the Parisian tenements, typified Paris and perhaps also France, especially its good nature, gaiety, glamour, and supposed naughtiness."

The same questions were asked in practically every other English-language newspaper: How could he do it? How could he be so stupid?

Maurice Chevalier was dead and the memory of his artistry was now tarnished. But people were jumping to conclusions. Maurice was still alive.

Before long the Fighting French (as the Free French had now become) headquarters in London issued a statement that they would be "very surprised" if Maurice had indeed been shot.

There were strict orders in operation that any suspects were to be arrested and taken for trial—not shot summarily. Before long an explanation became apparent for the "mistaken execution." It turned out that once again the common Chevalier name had been responsible. The collaborator-mayor of a tiny French town *had* been shot—and his name was also Maurice Chevalier.

Maurice's friends were the first to report that Maurice was still alive and well and living at La Bocca. He and Nita huddled together in their villa, expecting any minute to be carted off by Resistance squads as the populace turned out to jeer.

Maurice was not arrested, but he was asked by the newly installed collaboration tribunal to see them. The Germans were glad of the opportunities provided for them by Chevalier's investigation, and in the summer of 1944, when they had already been driven out of most of the country, they gave more lurid descriptions of the way they said he was being treated by the Maquis. Later that year they again announced his death. The previous report of his passing having been highly exaggerated, they wrote he had been actually bludgeoned to death by Resistance men using brass knuckle-dusters and other blunt instruments. The story spread like wildfire, but while it was in circulation, Maurice was plainly seen talking to members of the very organization said to have executed him.

"I did not collaborate," he told the tribunal when he came before them. "The Germans asked me to go along with them, but I refused." They listened to him, weighed the facts, and dismissed him from further consideration.

He was free, but Maurice was not satisfied. He was not free from his conscience. The mud still stuck. "I want to be able to *prove* to you that I did not collaborate," he said, but people were not listening.

One of his strongest opponents at the time of his collaboration trial was Josephine Baker, by that time much better known in France than in her native America. Their affair was long over but, acting like a woman scorned, she continued to spread the story of his "collaboration" vengefully even after the official cleansing operations of the tribunals had done their job.

"*Elle est une vache,*" Maurice said. "I have known many cows in my time, but she is the biggest cow of the lot."

Others in show business like Claude Dauphin, who had also previously accused him, now found ways to apologize, either privately or publicly. Miss Baker never did, and Maurice, who could bear grudges as well as he wore a straw hat, never forgave her.

The vituperative anti-Chevalier campaign continued in parts of the British press. The London *Sunday Pictorial* reported: "Living in comfortable luxury in Paris, he is working overtime trying to convince his countrymen and the rest of the free world that he is all on the side of de Gaulle and never ceased to work for a free France.

"So far, he's been left alone to his conscience. But there is in cold storage a bunch of gramophone records that may be played over one day to show that Chevalier did quite a lot of work for the Germans. Of course, he may be right and the gramophone records the work of some impostor." If the records existed they were never released.

The United Press wire service called him "the well-known collaborator." These reports appeared the same day that newspapers recorded that snipers were attacking General de Gaulle as he led his troops down the Champs-Élysées, and the Americans reached the Marne.

Chevalier was allowed another hearing, and this time it was officially stated that he was not a collaborator. He was cleared by the Comité d'Épuration. Similar hearings were held for Edith Piaf, who had also been to Germany to entertain prisoners. She was cleared "with congratulations." The Comité d'Épuration refused to add those two words to Chevalier's cleansing document.

The old insecurity welled up inside him once more. It was true that doubts still did remain in people's minds. Those who were in the Resistance argue over him to this day. Twenty years after the war had ended, the Duchess of Bedford—who, as Nicole Milinaire, had been a Resistance heroine—refused to invite him to her home, Woburn Abbey, "because he was a collaborator."

On the other hand, a Mr. P. J. Philip wrote to *The New York Times* from Ottawa, Canada:

"I should like to pass on this last conversation I had with him in the Rue Daunou in late May 1940 when everybody in Paris knew that the first phase of the war had been lost.

"I was surprised to see him, for the reports had been published that he was being asked for in Hollywood and that the French Government had recommended that he should do a propaganda film there. Very quietly, he answered: 'Yes, that is true but one does not abandon one's country at a moment like this.'"

The hardest people to please after the war were the French Communists. If an alleged collaborator could satisfy these arch-enemies of the Nazis that he was "clean," then he would really be above suspicion. Chevalier's mistake was to take what may have seemed at the time an easy course, a gift from heaven: The Communists agreed to promote him as an anti-Fascist. What he did not realize was that he was holding himself open to political blackmail. Their gesture, with one stroke, cleared him of charges of being a Nazi but at the same moment branded him as a Red. If he did not appear on their platforms, they would say he really was a collaborator. So Maurice marched in a Communist-run parade. He sang at a Communist-sponsored charity rally. And he gave a long interview to the Communist paper, *Ce Soir*, in which he laid his wartime cards on the table:

"I always refused to take part in all the shows the Germans organized and I had a heavy heart when I read in the Paris press, which was under their control, that I was collaborating with them. Nobody believed these lies for a moment. The provincial press and the foreign newspapers welcomed this news and spread it in vain. I was sure that all my friends kept their faith in me."

The thing that surprised people was, on the one hand, that *Ce Soir*, of all papers, would so willingly buy the Chevalier line and, on the other, that the originally Pétainist Chevalier should sympathize with the extreme Left. The Socialist paper, *Le Populaire*, said as much. Sam White, Paris correspondent of the London *Evening Standard*, told me:

"I met Maurice a long time after this and he was still dreadfully unhappy about the way he felt he had been blackmailed."

It was not an emotion Chevalier wanted published at the time, but its fruits would be harvested in years to come. What no commentator seemed to have grasped was the fact that Maurice

Chevalier, nearly five years after the war had begun, was still a symbol, to be cultivated by the victors now as much as by those who thought they had won in 1940. In 1944 rehabilitating Maurice Chevalier was a means of rehabilitating France. With him back in business, the country could get back to its business, too.

15.
Count Your Blessings

This is not a singer . . . this is not a conjurer of the fantastic, this is not a comedian, this is a creator of personages.

—Marcel Pagnol

It would be too simple to say that with the Liberation and the coming of peace the following year, Maurice Chevalier put behind him both the war and the problems that he had brought upon himself. They haunted him. To make life more palatable, friends planted stories that Maurice had acted as a "letter carrier" for a Maquis group called "L'Étoile." For years these stories were reprinted in feature articles, but they don't appear to have had any more substance than the tales about his collaboration.

Undoubtedly there had been a great deal of professional jealousy in the charges levelled against him. A lot of the flak directed at him between 1944 and 1946 came from other performers who would have been very happy to see him out of the way. In an attempt to get himself off the hook, he began giving a series of press interviews in which he stressed how he had turned down the Germans' offer for him to be able "to live the life of a king." He talked about how he had spent the war at La Bocca. "I only earned a twentieth of what I could have got had I chosen to leave my people and accept offers from America," he said. His message at first appeared to be accepted. The songwriter who had attacked Maurice on the BBC came to see him, Maurice said in several of his books—he repeated the story at every conceivable opportunity —and begged him to accept his apology. Maurice said he would think about it.

Everybody wanted to know when he would appear on stage again. There were rumours that he and Mistinguett would get together at the Casino, but this was mere wishful thinking, mostly on Miss's part. "Chevalier is in hiding because he is jealous of me," Miss said, "because I always get more applause than he does."

Soon after the news of his acquittal came through, Maurice made a tour of American military bases in France. He began slowly, his body riddled with nerves. How would the audience react? Would there be any catcalling? Would they—and this fear haunted him—start throwing things? In makeshift theaters in army camps, in drill halls, in the open air with white-helmeted military policemen ringing the temporary auditoriums, Maurice Chevalier went back to work.

It was harder than returning to the Casino. Even harder than after his nervous breakdown twenty years before, because now his audience knew all about his problem. It was not something he could keep to himself.

He only had a pianist on stage, but to say he was a success is to understate the emotion his appearance generated. Without his having to sing a note or even open his mouth, the applause for one of his first shows was deafening and lasted a full five minutes. At another camp, when he mounted the trestle tables that had been rigged up to form a stage, he tried to sing and found that his voice wouldn't leave his larynx. He coughed and tried again. Eventually, his voice returned, but it was not until he realized the G.I.s out front were eating out of his sweaty palm that he attempted jutting out his lower lip and giving the half-laugh which was his trademark. His repertoire was mostly nostalgic: the old songs that the Americans had liked so much in Hollywood— "Louise," "Mimi," and "Valentine." He also returned to his youth in "La Marche de Ménilmontant," about a young man who tries to be happy and flippant but is really much more concerned about the realities of life. It was perfect for him.

He followed the army shows with a comeback at the ABC music hall in Montmartre. As soon as he opened his act with the familiar "Bonsoir, Messieurs et 'Dames," the audience was all his. At one of those early performances was the American impresario and columnist Billy Rose. Shortly afterwards Rose reported in his column:

> I caught his show on a bitter night in November. None of the theaters was heated. No one would trade coal for money. I sat there in overshoes, overcoat, woolen mittens, hat and a fuzzy muffler up to my eyes—still feeling like a robed banana in a deep freeze. It's not easy for a performer to work to an audience whose view is obscured by the vapours of his own breath. But when Chevalier strutted out on the stage, the temperature shot up thirty degrees.
>
> There's plenty of grey under that jaunty straw hat now, but when he begins to sing, he's still the gay young man of France. Like Caruso, like Harry Langdon and like Astaire, when Chevalier is on, the other actors might as well be dealing pinochle in the dressing room. I think he's a cinch once more to stand the whole country on its head.

Indeed, Maurice now wanted to do just that. To be on the stage by himself and to tour America and Britain. He told *Stars and Stripes*, the American military newspaper, that he yearned to get back to films, and "I hope soon to get some good American food and a room with steam heat."

He didn't anticipate that his war record would intervene.

In March 1945 the British impresario Jack Hylton announced he was bringing Maurice over to England for a ten-week tour of London and the provinces. The Aliens Department of the Home Office was less enthusiastic and, without giving any reason, refused to give Maurice a visa.

When a French film company planned to do a movie about

the American leave center on the Riviera, the U.S. Army refused
to allow its troops to appear on camera with Chevalier. No reason
was given, but this time the studio asked the French government
for an official report on Maurice's war activities, and when this
showed that he was in the clear, passed it on to the Army.

"We have now received this denial," said an American military
spokesman. "We had to get it because we couldn't have American
soldiers collaborating with a collaborator." With the help of the
French statement, production of *Seven Days in Paradise* was allowed to continue.

If anyone doubted that Maurice was back in favour, a sharp
eye at the Peace Parade down the Champs-Élysées would have
confirmed the fact beyond all doubt. Together with the armed
services and the Resistance squads, there were also figures from
French public life, among them Maurice, who received the loudest
and the longest cheers of the whole spectacle. It was a gesture that
served to give him back his dignity.

The most welcome opportunity to try to clear his name before
American and other English-speaking audiences came from Paramount News, which allowed him to state once more exactly what
he had done during the war. The newsreel footage was later
featured in Marcel Ophüls's marathon film of the occupation of
France, *The Sorrow and the Pity*. In it Chevalier seemed to typify
the attitudes of most of his countrymen.

He was popular with the G.I.s in Paris, as well as with Marlene Dietrich, who was in the city to entertain troops. She was
out on the Champs-Élysées signing autographs when she heard
that Maurice was in a nearby restaurant. According to press reports, she immediately apologized to her admirers and went along
to see him. When Maurice saw her, his eyes filled with tears and
they embraced. One of the most popular entertainment centers
for Allied troops was the Stage Door Canteen, where Marlene was
appearing. Maurice immediately volunteered to take part in their
shows, too.

There was no more likelihood now that he and Marlene would
form a permanent liaison than there had been ten years earlier.
He was still in love with Nita, and they were living together—
although there were a number of stories circulating now that the

two had split up. It was true, however, that they were no longer in a state of idyllic happiness. Nita wanted to resume her stage career and Maurice was determined she should not. Possibly he thought she might become so popular with the public that his own fame and success would be eclipsed.

With the Liberation, Maurice was asked to think again about publishing his memoirs. The idea came from René Laporte, who was now a historian of the Resistance movement—a fact which endeared him to Chevalier. When Maurice told him he was already quite far along in his writing, Laporte insisted on seeing his work and liked it so much he asked his editor, René Julliard, to see the chapters.

The result was Maurice's first book, *Ma Route et Mes Chansons* (*My Way and My Songs*), the Chevalier story from his childhood up to the Liberation. It quickly became a best seller. "A new Dickens," declared one critic. Maurice loved that and the opportunity to open his heart to his public. He rode on a new cloud of success, touring France, signing copies every time he came down to earth. He sent a copy to his friend Georges Carpentier and inscribed it with typical immodesty: "To our Georges—from *their* Maurice."

"I'm very proud," he said as he scrawled his name over a pile of title pages. "I have great emotion about it. This is one of the most beautiful things in my life. It's a shot in the arm."

Maurice had recently renewed his friendship with Charles Boyer. For a long time Boyer had discussed books with Maurice, and now whenever they met, they each talked about their latest literary find. The two men felt a great warmth for each other. And it wasn't simply because they both were French born. "They were very great friends," Rouben Mamoulian told me, "because they found they simply liked each other. Sometimes counterpoint can be a lot more effective than harmony."

Chevalier and Boyer planned to see each other early in 1946 when Maurice was due to open in a series of one-man shows in the United States for the Shubert Brothers. But Maurice's optimism about himself was not completely shared by the Americans. Just before signing, the Shuberts changed their minds; they said they didn't think any man could hold the stage alone for an hour. Maurice replied that he would show how it could be done when he made his forthcoming tours, first of Switzerland and then of Brazil and Argentina.

Within a year of the Liberation, and only weeks after V-E Day, Maurice confirmed loud and clear that he was in his old form. He moved into the Pathé film studios and started work on a movie for René Clair, *Le Silence Est d'Or*. RKO, instead of literally translating the title as *Silence Is Golden*, which would have been appropriate since Maurice was featured in the picture as a silent-film director, called it *Man About Town*.

At first, M. Clair had to be persuaded to give Maurice the role. "I can't see you playing a man that old," he told him.

"But I'm fifty-eight!" Maurice pointed out.

When it was released two years later in the United States, *Life* magazine featured it as the "Movie of the Week."

The tours of Europe and South America did precisely what Maurice hoped they would—they proved he was once more going over with foreign audiences.

16.
Man of the Hour

When I do a one-man show on stage alone for a whole evening, I feel I'm hugging the crowd in my arms and that they are hugging me. It's pure love.

—MAURICE CHEVALIER

It was not until March 1947 that he and Nita returned to the United States to make the "beeg" comeback.

He couldn't completely forget the war and all its associations. When he boarded the *Queen Elizabeth* at Southampton—no problem with entry to England now—for the beginning of the voyage to New York, the first question people asked was: "Has your wartime record affected your position?"

Maurice replied: "I've never been so popular with the French crowd as I have been since the Liberation. That is the answer."

He carried a straw hat for the inevitable pictures, and made sure that none of the cameramen missed the Croix de guerre and

Légion d'honneur ribbons in his buttonhole. All the journalists noted that the fifty-nine-year-old Maurice's hair was now completely grey. He said he also hoped they wouldn't forget the fact that he still had a lump of German shrapnel embedded in a lung.

In America there were many lumps in the throats of the people who thronged the Henry Miller Theater on Broadway the night Maurice made his comeback performance. It was his first in the United States for twelve years. They came in droves to see him, the sort of people who could be sure of getting their names in the papers whenever they went anywhere. The curtain was due to go up at 8 P.M., and the audience was advised to be seated by 7:45, but people stayed in the lobby just the same to watch the spectacle of the crowd. Financier Bernard Baruch came and writer George Jean Nathan was there. So were Joseph Cotten and a number of the glamourous women of the contemporary stage, cinema, and cabarets—like Claudette Colbert, Hazel Scott, and Hildegarde. So was Billy Rose, who once again proved how devoted a fan another man of the theater could be.

"Instead of backing himself up with $20,000 worth of gingerbread and feathers," he wrote, "[Chevalier] appeared on a stage with nothing but some old portières and a fellow at the piano. . . .

"For a change, here was a man who could really wear a top hat, white muffler, and a blue coat. A lot of actors I chum around with won't like this statement, but I don't think there is a man in the American theater with half the talent and class of this kid from France."

Bing Crosby asked Maurice to appear on his *Philco Time* radio show and did a number of duets with him, including "Louise," "Valentine," and "Mimi," although he kidded his French guest about having "learned his English from Jimmy Durante."

To the audience at the Henry Miller, that was one of Maurice's most endearing charms when he finally came on stage on the show's first night. His pianist had already gone through an overture, when Maurice, to a mixture of applause and female sighs, finally slid onto the stage, his straw hat at a rakish angle over his right eye and just the correct amount of lower lip protruding. The tuxedo was midnight blue; the Croix de guerre and the Légion d'honneur were again very much in evidence. Maurice looked especially handsome as he stood with the spotlight playing on him, giving a sheen to his clothes and a sparkle to his face, and his famous charm was never more in evidence.

His own "Bonsoir, Messieurs et 'Dames" was again the song with which he opened his performance. It wasn't a clever move—"Chevalier was always a lousy songwriter," Charles Aznavour later told me—and the applause at the end of the number was not nearly as strong as that which had first greeted his appearance. He would have done much better with "Valentine." Except that the songs were not the most important part of his act.

His success lay in that the scripted part of his performance was the icing on the cake. Looking down towards the second row in the stalls, he called out: "How do you do, sir?" All eyes followed his and although there was some uncomfortable shuffling in the row, no one was sure whom he was addressing.

"I don't know your name, but I have the impression you are my friend because the first time I sing here een New York, een the Fulton Theater, you were sitteeng een the same seat. And your wife—I remember her, too, yes. Oh, that's very nice to see you both here tonight."

The audience laughed, still not sure whether there was really someone out front whom Maurice recognized so perfectly.

"You have not changed at all, you know. Oh, you have got a bit grey-er over there—but so am I. I don't know anyone who gets younger each year. Remember Baby Le Roy? I understand he is now a general in the American Army. Everybodee gets older. Of course . . . except your wife. Only your wife—your wife has not changed at all. . . . What do you say, sir? . . . [pause, with hand cupped to ear] It's not the same wife? Oh, I am sorree. I didn't know these things happen in America . . ."

He seemed nervous. He kept running his thumb up and down the silk stripe on his trousers.

"I've brought you all my best French songs . . . I can assure you, ladees and gentlemen, that every night I will try to poleesh my work a little more, try to understand you a little more so that we will get along better."

It was a promise well kept. But there were still some people who left the theater more aware of what had gone on before Chevalier's visit than perhaps they should have. Brooks Atkinson wrote in *The New York Times*: "To begin with, the most profound observation—Maurice Chevalier is a nice guy. Nothing has altered that winning fact. Now that the Germans have left Paris and the shooting is over, Maurice Chevalier has come back to New York with a bundle of nightclub songs which he sang at Henry Miller's last evening."

But, as he saw it, there was a big "but."

"Like all the rest of us, Maurice Chevalier is older and with so many bitter memories from the last eight years, none of us can recapture the gaiety that seemed like a permanent frame of mind thirteen years ago. In fact, there is something a little sad in seeing him again. There are too many ghosts in the wings and backstage."

After the season at the Henry Miller, Maurice began a coast-to-coast tour. He wanted to prove that he hadn't been forgotten. When he arrived in California, he was greeted by state officials —with a bill for $20,918, money he owed in income taxes from 1935. He apologized and immediately wrote a check—probably because he was only too delighted to be back, to say nothing of being able to perform again. "I can't complain," he said. "California has been good to me."

Maurice took advantage of his stay in California to go into the RKO studios to record a special prologue for what RKO persisted in calling *Man About Town*. It was a good way of getting into the story, to make certain that no English-speaker would feel left out of the action. He also sang his only song of the movie in that prologue—"Place Pigalle."

Chevalier was like a rocket in the film studio, as well as on and off stage. Impresario Arthur Lesser, who organized his tour, said at the time: "Maurice would go to the ocean each day before nine for a swim. Then he'd go to the solarium for a rubdown. Then breakfast. Then more swimming or tennis. After lunch, he'd work on his autobiography." There was another installment of those memoirs on the way.

In San Francisco he delighted another straw-hat wearer, the young Cuban-born musician-comedian, Desi Arnaz, when he met him. In his own autobiography, *A Book*, Desi recalled Chevalier told him: "You know, that is very good, what you do. How you throw the hat to the back, catch it with one hand and then push it down over your eyes. How do you do that?"

Arnaz, husband of Lucille Ball and shortly to be her costar in the *I Love Lucy* series, looked at the Frenchman whom he had always admired. "Now wait a minute, Mr. Chevalier," he said. "Don't put me on, please. You use the straw hat better than anybody in the world. You are the master, you're identified with it. What do you mean, how do I do that?"

"No, no, no," Maurice replied. "I'm not putting you on. I just don't know how you do it so that it doesn't fall off."

He learned the technique and subsequently added another facet to his repertoire. (A number of years later, Maurice invited Lucille and Desi to his home in Paris. They were astonished to see their photograph at the top of the staircase, but decided that he probably changed the pictures for each guest he received —which he did.) Maurice told Arnaz he admired his art of being able to go to a couple sitting at a table and "make love to the girl, but the man who is with her does not get mad at you. That's very good. I do the same thing."

Maurice also did a TV show with Lucille and Desi. Arnaz recalled being amazed how Maurice would relax until it was just time to go on the air, and then "it was as if someone had plugged him in."

Maurice was always plugged in to the varying needs of his audiences, and he proved it on the 1947 tour. Before he sailed home on the *Mauretania,* he gave a lecture in New York to the faculty and students of Columbia University at the Maison Française, the university's club for students of French. His subject: writing an autobiography. He had come a long way since leaving school.

Perhaps the most remarkable thing about the tour was the emphasis he was constantly putting on age. "Vingt Ans" was the title of his hit song. "When I say twenty years old," he said, "I can't help looking at the ceiling because that is exactlee how old I would like to be . . ." And he went on to translate the French lyric: "When you are thirty, you find one white hair. One!" They grew with age until "Seven-tee, when you are getting nearer the beeg silence!" He looked at the audience again: "You in the audience who are lucky enough to be twenty, don't waste one minute! Love! Love! Love!"

Maurice kept fairly quiet about his own love life now. Although Nita was with him on this trip, it was obvious they weren't together as often now. Anyone who didn't know Maurice very well would think that he was more interested in making money than girl friends.

Early in 1948 he invested money in a film called *Meeting the Stars on the Côte,* which featured candid shots of people like Rita Hayworth and Prince Ali Khan, Lana Turner, and Sonja Henie sunning themselves on the beaches of the Riviera. Maurice said he hoped the picture (which vanished without a trace in the midst of feature bills) would make him a lot of money

He was on a more sure footing when actually performing. And he demonstrated it time and again—at his comeback performance in the Champs-Élysées Theater, or at a charity show in Cannes and in London. When he took his show to the London Hippodrome later that year, *The Times* commented:

"The success of the entertainment is not even momentarily in doubt. Clearly the artist himself is confident that he is extremely unlikely to put a foot wrong and we know that he will not. His mastery of the comical trifle is indeed so complete that it implies that much greater thing—mastery of the art of the stage. M. Chevalier is a realist. He was wont to be the dashing young dog of the boulevards. He is no longer quite like that. Every gesture is precisely the right gesture. Every strut is an engaging strut. *'Vive la bagatelle.'* That's all he says. But he leaves us saying it, too."

He also went back to what he rightly termed "the good old U.S.A." His 1947 tour had been so successful that it was inevitable he would be wanted for a rerun, and not just on stage. A dozen luncheon clubs feted him as their guest of honour, and he enjoyed the role of after-lunch speaker immensely.

But he was not so sure about the reaction of his audiences. Was the length of the applause just a little bit shorter than on the previous tour? Certainly the reviews weren't impressive. *The New York Times* took up where it left off in 1947 and found his performance even more lacking. It did grudgingly admit: "Give Maurice Chevalier his due. He is an ingratiating entertainer. His smile is blinding, his manner is insouciant, he has a genuine comic gift of mimicry and an attractively uninhibited way of throwing himself into a song. He is an affable guide on a tour of 'Place Pigalle,' a number in which he sings of the G.I.s' celebrated 'Pig's Alley.' . . . But it all spreads pretty thin when you devote an evening to it. You begin to note what even M. Chevalier's charm cannot hide—that his English spoken material is stale for the most part, that some of his songs draw upon more energy than they are worth. . . ."

"A good part of the jaunty Frenchman's total effect probably lies stored away in the minds of his audience, memories from the era of the cloche hat and the cordial shop and the European grand tour. With these as props, M. Chevalier unquestionably can evoke a nostalgic jag. For a newer generation, however, in a uranium-tainted world, the result is likely to seem trivial."

Maurice looked at his act and tightened it up. There was, how-ever, an undeniable suggestion of a wavering in his popularity, not enough to cancel shows, but sufficiently strong for him to ask himself: how long? He had purged himself of the taint of col-laboration, but he wondered whether the weight of being nearly sixty wouldn't be harder to shake off.

And yet Al Jolson, whom he had seen and admired so much in the late 1920s, who was so much like himself with the same "punch" and equal self-esteem, was now riding the crest of a huge wave of new popularity in America. After being in the show-business doldrums for a lot longer than Maurice, a whole new generation was cheering him following the success of his filmed biography, *The Jolson Story*. He was at the top of the record charts, and a new film called *Jolson Sings Again* was in the works. A magazine article appeared in the States about this time headlined "Chevalier Sings Again," but people doubted just how true that statement was. He was singing again—but for whom?

There was a sharp boost to Maurice's ego when the Kraft Com-pany (the cheese manufacturers) suggested he might like to host their prime-time radio show, *The Kraft Music Hall*. The idea seemed tempting enough—until none other than Al Jolson was also asked to do it. Jolson jumped at the idea, signed the contract, and was once again the most popular radio star in America.

Maurice felt very anxious about the future. Jolson made things a little easier by sending Maurice a picture of himself with the message: "Outside of Lafayette, you're the best thing to come out of France."

For a time in 1948 Maurice talked about retirement.

"I'll bow out in 1951," he said. "I'm tired about worrying whether every performance will be a success. You hit a man on the chin so many times that finally he falls down. I want to stop while my work is good. To do badly after a success is like a painter throwing mud on his pictures."

But work didn't seem very good, and if he really meant to retire it was probably more sensible to do it now than to wait another three years. He did, however, begin to think again about the subject that concerned him most—security. To a startled public he announced in America that he was going to marry Nita.

"She offers me what I seek most—understanding, companionship, and sincerity. I have a better chance of making a success of marriage with her than with someone I don't know so long. Love is love, but life is life."

As he approached his sixtieth birthday, she was just thirty-one. "Nita is used to my ways and my views," he said. "I won't take a chance with a too young woman. Nor would I marry a widow or a divorcée. They are already formed in their definite views of life . . . while Nita has been formed to me."

This statement wasn't very complimentary to Nita; it seemed he was using her simply because she was around. She professed to be fairly happy about the way her name was coupled with the idea of marriage. "We have a tender feeling for each other," she said. "It was Chevalier who discovered me, launched me. I owe him everything and he is the center of my life. To speak to you about me is to speak about him."

Certainly, Maurice was aware of the pitfalls. "Marriage," he admitted, "is sometimes impractical in our business. We have too many diversions, too many things to distract us. Nita plans to leave the profession entirely. She wants to give up her work and try to be happy with me."

That didn't mean, though, that he had stopped looking at other women. On the contrary, he seemed to notice a beautifully curved figure more these days than he had for years.

"You've got to be so cold," he said at the time, "not to get a shock when you see an attractive woman. You see I'm associated with romance probably because something comes out of me that makes people think about it. There is no doubt I have to fight not to show my liking for women. If I didn't—why, it would be almost impolite."

Who was more impolite, no one can say. No sooner had Nita and Maurice officially announced their engagement than the twelve-year-long romance was over. Nita decided that she didn't want to give up having a career of her own, added to which she had found a new love.

Maurice was once more on his own.

17.
The Big Pond

If I went to a party, I'd bring him with me like I would a schoolboy. And he always accepted very readily and participated emotionally.

—ROUBEN MAMOULIAN

As he always had and always would, Chevalier found solace in his work, even if it was not quite as rewarding as it had been. The more he thought about it, the more he convinced himself that his profession was the only wife he really wanted. But that did not mean he intended to be alone.

He was an immensely dignified, trim figure and, as ever, he needed to have a woman in bed beside him. The females he met at the end of 1949 no longer shared bills with him—he was always on stage on his own. He was the center of a social whirl whenever he wanted to be. At a party his eyes would still focus on the prettiest unattached woman in the room; not necessarily the youngest but always the most chic, the best groomed, the one with the smoothest skin, the most seductive curves. Women found it a great compliment to be swept off their feet by the great Chevalier. He was not unlike the character he played in his film *Le Roi*, an Edwardian-era king who made it difficult for beautiful women to resist his seductive power. His grey hair—now attractively white at the temples—suited both him and the part to perfection. Was this, though, the right sort of behaviour for a man of his age? The thought now began to haunt him, and at sixty-one he made up his mind that he should know where to stop. Unless his career were to suffer, the curtain had to come down on his sexual life. But when he realized that this was a part of life too precious to discard casually, he told himself he should at least think about it—but not when the temptation was strong.

Soon after Nita left, Maurice met a beautiful young dancer called Jacqueline Noël. She inspired precisely the same reaction in Maurice as Nita had in her most beautiful and seductive youth. He fell for Jacqueline like a teenager. She was flattered by his attentions. He was overwhelmed that she should apparently find him so sexually desirable. There was plainly a lot of life in the old *canotier*.

Jacqueline became an integral part of his existence and occasionally even more important than his work. But he was still a man around whom everything had to revolve, and it was vital that the women who shared his bed realized it.

Jacqueline couldn't accept life on his terms. She was an intensely desirable girl. When she and Maurice were together, it was she who was at the center of their circle—a position in which she felt distinctly comfortable. As many girls so obviously in demand would, Jacqueline flirted with other men and thoroughly enjoyed it.

Maurice was consumed by the fear of losing her. She had only to meet another man for him to become hideously jealous.

Jacqueline decided that her life would be better without Chevalier, and she left him. Nita had gone by mutual agreement. But Jacqueline was completely different: She was the first woman in his life to discard *him* as unsuitable. His days as a Don Juan were over.

The depression Maurice felt now was worse than anything since his days at the sanitarium. Nobody at the time knew just how deep that depression was: As at the sanitarium, he planned to commit suicide. He spent days at La Bocca, locked in his bedroom deciding which method he should use to end it all.

Then he met Janie Michels. Janie was a sparkling young redhead, an artist who had been a pupil of Matisse and whose work some of her paintings resembled. She was married to the Comte de la Chapelle by whom she had one daughter. Thirty years later, still attractive and still painting, Janie Michels told me about how she had come onto the scene at just the right time. He spilled out his heart to her and told her how close he had been to taking his life. "At the time of the Liberation, people thought I was a collaborator," he told her, tears in his eyes. "Now I have had a very sad story with a woman I love."

Before long Janie was having an exceedingly good effect on Maurice. "You know," he told her, "you give me strength."

Looking up at him, she replied: "Maurice, you help me, too."

Maurice and Janie kept their relationship discreet; her talk with me was the first time she had ever discussed their affair. When reporters came round to see him at La Bocca, he confined his stories to his work or how he had given up smoking. The only woman strangers saw him with was his housekeeper, whom he called "my governess," or sometimes "*Maman*." When they called on him at his small home on the avenue Foch in Paris, he referred to it as his bachelor pad. "I'm almost sure I won't get married again," he told them. If it sounded like doubt, it wasn't what Maurice really felt himself. He wanted no formal ties which would lead him to question the strength of a relationship. He wouldn't risk making comparisons with the past, or court another failure.

With reasonable if not brilliant success, he continued the one-man shows. The only concession to his age was that he sometimes wore a plastic straw hat, which was considerably lighter under the hot spotlights than the real thing, batches of which had been made specially for him for the last twenty years by A. E. Olney & Company in England. This was the only company in Europe still making the hats, and they used to let him have a dozen or so at a time, always free of charge.

In 1950 Maurice celebrated his fiftieth anniversary in show
business by continuing to work. That year he sang one of his
favourite songs, "Ma Pomme," in a film of the same name. Had
he not done so, both he and a lot of his sincerest fans might
have been a great deal happier. It was a terrible film. "Ma
Pomme," which was translated as meaning "Just Me," was featured for a time in all Maurice's live shows. "I'm just a bum—
a b-u-u-m-m," he sang, a tune reminiscent of so many numbers
in prewar America that it made him look stale. It was also the
theme of the movie—the "king of the tramps" who just wants to
be with his fellow hoboes. Jolson had had a remarkably similar
role seventeen years before with *Hallelujah, I'm a Bum*. *Newsweek* commented: "Its thought content is terribly weighted
by unfunny ballast and music very far from the Chevalier standard."

There were other more unfortunate results from that film.
While he was making the movie, some technicians came to him
with a request which at the time he found no reason to refuse.
"Would you kindly let us have your signature?" they asked, and
Maurice put his name to the Stockholm Peace Appeal petition.
The petition had been launched by a number of the world's leading political and scientific figures. "They said to me," Maurice
recalled for me all those years later, "are you against the atomic
bomb? I said, yes, I was against the atomic bomb, so I signed."

Maurice did not realize that he was lighting a fuse for another
kind of bomb—one that would threaten his career as much as
had the collaboration rumours during the Nazi occupation. To
Americans the Peace Appeal was nothing more than a Communist propaganda document and, coupled with the interviews
Maurice had given right after the war to *Ce Soir* and the parades
in which he had marched, absolutely confirmed that he was a
Communist. As such, he was definitely not welcome in their
country.

Billy Wilder had planned to star Maurice in a film he was
going to call *A New Kind of Love*. It had to be called off. A tour
of the United States which Maurice had planned was abandoned.
He had to content himself with Canada.

Wherever he went the straw hat went with him—except to
Quebec, a city he always loved, since it represented the meeting

point of his two cultures, French and English. On this trip, however, he discovered that the two hats he had reserved for the show were missing. Chevalier without a straw hat? The idea was unthinkable, but there were no stores in the city that sold them. So he put an advertisement in one of the Quebec newspapers, a fact that received the predictable amount of publicity. The thief relented and anonymously sent the hats around to the theater.

After that, Maurice decided to take no further risks. A reporter asked him when he was going to retire. "You figure it out," he replied. "I've just ordered three dozen more straw hats."

The tour grew to include Scandinavia and virtually the whole of Europe. A lot of the old magic seemed to be coming back. *The Times* noted that in London: "His method is still to explain the meaning of each little French song in excellent English. An instance is his extraordinarily funny account of how young people nowadays are almost automatically raised to inarticulate cries of ecstasy by 'hot' music."

It was "Valentine" and "Louise" that audiences wanted to hear, although they were amazed by the way he mocked half a dozen European languages—reciting them as they appeared to him. *The Times* showed considerable understanding of his power. "The climax, when it comes, falls just short of the superb and what in another artist would be success is, in him, a failure. M. Chevalier can stand up to the highest standards of criticism and come through an evening triumphant."

Later in the run, the paper noted that "his accent . . . gets steadily and deliciously worse . . . his act is one of extraordinary virtuosity, for he can, with the thinnest of material, enthrall an audience by himself for an entire evening."

If he was virtually by himself on stage, he could exist only if there were people behind him to provide comfort and—more than occasionally—act as props.

Janie Michels, whose own career was rapidly expanding, was certainly one of these. Her artistic temperament was an important consideration in their relationship—helped, undoubtedly, by the fact that they complemented each other. Her paintings offered Maurice no kind of competition. Had she been a dancer or an actress, their relationship would have been very different.

Another vital ingredient in the Chevalier success recipe was the young man who in 1951 became his secretary, François Vals. Vals told me how at the age of twenty-one he had met Maurice in Bordeaux. He was just one in a long queue of people waiting for autographs. He had been collecting memorabilia on Chevalier for years, and on this occasion he had some of his material with him to show his idol. Maurice was impressed and took the young man's name and address. Later that year he wrote asking him if he would like to be his secretary.

He was so busy that he needed the sort of help which only a caring aide-de-camp could offer. François would play an ever-increasing part in Chevalier's professional life, smoothing out difficulties, helping arrange tours, finalizing arrangements with impresarios.

One show at the Champs-Élysées Theater ran for 131 standing-room-only performances. But that kind of success didn't last. He was at the Empire, as part of the theater's *Pleins Feux* revue, and went down with the rest of the show. He didn't like that happening now any better than he had when it occurred before the war.

Was he losing his touch? Maurice thought the answer could lie with the Americans and asked François Vals to try again to break through the U.S. government's embargo. But the Americans continued to ban Maurice from their shores. At another time he could have accepted it as a quirk of fate which could be overturned at a later date; now he needed the reaction of an American audience more than that of any other. If they still liked him, he remained a top entertainer. If he flopped in the States, he knew that the time had come to pack up. But nothing he said could persuade the U.S. government to allow him into the country, not even for a movie to be made of his life. Such a film could have been the crowning glory of his career and do for him what *The Jolson Story* had done for his American friend.

A film of his life would have been an exciting project and Maurice was thrilled by it, most of all, perhaps, because the man he admired as being the greatest of the contemporary American entertainers was going to play him—Danny Kaye. He knew what the comedian would have made of the role. He would have put a lot of Danny Kaye into it, but he would also have looked marvellous with the straw hat. The Chevalier accent would have melted like butter on his lips. "Anatole of Paris" had already proved that both on the screen and on the stage. But the American Attorney General, J. Howard McGrath, was unimpressed and so were other branches of the government.

"It is not in the interests of the United States to have Maurice Chevalier come to this country," said the State Department, and the film had to be shelved. For Paramount to make a film about Chevalier during the McCarthy era would be to consign the studio heads—to say nothing of Danny Kaye himself—to the line of people waiting for admission to the hot seat of the House Un-American Activities Committee.

"It is an immense injustice," said Maurice. "A lot of Frenchmen signed it [Stockholm Peace Appeal]. Nobody likes the atomic bomb."

He was shaken that the studios didn't back him up. He expected loyalty from "the profession," and it was to that profession that he appealed in a letter printed in the April 1954 issue of *Variety*.

"I feel certain," he wrote, "that they won't be able to keep the hand of suspicion about me for long. It is too cockeyed."

He went on:

> I worked 1946 and 1947 [actually it was 1947 and 1948] on Broadway and in the big cities of the United States. The U.S. police must have seen during those two years that I was not doing anything else than working hard, with a recital every night.
>
> Then in France, much later, like millions of other people I signed on an international list, absolutely in good faith, saying I was not for anything atomic falling on the world. And that, only that, did it.
>
> For it was only later that it was made public that the Stockholm petition had political roots. Had I known it in time, I would not have signed it because my policy has been not to mix in any kind of politics whatsoever. I have been for more than fifty years at the top of my profession

in France and this was only possible *because* I had never been in *any* politics. French people know that and every other country in the world knows it, too.

I hope that there is no personal malfeasance against me in some office of Washington. But I know that one day, the truth will come out as it always does in the long run.

Meanwhile, *Variety*, will you please tell all those of our beloved profession that although I have been humiliated in front of the whole world, I keep no sourness against America.

I wish for the U.S.A. that no more dangerous Frenchman than I am will ever work in your country. This kind of injustice can only happen in the chaotic times we are living in and what can one do but keep on proving by one's behaviour that it was all nonsense?

Best of luck, America and the regular ones of show business in spite of that one office in Washington being the *only spot* in the world where my name is not trusted.

> *I remain yours,*
> Maurice Chevalier.

Variety then published an editorial backing Maurice and criticizing the government.

"I'll always remember your amiable gesture," he wrote back.

He worried about it all tremendously. He kept saying that jealousy had been responsible for putting a giant banana skin under his feet. Whenever there was anyone around to listen, he put forward his case. To a group of Canadian sympathizers he said: "I swear by all that is most sacred to me, God, that I have no political interests. I am a singer. I sing to make people forget things like politics."

And he tried to prove it by singing, performing usually just with one accompanist, Fred Freed. He also continued to make films. Maurice may not have been totally enraptured at all times by some of the pictures he made, but he liked the money they brought him. In 1953 he made his first and only German movie, with a guest appearance in *Schlager Parade* (*Hit Parade*). The film was soon forgotten. The same fate was in store for his next picture, *Cento Anni d'Amore* (*A Hundred Years of Love*), made in Italy.

J'Avais Sept Filles was a different story altogether. Billed in the English-speaking world as *My Seven Little Sins*, it was about a man with a history of romantic conquests who uses a card index to help write his memoirs—and discovers too late that the cards have fallen into devious hands. They are being used by a troupe of girl dancers, each of whom claims to be his daughter by one of the women on the cards. Maurice formed a close friendship during the making of this picture with Louis Velle, who played his son in the movie. Velle had just left the *conservatoire*, and was only just embarking on his acting career. He had also just completed a novel. "I am so proud," Maurice told him, "to have a son who writes books!"

He also struck up a close friendship with Velle's wife, Frédérique Hébrard, also an actress and writer. He always enjoyed the company of a pretty woman—it is an undisputed fact that he found it difficult to spend any length of time with one who was even slightly unattractive in his eyes—and Frédérique was very attractive indeed. But it was her writing that helped put her on a pedestal for him, and with that advantage, he did not need to seek any kind of sexual relationship. She would bring him cups of tea between takes. "You know," he said, "I will give you my own special name because everyone calls you Frédérique. I have decided to call you, in my own way, Frédériquette. . . . No, we shall make it just 'Riquette, which in the south of France is a nickname for little girls."

He used the familiar form, "*tu*," with her, a special compliment. One day, over one of those cups of tea, he told her: "My dear 'Riquette. You are so cultured. You know so many things and I know nothing."

It was not modesty. He really meant it.

And as he regretted his lack of culture, so he was upset by the undeniable fact that he was, nevertheless, no longer the Parisians' most exciting star. After fifty-five years in the business, he was beginning to be taken for granted by his countrymen, rather like the Arc de Triomphe or his near contemporary, the Eiffel Tower. And like the Eiffel Tower, he seemed to appeal more to foreigners than to the French. There were empty seats at his shows. For the first time for thirty years, there was no difficulty in booking seats for Chevalier performances.

Being Maurice Chevalier, he developed still more anxieties about this. He said to François Vals: "You know, I think I *have* to go back to America to know if I am still big."

This time when he applied for his U.S. visa, it was granted. The American government raised no objection to his coming over.

A season was booked for him at the celebrated Ciro's nightclub. Soon after landing in New York, Maurice breathed in the heavy Manhattan air, looked at François Vals, and said: "You know, François, America is the place where all the champs of the world fight. Here you know what you are and what your name means."

Chevalier's name still meant a very great deal. The Ciro's cabaret performance was a huge success. He did two shows a night, and it seemed that each one was bigger than the one that had gone immediately before it. It became the "in" thing to watch a Chevalier performance and, perhaps even more important, to be seen at one. Among those who came was Vincente Minnelli, the Hollywood director.

"Would you, Monsieur Chevalier," Minnelli asked, "be interested in starring in a film of the Colette story, *Gigi?*"

18.
Gigi

*The first time I met him I was almost like a starstruck
girl. It was something of a conquest if you got a cup of
coffee out of him. But with his hand-kissing, his compliments, what a Frenchman! He always looked as if he
had just stepped out of a bandbox.*

—HERMIONE GINGOLD

Maurice, fast approaching seventy, was embarking on what
would perhaps be the happiest time of his life. After more than
twenty years he was going back to Hollywood, the place where
he had once been the most important of all its stars. The idea of
starring in what was going to be the biggest film of his career
stunned him. *Gigi* was the old story about the young girl schooled
by her grandmother to become *la grande courtisane* of her day.
For Maurice, Minnelli had the idea of building up the character
of the grandmother's former lover and turning him into an old but

dignified and wise roué. No straw hat this time. Instead, a series of elegant top hats to match the long frock coats he would wear; and three songs that would fit him like his tailored white gloves.

He didn't need much persuasion to take the role, but it would be two years before his work on the picture could begin. It would have a huge budget, there would be filming both in America and France, and since this was going to be a musical, a whole score had to be written. Arthur Freed, the genius of MGM musicals, decided there could be only one team to do the job justice—Lerner and Loewe, who had just had such a miraculous success with *My Fair Lady*.

In the meantime, Maurice had plenty with which to occupy himself. There was the title song to record for a Gene Kelly film called *The Happy Road* and a leading role in a picture with Audrey Hepburn and Gary Cooper. This was *Love in the Afternoon*, in which Maurice played the father of a young girl who falls in love with an aging playboy. Most of the critics agreed that it was Chevalier who stole the show—although Audrey Hepburn is on record as saying that she thought the picture would have been more believable had Maurice and Cooper switched roles.

Chevalier too wished that Gary had not played the part. "It was ridiculous," he said afterwards. "He was supposed to be in love with Audrey Hepburn. He looked as old as I did and people did not like it."

Cary Grant, he thought, had the right idea. "He is allowing his grey hair to show."

Maurice himself was very conscious of his age, and like a lot of elderly people—he was now sixty-eight—he thought a great deal of the past. Never more so than when he heard on the radio that Mistinguett, the Miss who had been so much a part of his most formative years, was dead. She had died of a brain tumour, lying on a satin bed surrounded by violets and azaleas.

He immediately felt compelled to put his thoughts of her down on paper. He said then:

"In the final reckoning, no one else has ever been what she was to me or done for me what she did. More than any other woman, she was what I mean by love."

Ironically, just before she had died, Miss had written yet again of the man she still considered her greatest love: "Maurice lives the way he dances. He doesn't dance. He hops. I'm glad for his sake that he had a fine career. It was what he wanted. I watched his success from afar with fondness and not a little pride. He worked very hard. He is quite clever. He's the conscientious one. I'm the reverse. I begin with the answers. . . . Explanations come later. Chevalier has never been like that and that is one of the explanations for his lack of style in his dealings with women. What's he trying to prove?"

What he tried to prove now that she was gone was the very important part she had played in his life. He wrote a poem in her memory:

> *You're not leaving.*
> *You've not gone away.*
> *You're changing, that's all.*
> *You'll always be where life leads me.*
> *Your face, your looks, your laugh*
> *Will break through the noisy shadows*
> *Of places where business tries to take the place of love.*
> *You are my girl, my mistress, my greatest woman friend.*
> *You loved my mother.*

For him there could be no finer compliment to pay anyone than those last four words.

As for himself, the best came from the newspaper *France-Soir*, when he opened at the Champs-Élysées Theater soon after his return to Paris. It seemed that his absence in the United States had made the French hearts grow fonder.

"We are very happy to have rediscovered this year, Maurice Chevalier, as good as ever he was," wrote the paper's critic. "For professionals, his work is an education. What he does, the way he presents, the way he brings on his first song, the speech which precedes the number one song is a disconcerting feat. He makes fun of himself, nicely underlining the little faults that people attribute to him and, without seeming to do it, cuts the grass under their feet in a friendly way, talking about his age, his silver hair, his slightly dark complexion. He mentions a stoutness you cannot see anymore. He alludes to a greediness which becomes unbelievable—all this with good humour, a knowing point, a dazzling smile . . . evil!"

He seemed to shine particularly wearing a ludicrous pigtail and a kimono; or sporting a Spanish matador's hat under which he called out "*olé*" and carefully avoided catching his nose in a pair of castanets.

"These different ideas let Chevalier renew himself," said the papers. "The compliment isn't small when you think that you're talking of an artist who is celebrating fifty-five years of success."

Whenever Maurice finished a tour or a film, he would go back to La Bocca, often with Janie to keep him company, to boost his ego, to make him laugh. Other performers would visit him there. Then when it came time to start work again, Maurice would be ready to move off. For a younger man it would have been a schedule leading to collapse. Chevalier seemed to thrive on it. His verve was the talk of French show business.

Patachou, then celebrated as the new Mistinguett, couldn't understand how he could carry on that sort of existence. The Riviera was fine, still as beautiful as it had ever been, but it was not exactly the center of the theatrical world, was it? "How can you cut yourself off like this?" she kept asking him.

At the time she was a great friend—a performer Maurice respected. They would later have a huge row and never return to speaking terms; even today she refuses to talk about him. In this instance he regarded her advice every bit as valuable as her talent. What she said was right. He had to move his base somewhere much more at the center of things.

He found it at Marnes-la-Coquette, a picturesque village about five kilometers from Paris. There a long, low house with beautiful grounds was up for sale. It was just what he wanted; it would be the new La Louque. The house was directly opposite the one in which General Eisenhower had lived when he was Supreme Commander Allied Powers Europe, and where General Alfred Gruenther now stayed.

The new house meant a great deal to Maurice, for it really symbolized the journey from Ménilmontant.

"It is an enormous house," he told Janie, "but it's a dream for an old man. As a reward for working so hard, so long, I had to have a beautiful house."

It had once belonged to Sir Richard Wallace, who had founded the famous Wallace Collection in London. More significant to

Chevalier, he had given Paris its street fountains. "When I was a street urchin," Maurice said to François Vals soon after moving into the new La Louque, "I depended on those fountains for drinking water. To buy the house of the man who gave us those fountains! That seems like a crowning achievement."

Marnes was a picture-postcard village in the woods of Saint-Cloud, and very much of Paris if not actually in it. So Villa La Louque was now much closer to where the original La Louque had brought him into the world. It brought her memory even closer, too—if that were possible because there was not a day when Maurice did not think of her. In the garden he put up a sculpture of his mother's head fashioned out of rough white marble, and next to it a bench from which he could talk to her when alone. The head was arranged in such a way that each morning it would catch the first rays of the day's sun. "They kiss her face," he told Janie.

Maurice was a man of mixed taste in painting. He hung pictures throughout the house—Cézannes, Utrillos, and a whole collection of paintings by unknown artists who were likely to remain that way. One of his favourites was a huge, life-sized portrait of himself painted by Janie. In fact, much to her regret, the house speedily took on the look of a rather uncomfortable Chevalier museum—wall upon wall covered with pictures of himself on stage, with General de Gaulle, with the Queen of England, and with Presidents of the United States, and photos of a dozen crowned and uncrowned heads of Europe and other parts of the world. Everywhere there were ashtrays shaped like straw hats. On a shelf was a slab of black marble bearing a "mask" of Maurice's hands carved in solid gold.

There were pictures of other stars—like the one Lucille Ball and Desi Arnaz saw of themselves; one from Doris Day inscribed: "To my rosy-cheeked friend," and one from Marlene Dietrich on which she had written: "I have always known you were the greatest. But since I have invaded your profession, I am on my knees—Marlinou."

The wall behind the desk in Maurice's study was covered with playbills. A matter of inches from the desk, there was a huge bronze statue of Georges Clemenceau, whom Chevalier had admired so much. Whenever Janie tried to make things less formal, he protested violently. His whole life had to proceed "to order," and his house symbolized the fact. He liked to give weekly luncheons, and when his guests arrived he would stand at his door, a gold pocket watch in his hand. He didn't easily forgive latecomers.

Maurice didn't doubt the wisdom of his taking the *Love in the Afternoon* role, although it was the first of his career in which he was not the top star. "I was glad to be able to do it," he said later, "because it was a good way to return to international pictures. I'm not worried anymore about being photographed in a light that makes me look as old as I am."

Like many things he said, it was only partly true. The director, Billy Wilder, for one may have found that difficult to swallow. Chevalier's charm certainly didn't come across to him. It became the custom when the film was in production for each of the leading players to take turns in giving a party for the technicians working on the project. Chevalier never would. Was this the old Chevalier parsimonious streak?

"He was the most unbelievably generous man you could meet," said Janie Michels who about this time, soon after the birth of her youngest daughter, became even closer to Maurice. But he loved her, and being generous to people he loved was second nature to him.

He made a home at the new La Louque for his brother Paul who, after spending most of his life taking advantage of his relationship to his younger brother, was now retired. For him Maurice was the epitome of generosity.

Hermione Gingold, who played the aunt in *Gigi*, found Maurice rather less than that. While making the film he stayed at the plush Bel Air Hotel, while she was down Sunset Boulevard at the slightly cheaper but still elegant Beverly Hills Hotel. "How much are you paying there?" he asked her. When she told him, he immediately arranged for his things to be moved from Bel Air and, he, too, checked in at the Beverly Hills. But she didn't escape his charm. With him she sang what was probably the best-loved song in the film, the duet, "I Remember It Well." It later became virtually a living motto for Maurice.

"It was my first American film and I was very nervous," Hermione told me. But Maurice put her at ease. "I had to sing and I hadn't got a great voice, but with him I felt the greatest prima donna in the world."

With Alan Jay Lerner, who wrote both the screenplay and the lyrics, Maurice went over the finer details of his part. In his own memoirs, *The Street Where I Live*, Lerner recalled that Maurice talked about his attitude towards life.

He said: "I'm much happier now than I have ever been. Every artist is a mixture of passion and reason. In my case I've been lucky enough to have had a little bit—maybe only just a half inch —more reason than passion.

"I grew older and suddenly realized that I have not the right anymore to play with passion. If I do, it will not be good, or it will be that worse thing, sad.

"I've had all that passion can give me, beautifully and marvellously. I've had my share of everything, but I've never overdone it. In exchange, I have a kind of serenity."

Lerner thought about that. Three days later he came to him with a new song idea. It was called "I'm Glad I'm Not Young Anymore."

It wouldn't be long before the question everyone seemed to want answered was: "Are you *really* glad you're not young anymore?"

"Well, put it this way," he said. "Perhaps if I had to live it all again, I'd not be quite so lucky."

Getting the numbers right caused a few problems. Maurice practiced his songs for hours—in front of a mirror and in the bathroom. Finally, after going through "I'm Glad I'm Not Young Anymore," Lerner told me that Maurice asked him: "Is it okay?"

"Fine," said the lyricist.

"And the accent?"

"Excellent," Lerner replied. "I understood every word."

"I didn't mean that. Was there *enough* accent?"

The accent was still Maurice's key to success in America—so much so that one wag let it be known that he was taking courses in French intonation at a Berlitz school.

But there was one problem in recording the sound track which neither he nor Lerner had antipicated. Hermione Gingold told me that for most of the time a dreadful clicking noise could be heard in front of the mikes. The electricians were called in and all the sound equipment was gone over thoroughly. The men even took the floor up. Eventually, the problem was solved—Maurice's false teeth were too loose. So a new set had to be made hurriedly for him before the production could proceed smoothly to its close.

Maurice, now much mellowed and very different from the way he had been on his previous abrasive excursions to Hollywood, brought his own standards of perfection to *Gigi*. He would always turn up on the dot of 5 A.M.—his punctuality was something of an obsession now, much to the irritation of his close friends—in a beautifully cut, perfectly pressed suit, while his fellow performers arrived in slacks and sweaters looking extremely bleary-eyed.

Janie told me that at this time she remembered his saying: "Imagine, when I first went into show business, the most wonderful thing was to stay in bed while my brother had to get up early to go to work. Now here I am, a top star, and I have to get up in the middle of the night!"

Maurice was more than just the wise man who tried to remember it well. He was also the narrator for the picture—which began with him standing in the Bois de Boulogne watching children at play and singing "Thank Heaven for Little Girls." That tune and "I'm Glad I'm Not Young Anymore" both became standards for him.

Leslie Caron was exquisite in the title role and Louis Jourdan suitably young and debonair as her suitor, Maurice's nephew. Eva Gabor played Hermione Gingold's accomplice in leading Gigi the wrong way up the garden path. Lerner and Loewe had found themselves just the suitably brilliant follow-up to *My Fair Lady* they had hoped for—even to the point of using a discarded number from that show, "Say a Prayer for Me Tonight."

"As might be expected," said *Daily Variety*, "Chevalier is the scene stealer, at once compelling and at all times the great prophet of French romance. His ageless attraction still proves to be overpowering, and his cocked-hat shuffle will endear him to variously aged women wherever he plays."

The film collected nine Oscars—including those for best director (Vincente Minnelli); best screenplay (Alan Jay Lerner); and best song ("Gigi"). Maurice himself was awarded a special

Oscar—for his "contribution to the world of entertainment for more than half a century."

He said after receiving the award: "I really felt so moved. I didn't know how to answer. Afterwards on the plane to Chicago, I didn't sleep. Not because I couldn't. I didn't want to. I wanted to savour and treasure every minute of that night."

The only place where *Gigi* wasn't a huge, instantaneous hit was in France. To the French it was all too modern. Colette was a national institution and the idea of sullying her story with music was like watering down champagne—or parodying Maurice Chevalier.

The brilliant success of *Gigi* in the English-speaking world and the immediate cry from MGM and all the other Hollywood studios for more of the same didn't stop Maurice from worrying about what was left for him. He certainly became no happier as he contemplated the lengthening roster of new stars in the late 1950s. To him each one was a threat. When Yves Montand first became an international star with his one-man show, Chevalier literally shuddered as he read reviews of his first-night performances. "My God," he told Rouben Mamoulian, "this is the end of me. Chevalier's gone—finished!"

When Charles Aznavour first hit the public's attention, he, too, was seen as the end of Maurice's career. They had first met at a time when the young Aznavour was more a songwriter than a performer. With Paul Roche, Charles had written a number that he thought Chevalier could use. The sequence of events, as Aznavour explained them to me, reads now rather like a scene from a mystery novel—just as the criminal is about to be apprehended. Maurice *was* interested and invited the two writers to his home. But when he tried the number out to Roche's piano accompaniment, he insisted that Aznavour leave the room. "He didn't want me to see him work," Aznavour said, "in case I picked something up that I would then copy. Later on, he got to like me—simply because he said I was the only one who didn't take anything from him!"

At a show Maurice paid Aznavour the supreme compliment by introducing him from the stage. He said he was like his son. "In fact," he added, "I would be very happy if he had been my son. . . . No. I would have been happier if he had been my brother. . . . No. That's not right either. I would have been much happier to have had him as a father."

He proved his affection by giving Aznavour one of his real straw hats—which by the mid-1950s had become the traditional Chevalier means of offering praise. For those whose achievements were not so highly recognized by the "master"—the threats—he gave instead one of his plastic straw hats.

Calling attention to illustrious guests from the stage could be a hazardous operation—as George Jessel once told me he had discovered to his cost. It was in the mid-1950s and Jessel, at the Broadway Palace, America's flagship vaudeville theater, greeted Chevalier who was in a box. "After that," said Jessel who, because of his after-dinner speaking, went on to earn a reputation as America's "Toastmaster General," "nobody paid any attention to me for the rest of the show because people kept watching him. Chevalier was on everybody's lips—including his own."

Maurice didn't recognize the hundreds of Chevalier impersonators for what they were—living compliments to his own uniqueness. For example, there was the musical clown, Zimbal, long since retired. Charles Aznavour told me that Maurice remembered he had always done the very best Chevalier impersonation of them all and the memory still represented as much of a threat as anyone up-and-coming in the business. Maurice couldn't even bring himself to say Zimbal's name.

Along with the fear he had of competitors, he was terribly suspicious of compliments, no matter how lavish they were and how sincere the source. When the Alhambra Music Hall management decided to rename their theater the Alhambra Maurice Chevalier, an opening concert was arranged starring Chevalier himself. Ginette Spanier was there that night and described to me what happened.

As usual, Maurice was so taut with nerves that he seemed about to explode. One after the other, the great French stars of the day went out on stage and performed as well as they knew how, each of them paying tribute to Chevalier's great artistry.

When Maurice saw the very young Michel Legrand, he decided that the man's charm, his appearance, and above all his youth were the final stamp ending his own career. He told the theater manager, waiting with him in the wings: "Tonight I am going on stage to announce my retirement. I shall not appear again." As he waited, he took a card from his inside breast pocket and scribbled a message of good-bye.

Finally, the orchestra struck up the opening bars of "Valentine," and Maurice jumped out on stage like a greyhound suddenly catching sight of the electric hare.

What he heard at that moment was not applause but audible rapture. The audience stood on their seats. They screamed. They shouted. They applauded. Retirement would have to wait.

19.
I'm Glad I'm Not Young Anymore...?

It's just a kind of exchange with an audience that gives it back to you in response.

—MAURICE CHEVALIER

Maurice marked his seventieth birthday with a special gala show at the Champs-Élysées Theater. The French still couldn't completely understand what all the fuss over *Gigi* had been about, but they appreciated the tremendous value he represented to national prestige.

In Britain and America, though, he was bigger than he had ever been before. On one tour of the United States after another, he would be feted like a visiting monarch. Harry Truman received him at his home at Independence, Missouri, and it was like a meeting of two elder statesmen. In Hollywood the film capital honoured him for his talent and for what he represented to the business. That did not stop the occasional teasing, usually by his contemporaries. Jack Benny was among the many stars with whom he appeared on television—with a few digs at his alleged stinginess.

George Burns told me that he knew exactly how to take advantage of Maurice's undeniable conceit. During a party at which Chevalier had—without any difficulty whatsoever—been persuaded to sing "Louise," "Mimi," "Valentine," and everything else the guests wanted to hear, George tapped him on the shoulder and made a request of his own. "Maurice," he said, "would you do a favour for my sister, Goldie?"

"Certainly, George," he replied and proceeded to take his gold fountain pen from one pocket and a photograph from another.

"No," George corrected. "I don't want your autograph. What I should like is for you to have an affair with her!"

But Maurice was still fully occupied with Janie Michels.

The great success he had was as much as ever in the way he sold a song, not the voice with which he did it. It was a point he explained to newsmen, who after *Gigi* flocked around him more than they had done at any time since the Liberation.

"Sincerity," he told them. "That is the secret. And love—you can't sell a song without love.

"Those great, round, solid songs that I've sung for many years now, I must mean them, feel them. After all, my numbers have survived swing, jazz, boogie-woogie and rock 'n' roll. They're the same now as they were twenty-seven years ago—healthy and strong. They are totally different from what is popular today, but they have the same appeal.

"It is impossible for me to sing only with my throat, because what comes out is not so lovely. So, I've found other ways to communicate."

And then he explained what had always intrigued the keen Chevalier watcher or listener: "I alter every song that I do, so that I can feel it belongs to me. If I can't feel, I can't sing, you see?

"When I sing 'Every little breeze seems to whisper Louise,' I mean just that. And the audience responds. You can only make contact with an audience by being honest. You get from an audience what you give them. Audiences are instinctively very wise about dishonesty."

He also said something that he—as the "champ" he had been

for so long—understood only too well: "An entertainer is like a fighter who must change his style in the middle of a bout when he discovers what his opponent's weaknesses are. My own method is to make friends with an audience. Americans trust you, but in France you must win over the listeners every time you sing."

Mary Pickford congratulated him on his recent triumph in *Gigi* and on his extremely trim appearance. In response there was the usual glum look on Maurice's face. "Mary," he explained, pouting out that lower lip as though singing "Valentine," "the trouble is, I'm not ambitious any more." Nonetheless, he still worried about what was left for him and Billy Wilder commented in 1959: "He is oblivious to the fact that everyone's mortal. He's making plans for thirty years from now."

Maurice began to see a changing world around him, and even though that world had made him the king of its entertainers— he had been a top-flight performer for longer than anyone else in the history of show business—it concerned him as only he could be concerned about changing events. Of course, he related it all to his work.

"Even 'Valentine' is not so young anymore," he said. "It is the story of a little girl who was so young and so sweet. The years go by and 'Valentine' is encountered again. But she is no longer petite and has grown a double chin into the bargain. It is a very human story."

Despite his triumphs, he talked incessantly of having to retire before the profession retired him, although a few days later he could take it all back and add: "If I had to fight to stay up there, I'd give it up. But I'm not fighting. It comes very easily. I'm still getting paid top rates." And that was what counted. With Jolson and Harry Lauder as his inspirations, he thought that what he would probably do before long was give up the stage entirely and concentrate on films. He would also continue his writing, which he said in 1959 was a "passion." He added: "I'm crazy about writing. It's a thing I can do as an old man without getting out of wind."

Newsweek recognized Chevalier's unique position in the world by featuring him on the cover in March 1959. "My real luck is to be my age and still have something to offer the public," he told the magazine.

That same year he appeared in a nonsinging role in a Jean Negulesco movie made in England and France called *Count Your Blessings,* in which he costarred with Deborah Kerr and Rossano Brazzi. It was a modern-day story of a rich uncle—this time a duke—trying to persuade his nephew (Brazzi) to take a mistress. The real blessing would have been had he turned down the role, which wasn't worth the effort.

But he still loved everything to do with his profession, including its people, especially if they hadn't all made it to the top.

In Las Vegas his best friends were a couple of French acrobats who never had the slightest chance of achieving top stardom. He felt a lot more comfortable with their vaudeville badinage than with the usual Vegas jet-set chitchat. He liked people he felt he could trust, and usually these were ones with whom he had worked. When he was back in New York and heard that his costar from *Gigi,* Hermione Gingold, was in town, he called her up.

"Would you like to come and see me?" he asked.

She said she'd be delighted.

"Come at one," he suggested.

"Oh good, I thought," Miss Gingold told me, "that means lunch."

She arrived, as she knew Maurice would wish, on the dot of one o'clock.

"We talked and we talked and we talked. At two-fifteen I looked at my watch and told him, 'You know, I'm getting pretty hungry.'

"'Are you?' he asked.

"I said, 'Yes. I think I'll be going.'

"At that point Maurice replied, 'Well, you must come again sometime.' Not a coffee or a Coca-Cola or anything like that!"

He may not have offered any food, but he was charm personified.

Money, of course, was still very important to Maurice. As he looked out at the manicured lawns that covered much of the two acres of La Louque, he often said to Janie: "Such expense! Every flower bulb. Every blade of grass, so expensive!"

Maurice was frequently bombarded with begging letters. He would ignore them all. It was more a sign of respect for the memory of having to do without than another example of his parsimony. Money, he believed, was a commodity that was earned by hard work, and there was no excuse for able-bodied people not to earn their own.

That was why when his New York producer, Arthur Lesser, in 1955 suddenly put up the seat prices for the Chevalier show at the Lyceum Theater without asking Maurice's leave, he showed his anger in no uncertain terms. "I won't take you to court, Mr. Lesser," he said, as François Vals told me, "because that is not my way, but you ought to be ashamed of yourself."

Later in the season Lesser sued Chevalier for $285,000 for appearing at the Lyceum without his "help." Lesser lost.

The show was a complete sellout, and Maurice indulged himself in his favourite New York pastime—walking around Central Park "just as I used to do with George M. Cohan when I first came here."

His success on these trips was in no small way due to François Vals and his wife, Madeleine, for whom he had bought a house close to La Louque. They usually travelled with him. He called them "my children." Later when the Valses had a daughter, he treated her like one of his own.

When Chevalier heard that a small-time singer called Félix Paquet was ill and in the doldrums, he invited him to come and work for him, too. Paquet, of medium height and pathetically thin, looked as though he had come through a crisis and was finding it hard to recover. His whole appearance was not helped by a poorly made brown wig which always looked as though it had been pinned on—and in a hurry, too.

Maurice told Paquet that he needed a driver. What he really thought he needed most was a pro like himself to whom he could talk about the old days of the music hall.

He liked Paquet's wife and he told them both: "Please come to my place. It will cure you with the good air and the good food and you'll soon be strong."

It was a cure for Paquet, who gradually became Maurice's confidant as he drove him to and from the theater, the racetrack, or anywhere else that he had to go. He did some secretarial work, too, and his wife became Maurice's housekeeper.

It was clear, Janie Michels told me, that Paquet adored Maurice, who in turn looked after him like a father. He saw that the younger man ate properly and did enough exercise, and he looked very seriously at the figure that Paquet cut in public.

"I think," he told him, "you would look better without that wig."

From that moment on, Félix's thinning grey hair was exposed to everyone whom he met.

"I like to grow old without worrying too much," Maurice said. Was he suddenly waking up to the fact that he needed to change his life-style?

His present work schedule was tough enough, and he needed the support of the Valses and the Paquets to put all his energy into public appearances. "You can't bluff a one-man show," he said at the time. "It's the most difficult thing to do and if successful it would be the most marvellous crown to my career."

In London he had tea with Queen Elizabeth. General de Gaulle, soon after becoming the first president of the Fifth Republic, invited him to dinner and, to underline the fact that he held no hard feelings over what had happened during the war, sent him a letter saying, "Thank you for all you have done for France." Sentiments didn't come much sweeter than that.

At a charity gala, De Gaulle joined Maurice in a duet—singing "Ma Pomme" for an enchanted but startled audience.

Maurice liked inviting celebrities to join him in his act, even if they weren't all as exalted as De Gaulle. At an "April in Paris" ball in New York, he and Elsa Maxwell did an impromptu version of the popular duet, "Baby, It's Cold Outside," and discovered only later it had been transmitted on TV throughout the world. The idea enchanted him. "Imagine that," he said to Elsa like an excited schoolboy. "At our age! Our age!" It wasn't like making a series of his own, with all the pressures that entailed.

"Maurice," reported Miss Maxwell, Washington's best-known hostess, "never makes the mistake of so many of our mature actors . . . he plays only men who are no longer young but whose hearts remember. . . . There are artists who work from the heart and those who work from the brain. From the brain you admire them but from the heart you feel them!"

He was often asked how he knew when to recognize the right time to start growing old on screen. "There are two ways," he said, "or rather combinations of ways. You look at yourself in the looking glass, then you look at the photograph on your passport which you have been using for several years. If there is a sharp contrast between the two, you know right away it is time to quit playing the lover, unless you are deliberately blind. It is difficult to fool yourself about such things, but you can do it if you do it with determination." People who didn't heed this warning were, he said, sad and embarrassing. "If not to you, it is embarrassing to your audience."

That did not mean that he had stopped caring for women he found vital and attractive. He never denied that even now when he did a one-man show he kept a watchful eye out for the most beautiful women in the audience.

Janie was still very important to him. Together they travelled to the United States when he appeared at the Waldorf-Astoria. Without giving any indication of his feelings for her, he announced: "I am delighted to welcome a wonderful young portrait painter called Janie Michels. Go and buy her pictures."

In an interview with *The Saturday Evening Post*, he said, "Let's say that I'm more selective about women than I used to be. There are some things which do not excite me easily anymore. But don't get me wrong, I can still get excited—even though I may have to send myself a telegram the night before to warn myself!"

Being virile was vital to him and he continued to do his daily exercises and to escape to the golf course whenever he had the opportunity. It wasn't that he loved exercise, but simply that he required, above all, the physical advantages he thought those exercises brought. He was proud of his appearance—the white hair and the finely proportioned features of his face, the still upright 5-foot 11½-inch-tall figure.

He honestly believed there was no point in looking at a pretty girl if the girl wasn't likely to look back at him—and not simply because he was a famous star.

"I think it is not good for any man, even a young man, to chase any girl. . . . Love is the same as success—one should meet it halfway. When it happens, you should clasp it to yourself in the middle of the road, if that's where you find it. It should be like the coming together of the negative and positive poles of a magnet. When you are going to fall in love with some-body, most of the time she has shown you already that she likes you. If you just fall madly in love with a person who does not even look at you—who, in fact, is high-hatting you—you are fall-ing in love with the wrong person.

"I still want to be loved," he said. "I think I am not too un-lovable. I remember Douglas Fairbanks, Senior, saying to me when he was sixty and about to marry Sylvia Ashley, 'Maurice. Do you think a woman can still love me?'

"He looked so wonderful, yet he thought he was too old to be loved. Me, I have never had that problem!"

If he had always spoken rather tongue in cheek about women, drink was a subject about which he could be more truthful.

When he had lunch with Charles Aznavour and *France-Soir* journalist Jacqueline Cartier, Maurice ordered both a white and a red wine. But instead of drinking them, he merely sniffed the aroma. "Wine is now for the nose," he said.

Show business, though, was still for his soul. After sixty years of leading the field, he knew exactly what he was capable of doing to perfection. Any other way didn't interest him.

"After this season," he said, "I'm going back to France, feeling the way Georges Carpentier would feel if he came back to America at the age of seventy and won all his fights. What has happened to me doesn't happen very often, and it makes me feel terribly proud. Maybe I'll be the Bernard Baruch of show busi-ness."

And he went on to prove it, making a three-album record set of thirty-six numbers, in which again and again he asked the musical arranger to change a bar here, a note there, an instru-ment every now and again. Sometimes he tried to make the musicians feel better by telling them: "I think I gave you the wrong feeling with it."

When he recorded the album—with enough extra material for MGM Records to cut an additional LP at a later date—it was like watching a Chevalier one-man show on stage. Recording "She Didn't Say Yes, She Didn't Say No," he seemed to be making what *High Fidelity* magazine called "little pleading gestures and [he] coquettishly pulled at his fingers in the manner of a shy young girl."

Maurice knew he had done well. When the track was finished to his satisfaction, he muttered to himself: *"C'est bon."*

Maurice explained why afterwards: "I don't know exactly what I'm going to do with the songs. You see, I must do a little something that has not been done before with American songs."

He was perhaps never happier than when he recorded a tune about a French-Canadian Indian, called "Nobody Throw Those Bull." Maurice bent down low, made rude faces at the microphone, and shouted at the ceiling. It would have brought the house down at the Waldorf-Astoria. At the MGM recording studios, it got a huge round of applause from an orchestra already showing signs of the fatigue of working a whole day on more conventional tunes.

It was the same with his own performances. When he made another cabaret appearance at the Waldorf-Astoria right in the middle of a musicians' strike, he was faced with the alternative of cancelling his show or appearing without a pianist. He chose to go on. It was perhaps one of his best performances ever—simply because he had no alternative but to make it the best. He couldn't afford making it seem that without an accompanist he was nothing.

"When I sense an audience is responding to the gaiety I'm trying to give out," he would say, "I feel gaiety coming back to me. It's like a boomerang, a blessed boomerang.

"A man goes to his office, he is always grumpy, growls a greeting to his secretary. She may have awakened spirited and jaunty, but right away, the ugliness is contagious. Or in reverse, he comes in whistling, maybe he's picked a flower from his garden for his buttonhole as he hurried to catch his train. He extends a merry greeting and it boomerangs. The office brightens. There are targets everywhere. I like to try to bring it out in bus drivers in big cities.

"People ask them long and involved questions, usually about how to get some place in the opposite direction. So I board a bus and give a greeting."

It was true, he did still ride buses. It gave further ammunition to people who suggested he did it because it was much cheaper than using his own car or a taxi, but he would say it was another good way of keeping in touch with his own kind of people. When he wasn't riding buses, he continued walking, and still liked no-where better than Central Park. On one walk he saw a girl, about nine years old, skipping past him. Nearby was a flower seller. He bought a corsage and handed it to the child. Now that his in-satiable urge for sex had finally begun to wane, Maurice was more aware of beauty for beauty's own sake than before. Never an in-tellectual, he was also able to appreciate forms of art that had escaped him previously.

At the age of seventy, he met Pablo Casals. The legendary cellist, then eighty-two, recalled having thoroughly enjoyed a Chevalier performance back in 1904. After they talked for a time, Casals said: "Now I'll play for you."

Chevalier was amazed. He couldn't believe his ears. He swal-lowed hard. When Casals was halfway through his rendering of "The Song of the Birds," a folk melody from his native Catalonia, Maurice was weeping unashamedly.

"*Quelle beauté*," he cried. "*Quelle beauté.*"

The recital over, the two men embraced, and the cellist pre-sented his guest with a signed autograph inscribed: "To Maurice Chevalier, whom the world loves and admires for his art, simple and touching."

20.
Break the News

I loved Maurice because he was straight, solid, and a very good friend.

— Thérèse de Saint-Phalle

It was clear that old age was resting on Maurice like a cool breeze on a calm sea. He may not have been glad he was no longer young but he wasn't allowing it to cause deep melancholia.

On his seventy-second birthday in 1960, he was asked what he felt about the advancing years. "Considering the alternative," he said, "it's not too bad at all." He was beginning to enjoy free time as moments in which to relax and not simply as wasted gaps between shows. What was more important, he liked being with a diversity of people—like Pablo Casals—whom he would have been afraid to meet before. Occasionally, however, he expressed reluctance if he thought they were too far above his own station.

As the little girl in Central Park discovered, one of the nicest things about Chevalier in old age was the appeal he had for young people—very young people at that. After one show, he found another little girl waiting at the stage door.

As he made his way through the crowds which still gathered for him, she forced her way through legs and feet and grabbed Maurice's arm. "I love you," she said.

"No, you don't love me," he almost scolded, amazed that there could be this mark of affection from one so very young. "You might like me, perhaps even admire me. But you're a little girl and you can't love an old man."

But she probably did. So did the very young girl whom he met in Vichy after attending the opera. As he wrote soon afterwards, the two, old and young, began talking. Since both of them liked walking, Maurice said he would take her home. He got within sight of her house, and then decided that the rest of the hill was too steep for him to negotiate. His friend thanked him warmly and skipped off home while Maurice watched till she vanished safely through her front gate.

One of his closest friends was Ginette Spanier, the director of Maison Balmain, whose circle extended far beyond the world of fashion. Her dearest friends were show people. Once she telephoned Maurice at Marnes-la-Coquette and asked him to her home for dinner.

"I should like you to meet Noël Coward," she said.

Maurice contemplated the offer for a moment and then told her: "I thank you for your kindness, but I think I shall not come. The great Noël Coward is too much for the boy from Ménilmontant. He is a man with a wonderful education."

"What are you talking about?" she said. "You come from Ménilmontant and Noël comes from Teddington. I'll expect you at eight o'clock." As the clock in her apartment chimed eight, Maurice was ringing the doorbell. He spent the next three hours in animated conversation with Coward, each quite truthfully telling the other of his admiration, Maurice calling Coward "a grand gentleman."

Maurice frequently went to the theater with Ginette and her husband, Dr. Paul Émile Seidman, trying to see everything that was not too intellectually demanding. But his insistence on punctuality brought problems.

He would always arrive at their home—usually wearing a beautiful steamed soft hat, a superbly tailored coat over trousers creased to a knifelike edge, and mirror-polished black shoes—an hour before the performance started and expect to leave for the theater immediately. In the end Dr. Seidman developed the habit of driving to the theater slowly through the park.

Ginette says that one of the reasons Maurice was so friendly with her husband and herself was "simply that we were working people who were not pretentious the way French intellectuals usually are. He was always frightened of pretentious intellectuals."

Maurice was as conscious now of new talent as he had ever been. When he saw performers whom he admired, he would climb the stairs afterwards to their dressing rooms to offer his congratulations. He wouldn't do it for the big stars or for those he still considered threats, but if there was someone he thought was on the way to success and needed only that little extra encouragement, he considered it right to offer it himself.

In 1960 everyone wanted to know what he thought about Brigitte Bardot. "This girl," he said, "is like a diamond, a little Parisian girl who can change the whole picture of Frenchwomen. She is beautiful like a heart—not at all a vamp. I look upon her a little bit like a daughter. I see her in a movie and it makes me very happy. Very content."

He was planning now to go back to the United States to make a new picture. "I don't know who the partner is that I'm going to have, but not Brigitte and that is a pity."

The new partner would, in fact, be Shirley MacLaine—and Frank Sinatra and Louis Jourdan, with musical help from Cole Porter, to say nothing of publicity assistance from Nikita Khrushchev. The picture was *Can-Can*, in which Maurice played a role not totally dissimilar from the one in *Gigi*, although Bosley Crowther in *The New York Times* noted:

"Maurice Chevalier totters meekly on the fringes as an elderly judge who is not so sure in this picture that God should be thanked for little girls, particularly when the creatures are as frightening as Miss MacLaine."

Certainly, there was nothing wrong with Maurice as the judge who, in contrast to his young colleague (Jourdan), values the importance of the cancan to the culture of his native city.

Khrushchev entered the picture when he visited the Twentieth Century-Fox studios to meet Marilyn Monroe, news of whose beauty had percolated to Moscow. He had come to America in the first place to harangue the United Nations, and now he wanted to see more of the country. Hollywood seemed the place to begin.

Since the studio wanted to show him some action, and the cancan number at the picture's end was being shot that day, it was presented as the spectacle of his visit. Comrade Khrushchev was not amused. He had already clashed at lunch with the studio boss, Spyros P. Skouras, on the merits of their two systems of government. Over vodka he later told the world what he thought of the cancan. It was, he said, "thoroughly immoral." It typified the decadent West. No one, it seems, bothered to inform him that the number was being featured in a film set in the late years of the nineteenth century.

Khrushchev was introduced to Chevalier, but didn't pretend to recognize him.

Maurice's only musical numbers, regrettably, were a duet with Louis Jourdan called "Live and Let Live" and his solo, "Just One of Those Things."

When he got back home, he decided that it was time to recognize the importance of a few ordinary people in his life. He gave a party for the entire village of Marnes-la-Coquette on the grounds of La Louque, climaxing it all with a one-man show especially for them.

"Today," he said, "to celebrate my great age I give to my village a present—this show in the open air. My secret is that the public gives me confidence and I'll do anything for them. This is a pact since I was twelve years old."

He was firmly established both in the village and in the house, which now resembled a Chevalier museum more than it ever had before. There was a magnificent new Utrillo, which Maurice took to his heart the moment he first saw it. The picture was called simply "Ménilmontant."

Complementing the collection of Impressionists—he had a number of Renoirs—were works by Picasso, Modigliani, and Dufy.

In the Chevalier gallery, too, was a nude portrait of Colette —the woman who through *Gigi* had given him new life in old age. He also continued to expand his collection of personal memorabilia, including not just a few straw hats but also about seventy walking sticks, a hobby he had picked up from Sir Harry Lauder.

And he collected overcoats, too. There were about fifty of them in special wardrobes. "I buy any unusual ones I see, simply because I like them," he said. They were, of course, irresistible to the man who remembered so well when he was not able to afford anything of substance on his back.

Maurice also made a special point of arranging his bedroom the way he wanted it to be—a place where he could spend his morning reading or writing letters. There were hundreds of books, many in exquisite bindings, lining the walls, and a number of personal pictures, too. On top of the bed was a huge fur rug.

The dining room, with a magnificent long table and a set of hard, uncomfortable chairs, was at its best when Maurice held his luncheon parties for the people he admired—famous musicians, or writers like Marcel Pagnol, or Hollywood stars like Douglas Fairbanks, Junior, or Gary Cooper. Cooper came to lunch, accompanied by his daughter, just a few months before he died, and Janie Michels was Maurice's hostess. She told me she remembers Cooper as "gay, charming, and always kidding Maurice, but not very impressive." Maurice enjoyed these get-togethers enormously and played the perfect host. But the slightest difficulty—a table mat misplaced or the wrong wine brought at the wrong moment was a tremendous problem to him, and he took a long time to get over it.

He was at La Louque for only six months of the year. The rest of the time he lived in hotels. "I am like a commercial traveller," he said. When he came home from an overseas trip, people around him would try to persuade him to rest. "You must be very tired," said Janie almost every time she greeted him at the house. "The first thing you must do is go to have a little sleep."

Inevitably, he would reply: "No, I will go first to my hairdresser and then to my doctor and after that to see a movie."

And he always managed to get all those things done, and in that order. His doctor was usually delighted with him. It didn't seem at all likely there could be any change in this seventy-two-year-old's life-style.

His public image and the real Chevalier were much closer together than they had ever been before, although he might not totally hold with that view himself. He once wrote: "Mistrust a comic who is too lively *off* stage. He'll lack sincerity *on* stage. No one's got that much to give. An artist gives his all to the public. There he becomes the being of his own dream. The rest of the time he's restoring himself, getting himself together. A singer of songs or a reciter of monologues has less danger of doing this than a cinema or theater actor or performer in opera or revue. He is responsible for what he chooses. He's master, while the others only serve. With more or less talent, but nonetheless, they serve."

No one would dare suggest that Maurice Chevalier was anything but his own master as well as that of everything he touched, but he still wasn't totally fulfilled. He desperately wanted the TV series he had previously turned down. *Gigi* had given him a taste of being a household name again. Unfortunately, all attempts to arrange a weekly *Maurice Chevalier Show* floundered because no company was willing to meet the sort of money needed to make him look as good as he really was.

So he contented himself with more guest appearances. He appeared with Sophie Tucker in one show and, with Ted Shapiro at the piano, they sang together an appropriate version of "I Remember It Well."

"Oh, Sophie," he said, "you're a real professional." Praise came no higher.

When he appeared on the Dinah Shore TV show, Jack O'Brien wrote in the New York *Journal-American*: "Maurice Chevalier's seventy-year-old charm was so marvellously and constantly present it was almost tangible. A great entertainer."

American critic Arthur Petridge wrote that a TV special called *Bouquet From Maurice Chevalier* was more than that. "It was a lovely reminder of what a great amount of joy this man has brought to millions with his charm and voice."

Maurice explained the secret of his success on "the tube." He said: "When I am in a theater I am performing for perhaps thousands all in one place. But television? Ah, that is different. There are many more: millions who see me at one time. But we must remember that they are not just in one place, but in their own homes and in each of such homes, there are not so many watching a show. Maybe two or three or four. That's it! That's it! So when I act and sing before the TV cameras I'm performing for just those three or four."

It was, of course, all due to his luck in making the right decision at just the right time, as when he thought of returning to America when he did.

He told me: "When I went back to America, I thought I must do something that is worth the name they gave me and that's when I did the one-man show. I think it has been the most beautiful thing I've ever been able to do in my beautiful profession."

His plans as always were to continue—more one-man shows, more appearances on TV, more records—he had now cut an album of songs that Al Jolson had made famous, like "April Showers" and "Sonny Boy"—and more movies. "But no more like *Gigi* or *Can-Can*, he emphasized. "They were fun to do, but I will not accept any more roles where I am just a charming old man on the screen."

He contented himself with other ways of showing his charm to audiences—like appearing at a Royal Variety Performance at the London Palladium and addressing a song directly at Queen Elizabeth, the Queen Mother. Pointing to her, he carolled, "You Must Have Been a Beautiful Baby," and the house roared, Her Majesty enjoying it more than anybody.

It all looked so easy—except that he laboured incessantly at making it seem that way. He practiced for a couple of hours before the performance in front of his dressing-room mirror. Then when it was all over, he went in front of the mirror once more and did the whole act over again for himself—to see if it had really been good enough.

The Queen Mother seemed to think it was. "My aim," he told her, "is to become a new kind of character actor with personality. I look on life almost as a spectator."

He hadn't quite followed that premise with his film *A Breath of Scandal*, which harked back to the Ruritanian pictures of the 1930s, with Maurice playing a prince, this time the father of Sophia Loren. But it wasn't good enough to justify the names of either Chevalier or Loren. Angela Lansbury was in the picture, too. She told me that she was not exactly overwhelmed by the Chevalier charm. Had it been there, she said, she was not aware of it.

Fanny was a different kettle of fish, since it revolved around a fisherman, played by Horst Buchholtz, who loses the girl he loves to an elderly shopkeeper played by Chevalier. The picture followed a highly successful Broadway musical based on the Marcel Pagnol trilogy, which had already been filmed as three separate French movies, *Fanny*, *César*, and *Marius*. This time the music was consigned entirely to the background without any songs either from Chevalier or anyone else. It was a happy reunion for Maurice and Leslie Caron, who played his young wife. But more important, it was the first and only teaming he had with his old friend, Charles Boyer, who played Buchholtz's father.

For them it was the meeting of two kindred spirits, although at times it looked more like the getting together of two school-boys intent on wrecking whatever had been set up in advance. Filming was at Cassis near Marseilles, and when they could, the two men would escape from the cameras and lights and take off for the nearest bistro or tourist attraction.

At the local flea market, a woman came up to the two men to ask for their autographs. They were standing by an empty stall. Maurice assumed she thought he was the proprietor and played along with her whim. So did Boyer, who sold her a beautiful antique candlesnuffer before scribbling an autograph.

They found a million subjects to talk about. But there were occasional moments of silence, usually in restaurants at the end of a meal—when neither of them would appear to be too anxious to pay the bill.

When *Fanny* was in production, Maurice said:

"I've learned it's nice to have money."

A newspaperman asked him if he were being paid as much as Elizabeth Taylor, Marlon Brando, or John Wayne.

"No," he replied. "But I hope they will earn my salary when they reach my age."

He liked his role as an elder of the cinema. "I'm too old for love," he said again, as though appeasing his own conscience. "Although I still like to look at pretty girls, I'm too old to go out drinking every night, but I'm not too old to recall with pleasure the nights when I did. The older I grow, the less bored I become and the more I value the things that happen to me."

Fanny had a wildly enthusiastic response in America. The *Hollywood Reporter's* James Powers said: "Maurice Chevalier gives the finest performance of his career, genuine acting abetted but not obscured by the fact that he is one of the greatest charmers of our time." Brendan Gill of *The New Yorker* described the film as "a rollicking picture about illicit love, bastardy and avarice, *Fanny* is ideal for children."

In France *Fanny* left audiences cold. Was it again the French people's instinctive resentment at one of their classics being adapted by the Americans? Whatever the reason, the picture flopped there.

The friendship between Chevalier and Boyer, however, remained buoyant for the rest of their lives, although, as always, Maurice was conscious of the effects of the aging process. Once he looked over at his friend and told Rouben Mamoulian: "He looks like an old Japanese."

Remarkably, Maurice still didn't look like an old anything. Nor, despite his many protestations to the contrary, did he behave like one.

Janie was with him on the *Fanny* location. They frequently travelled together although mostly between working engagements. In Cassis, Janie stayed with her children at a local hotel. At the end of a day's filming, a tired and usually worried or anxious Maurice would join her there and together they would have dinner on the terrace. "It was enchanting," she recalled for me. "He was so pleased to be with us."

One of their favourite holiday places was Deauville, where they would stay at the large and elegant Hotel Normandy. Usually, there were invitations to parties to accept or show people to meet. But he was never happier than when they were alone, and when there were no invitations to answer or things to do. Then he would say: "Oh, Janie, tonight, we will see a bit of television and go to bed early."

She didn't go to Sicily with him when he made *Jessica* there in 1962, mainly because it was going to be a working trip and he wanted to get home as quickly as possible.

For the first time in this movie with Angie Dickinson (later to become known for her title role in the *Policewoman* TV series), Maurice played a priest—but did it so well that he could have gone on playing priests for the rest of his life. He may have looked old and pure—no one had the temerity to mention the strangeness of Maurice playing a celibate—with steel-rimmed spectacles on his nose and specimens of needlepoint at his knee, but when he took up a guitar to sing three or four songs, the cassock-wearing Chevalier was perfectly in tune with the lovable rogue from *Gigi*.

Maurice's name was still one to reach the headlines whenever a publicist could come up with the right idea. In 1962 someone leaked the "fact" that he would be playing the dirty old man in *Lolita*. Maurice said he was shocked.

In his next film, *In Search of the Castaways* for Walt Disney, he had all the fatherly love he could handle, wearing somebody's idea of a scientist's outfit, including a spotted tie. It was a story replete with crocodiles, cannibals, and children (the leader of whom was played by Hayley Mills) travelling the world in search of the kids' shipwrecked father. It was marvellous Christmas stuff in 1963 and remains so today. Hayley described him as "no doddering old man—but a charmer who loved young, attractive women." He was, she said, "the most exciting person to be with."

Maurice had passed through the watershed of no longer need-ing top billing at all times. It made things a lot easier for him. It was also why he had been so happily able to play cameo roles, usually with his old straw hat askew—in musicals like *Black Tights*, an anthology of ballets featuring Cyd Charisse, Roland Petit, and Zizi Jeanmaire; and *Pepe*, starring Cantinflas, Dan Dailey and a whole string of other guests. He did it again in *A New Kind of Love*—which had nothing to do with the picture Billy Wilder would have made with Maurice in the 1950s had

the Stockholm Peace Petition not intervened—with Paul New-
man and Joanne Woodward in the leading roles.

Maurice wasn't any more concerned about the pressures of
filming when he and Hermione Gingold teamed up again for
I'd Rather Be Rich in 1963. When people wondered how this
Peter Pan of performers could still give so much, he usually
answered that it wasn't hard at all. He spent virtually the whole
picture in bed. He wasn't reverting to type, he was simply playing a sick millionaire. Miss Gingold was his nurse. She seemed
to think that Maurice didn't know his lines very well while making the picture, so offered him the occasional prompting. He was
gentleness and charm personified for her. "You must be tired,"
he said to Hermione between shots. "Come and have a lie-down
with me on the bed." And she did, at every possible opportunity.
"Why not?" she said, recalling that moment. "It was hot and
tiring." And she added: "He behaved immaculately."

Afterwards, Maurice said it was the nicest movie he had ever
made.

Certainly, it was more notable than *Panic Button*, which came
and went at about the same time. Maurice worked with Jayne
Mansfield in this movie about a back-number film actor who
suddenly hits the high spots again. He described working with
Miss Mansfield as being "most enjoyable—particularly the part
where her bra broke in rehearsal."

He was now seventy-five years old, and a gala at the Champs-
Élysées Theater was arranged to do him honour. His own performance, it was generally agreed, was better than the earlier
one on his seventieth birthday. The whole of Paris society was
there—including the Duke and Duchess of Windsor.

It was, Thomas Quinn Curtiss wrote in the *New York Herald
Tribune*, a "demonstration of public affection" for a man with a
"vitality and a sense of fun [that is] boyish and one wonders if
he was not very much the same when he first ventured down
from Ménilmontant."

Not only did Maurice sing and imitate some of the people
who had watched him perform—from a clergyman to a drunk at
Las Vegas—he danced the Twist and sang a Gershwin medley.
Most exciting of all, though, was just to watch Maurice Che-

valier being there. Janie was in the audience, too, and that night she was sharing her love affair with the world.

Everyone, it seemed, wanted to say thank you to their favourite entertainer. France showed its appreciation by awarding Maurice the Ordre National du Mérite, a distinction that came to very few. He was probably even more touched by the gesture of his favourite charity, Ris Orangis. They put up a statue to him. Radio Monte Carlo paid its own tribute with a TV special called *La Joie de Vivre*, which Maurice in no uncertain terms exemplified.

For once in his life, everything seemed to be going so well, particularly with Janie, who was still the sophisticated red-haired beauty with whom he had first fallen in love. He was fond of quoting Napoleon: "In love, even retreat is a victory." Although he had no wish to retreat from his affair with Janie, when her husband, the Comte de la Chapelle, died in 1965, he did not want to marry her. This chapter in his life has never before been revealed.

"If I marry you I shall have to get divorced from Yvonne," Janie told me he said. At first, it seemed he was trying to hide the fact that he and Yvonne really had been divorced. But she knew what he meant. He was partly referring to the fact that the Catholic Church would never recognize the end of the marriage; he also meant he was still tied in his mind to one of the unhappiest periods of his life. As they curled up together in front of the fire at La Louque, Maurice told Janie: "One of the most unfortunate things in my life was my marriage. When I met Yvonne, she was cute, nice. She was adorable. For a time we had a good performance together, but she was so jealous. Our marriage was hell. When Yvonne was in my bed, I felt poison all over me. I've had some very bad adventures, but this was the worst."

It was that memory which had persuaded him not to marry Nita, and now it was the reason why he didn't want to marry Janie. She, however, was content with the arrangement they had.

"I was really married to him," she told me, "in every other sense. I'm not someone who is interested in marriage. It is nothing for me. I don't care for it. When you're younger, young people together, and with a view to a future, that is very nice.

I'm not against it at all, but if you're good and understanding with someone, it *is* a marriage really. Seeing a priest doesn't change anything. When you're not young it makes no difference."

She and her children moved into a house on the La Louque estate.

For Maurice and Janie their relationship was idyllic, except that behind the scenes there hovered an influence which Janie didn't consider entirely healthy. Félix Paquet was taking up more and more of Maurice's time and it began to worry her. At first, Paquet would constantly show his gratitude. "Oh, Maurice," he said quite often, "you've been so good to me. You have given me hope. I was so weak and yet you made me strong." Too strong, some people think now. Paquet began to see Maurice as an extension of himself—an intelligent and important extension. Sometimes against Maurice's will he would invite more literary or artistic figures for lunch.

Much of the time, Maurice would have preferred being with the few real friends that he had. But Paquet continued to invite international celebrities on Maurice's behalf—an ambassador or an actor like Yul Brynner. The invitations were issued, Janie insists, without Maurice knowing about them until the day of the function.

"I wish Félix wouldn't do this," he told her. "They cost so much. They make me so tired."

Maurice admitted that he was being pushed in directions he would have preferred not to go. "I am strong and I am weak," he told Janie ambiguously.

She worried about that, but at first Maurice didn't seem to be any the worse for it. And it certainly didn't affect their own relationship. Together they would talk about their time apart from each other; Maurice about his latest expedition as a "commercial traveller" and she about the customers who came to her art studio.

At La Louque, Janie had turned a small room into something that more closely resembled her idea of warmth. And in the comfortable chairs amid the soft cushions, they would talk and plan. There never seemed any reason not to think of the future.

Occasionally, Maurice revealed that he hadn't been quite as

indifferent to a pretty girl as he now claimed to be. "Today," he would tell Janie, "I've been a little devil!" Both of them would laugh, but she knew exactly what Maurice was capable of. Making love to a girl he found desirable was still quite within his grasp.

And yet he still liked it to be thought that that side of life was all in the past for him.

As Thérèse de Saint-Phalle, then an editor with Maurice's French publishers, Presses de la Cité, recalled, he told the head of the firm, M. Neilson: "I gave up sex at sixty-one because it is not good for an older man to make love." Neilson, who was sixty-five at the time and enjoying, so he thought, a normal sex life, wasn't very pleased.

Everyone knew that Maurice's first love was still his profession. Very few suspected there could be anything or anyone else. Before long, however, a newspaper photographed Maurice and Janie together and suggested that her children were Chevalier's. Even so, they kept their relationship as discreet as they wanted it to be, and little was said about them, although occasionally, papers printed pictures of Maurice with his "son." But he did think of Janie's children as his own; he was godfather to the younger two, her son, Jojo, and her daughter, Marie-Noël. They, together with his three great-nieces and François Vals's daughters, were he often said "my babies."

When Maurice went away on tour, he wrote Janie letters in which he expressed his devotion to her. In one from Long Island, New York, he wrote: "I am with you in your torments as I am in your joys. I hold your hand. I admire you. I love you." And in the same letter he added notes to Jojo and Marie-Noël, saying: "I think of you without ceasing."

When he heard that Jojo was thinking of one day becoming a farmer, he sent him a postcard from Atlantic City saying he knew he would be "the best farmer in France."

One didn't have to know Maurice terribly well to realize that he loved children. He took his nieces and Janie's youngsters to puppet shows, and on Sunday afternoons he gave tea parties for them at La Louque. There were always the best cakes to the accompaniment of the latest pop records for the children and, afterwards, pocket money for each. He would bring them all back presents from his overseas tours. When he decided on American Indian costumes for all the children, he donned one himself to get into the spirit of their game.

He kept photographs of the Michels children by his bed. When he went to the hairdresser, he always took his godson with him—although at first much against his mother's wishes. Jojo had long hair which Janie thought made him look lovable. "Ah, yes," said Maurice, "but he should be like a lovable little man, not a lovable little girl."

He extended that kind of love to a wide circle of friends and admirers. When Louis Velle disappeared for several weeks while on location at a remote spot, Maurice was a constant source of comfort to Frédérique Hébrard, whom he still called 'Riquette.

The public didn't hide its own love for Maurice. When in 1965 it was revealed that a French film would be made of the Chevalier life story, it seemed only appropriate. Alain Delon was chosen for the title role, and Maurice let it be known that he was well satisfied with the choice. Charles Aznavour and Yves Montand were mentioned, too. Unfortunately, like so much else in show business, it never happened.

When talking to fellow professionals like Aznavour, Maurice revealed what his priorities were. On one occasion, he told him: "Charles, next week I'm going to Monte Carlo. All I'm going to have to do is introduce Marlene Dietrich, but they're paying me good money!"

He and Marlene were together whenever she appeared in Paris, too. Every time she did, he would go to her dressing room, kiss her, and say: "I have never seen you so sexy and so wonderful!"

That part of the story is well known. What has never been revealed before is the almost teenager-like attachment they had for each other. Once, Ginette Spanier recalled, Maurice told her how he and Marlene had walked to an old house in Hollywood, then owned by a married couple working in television. It was where they had spent much of the time when they were first in love. Amazingly, they were not recognized when Maurice said to the owners: "May we come and look around your house? We used to spend many happy times here."

Now their love had turned into sincere friendship and affection. But that didn't mean he couldn't tease her. Janie Michels heard him tell her:

"Marlinou, you are the queen of the quick story."

"Yes, you were in love with me," the star replied, "but as soon as you could, you left me."

"No, Marlinou. I'll never forgive you for preferring Jean Gabin to me."

"Ah," she returned, "Jean is so French. But it was not Jean or you. I had but one love in my life and this love was never realized. It was for Orson Welles. He is the love of my life, but he never realized our love. Every time I know Orson is free, I ring him and say, 'Orson, this is for us.' He would always reply, 'Marlene, too late. I have a new one.'"

These were private moments. In public it seemed now there could be but one question for Chevalier to answer: "How long can you carry on?"

His reply was always the same: "As soon as I feel that it is not so great, as soon as I feel that I do not give what I want to give to an audience, as soon as I don't feel proud of what I'm doing, then I could retire in one afternoon."

On a good day he thoroughly enjoyed talking to newspaper people and those close to them. Once, around this time, he drove from Marseilles to Paris with a film publicity writer—for much of the journey entertaining the writer with a nonstop selection of his songs.

In 1965 Maurice was back in New York performing at a sellout engagement for impresario Alexander Cohen at the Alvin Theater. Cohen took Maurice's advice and billed the show as *Maurice Chevalier at 77*. He was booked for six weeks, but because it was doing so well, Cohen decided to extend the engagement by another two weeks. But this idea misfired somehow. For reasons that were never properly explained, the extension was disastrous. Maurice wrote Cohen a letter saying how sorry he was that things hadn't worked out. He enclosed a check for $12,000—his fee for that last two-week period. But he didn't mention the money in his letter.

Soon afterwards Maurice made what would turn out to be his last live film appearance, playing a priest again in an inconsequential Walt Disney film called *Monkeys Go Home*. Everyone agreed that Maurice stole the picture from Dean Jones and Yvette Mimieux. He had a similar effect on Disney himself. Before beginning production of the film, he called to see the cartoon mogul, one of the men he admired most in the world of films. When he and François Vals stepped into Disney's office, they were astonished to see two pictures framed behind his desk. One was of President Eisenhower, the other of Maurice.

For the rest of the day, he kept saying to Vals: "Imagine, Walt Disney has my picture! My picture! I still can't believe it."

He once wrote: "I don't intend to stop until I figure that I am no longer a credit to the memory of La Mère Chevalier or the profession which adopted me as a child and gave me its backing." And he told friends: "I want to go on for as long as the people come out of my show feeling happy, feeling they have spent a wonderful evening."

And miraculously that is just what they did still feel. In June 1967 he went on a tour first of Canada—beginning with Montreal, scene of Expo 67, where he received the biggest fee of his career to date—and then of the United States. He again met Harry Truman in Independence. At the "April in Paris" ball at the Waldorf-Astoria, he was guest of honour and came back to play the hotel's famous Empire Room.

Maurice still liked calling out names from the stage, despite that warning from George Jessel. While he was at the Waldorf-Astoria, François Vals sent a message to Rouben Mamoulian who he knew was in town.

"Would you like to see Maurice's show?" Vals asked.

"Of course I would," Mamoulian answered.

The director, whom Maurice had admired more than most of those with whom he had worked, was placed, together with his wife, close to the floor show. Maurice came on stage, looked around him, came right by the Mamoulians' table, and appeared not to recognize them.

Then he said: "I would like you all to know that this is the greatest evening of my whole life."

"I said to my wife," the director told me, "Oh, come, Maurice. Too much. It's not true. Why go so far?"

As though he had heard what his friend said, Chevalier went on to explain: "I'll tell you why: There are three people here who make it this important evening. One is Benny Goodman. . . . The second is a man who once directed me in a movie, Rouben Mamoulian. . . . The third is President Eisenhower." Nobody had noticed the ex-President and his wife, Mamie, sitting incognito in the audience. Certainly, distinguished guests did not come more important than that.

The Waldorf rewarded him accordingly for this new stint. They paid him $14,000 for a week's work.

Later Maurice attended a retrospective season of Rouben Mamoulian's work. Mamoulian told his audience on opening night: "One of the great pleasures of a director is when he discovers a promising new talent. It so happens that on this visit to New York, I found such a young talent. His name is . . ."—at which point Mamoulian with a worried look on his face seemed to reach for a piece of paper—". . . Maurice Chevalier!"

Maurice sauntered onto the stage and then brought the house down with an amusing speech in which he said all the right things.

This tour was promising to be one of the most successful of the Chevalier career. In October 1967 he made the decision that it would also be his last. At first, the only people he told were Janie and François Vals. In New York he told them: "You know I am tired. At the end of my show in Paris, I am going to quit my profession."

Vals, who had been preparing Maurice's tour for the best part of twenty years, wasn't exactly delighted at the news. "Monsieur Maurice," he said, using the term he always had for the boss, who still seemed something of a father figure, "it's always better for you to be able to come back if you want to."

Maurice replied: "François, you are always very kind. But I am the champion and I know what I'm doing."

But why was he taking a year to retire?

"I need time to say good-bye to all my friends," he told François.

There were few people who agreed with his decision to pack up and go. He told them: "*Apprends le renoncement* (Know when to give up)."

For the moment the decision of his pending retirement from

show business wasn't announced. But the intention was very strongly there.

Maurice knew that he had made the right choice to have a long farewell tour, although the strain began to show very early on. Within weeks of its start, he said he was very fatigued and could plan no further than a few days ahead. At Pittsburgh he felt "drained and exhausted" in a town that had begun to affect his nerves—because he knew that the locals were afraid to go out at night. Three thousand people filled Penn Hall just the same.

"My motor is beginning to grumble," he wrote later, "but at least it continues to turn over."

While in America he saw a colour telecast of himself at home which had been produced by Frédérique Hébrard. "I saw a kind of singing actor who basically is neither an actor nor a singer," he wrote a short while afterwards in his book, *I Remember It Well*, "but rather an attractive old man. He walks more slowly than he used to, but his face still reflects inner freshness and youth. As for his delivery, it has more sincerity than technical perfection."

But sincerity still wasn't enough for him. Even now he sought the technical perfection, too.

As weeks went by, there was always the fear that the shows wouldn't work out the way he wanted them to. That feeling of inferiority which had pervaded notions about his education seemed to infect his work. Every morning he would ask the same question of François: "What can I do today?" Vals told me: "He knew his songs were inferior and that his voice wasn't so great." How could he be sure that he still had something to offer? And because he worried he worked harder. The trouble was, he didn't always take account of his age.

In twenty years Maurice had only cancelled four shows, and he wanted to keep the figure at that. At the Greek Theater in Los Angeles, he felt so ill that he had to take antibiotics, but he went on just the same. "You owe it to your audience to do your best even if you're not feeling up to it," he explained to Vals.

Then he developed a blockage in his left ear, which affected his balance, and a short while afterwards had to cancel a performance in London. But the trouble did not recur.

In December 1967, after a two-month tour of twenty-two cities, he was back at Marnes-la-Coquette. But now when he went there, he was indeed going to La Louque, for he had brought his mother's body to be reburied in the village cemetery. After so many years apart, they were close again. He had plans for them to be closer still.

But things were beginning to happen that signified the big change to come. At the Ris Orangis he handed over his duties as honorary president to Charles Aznavour. It made him more than just sad; it meant the curtain was really coming down and when it registered, it hurt.

Soon, though, he was off again—to Scandinavia, where he was greeted with flowers and other gifts but, most important of all, by applause; and then to Vienna, the city that now resembled an elegant old lady all dressed up but with nowhere to go. At the Hotel Imperial he said he felt foolish in a suite which looked as if it had been created for one of Ernst Lubitsch's pictures. Although he tried to smile for photographers—and sometimes it didn't come any easier in the late 1960s than it had in Hollywood some forty years earlier—there were occasions when it showed that he merely tolerated the need to be friendly to newspaper-men.

At a press conference in London, he was asked to put on a straw hat. "No," he replied, "it's upstairs in my room, ready to use in Manchester, not for now."

He played the Palladium and at first was disappointed by the English reserve before his show opened. If he flopped here, he decided, he had better go straight home to Paris. But London, which had been so formative for him, was loyal. He was a sellout there and everywhere else he played in the country. "My only worry now," he said afterwards, "is making sure my popularity doesn't go to my head."

After a stopover at La Louque, it was back to America again for the spring of 1968—to receive a special Tony award at a ceremony in New York. It was his last appearance on the New York stage. George M. would have been proud . . . and jealous. Later in the year he was off to Latin America and Canada. He told everyone he had never been happier, though when he returned to Paris, he said it was "a kind of happy nightmare." There was, however, the compensation of being overwhelmed by the way his native city poured out its Gallic heart for him. At the Lido a star-studded crowd gave him an eightieth birthday party. Maurice sat between Claudette Colbert and Noël Coward, and everyone who was anyone in Paris was there—except Marlene Dietrich, who was invited but didn't turn up.

The pavements and service road outside the Lido were jam-packed to the point where it was impossible for any of the people to move. They watched, excited, at the celebrities drawing up. But there was one man they were waiting for more than all the others put together. Finally, the word spread through the ever-thickening throng: *"C'est Maurice! C'est Maurice!"* Dozens of people managed to break through the human barrier of *gendarmes*. Mercifully, no one was hurt, although Chevalier himself had to acknowledge that the women jostling him wanted nothing more than to give him a hug and a kiss, which many managed to deliver before the police dragged them away, satisfied.

Inside the theater there was a vast cake and the food was sumptuous. But what was most delicious of all was the flavour of an evening when his own fickle France was quite clearly paying its unique tribute. There was a film that flashed back to various episodes in Maurice's career—it didn't mention the war—and entertainer Jean Yanne affectionately pulled the leg of the guest of honour. For days afterwards there were Chevalier records on the radio and Chevalier interviews on television and in the press. The Musée de la Chanson organized an exhibition in his honour.

Maurice made a brief tour of Spain and then it was back to Paris again. At the Champs-Élysées Theater, the Begum Aga Khan, Marcel Pagnol, and M. and Mme. Hervé Alphand were present for the first of three weeks of shows that were quite the most spellbinding of his sixty-eight-year-long career.

Sentiment doubtless played a very important part in it all because, as he always said, the audience was a very warm radiator. But he was in this swan song performing perhaps better than ever before.

Finally on the last night of the scheduled run of the show,

with an adoring crowd waiting for yet another encore and more news of his next performance, he moved to the footlights, held out both arms to call for silence, and began a speech which only a minute or two before he had still been unsure whether or not to deliver:

"In my French suburb when I was just a kid, I dreamed to be on the stage. Now I can't believe, standing in front of you, that my great big dream came true.

"But now it's time to say *au revoir*. With a smile of hope, yes, *au revoir*."

The sounds of an audience suddenly realizing they had heard the very last live Chevalier performance echoed throughout the theater.

"My hope is that next time we all can meet again, even if I'm out of this game, at the end of my poem.

"Who can predict? Who can foresee? First, I have something to say, you see. Thank you for the long ride. Thank you for the great nights."

He spoke of the "mysterious contact of the heart" with the international audience which had cheered him as the people of Paris were cheering him now. And weeping, too. "To them all, I will say *au revoir*," he repeated.

Again Maurice looked around him, a lump as big as an almond in his throat. But he managed to choke out words that sounded all the better for that extra dose of emotion:

"I started my career in a low dive in Ménilmontant. I finish it here in this beautiful Champs-Élysées Theater, after sixty-eight years of good and loyal service, and it's good like that . . . The word *adieu* is too sad. I'll say then that it's the last time I'll appear on any stage. . . ."

To his mind came the memories, the triumphs, the heartbreaks. Instead of his adoring audience that night, he saw shadows of a small boy singing in the wrong key at the café-concert; and of the proud young romantic dancer curled up in a rug with Mistinguett. One second he was standing in front of the camera singing "Louise," the next—and he shuddered at the memory— at Alten Grabow. He thought of Fréhel, of Yvonne, of Nita. And, superimposed on them all, the constant, overwhelming presence of La Louque. Was she calling louder than usual that night? Or just proudly cheering with the others?

Next to her those people who counted for most in his life were with him, too, in that theater, standing as they clapped and wept. They always had been.

As he told them then:

"It's been a long, long love affair."

21.
Un, Deux, Trois, Quatre

If really I've given you half the happiness you have given me I think it's right to say "there's no business like show business."

—Maurice Chevalier

Retirement had turned Maurice Chevalier into two different men. Vals told me later that he thought Maurice began to die when the last vibrations of applause finally stopped echoing in his brain. Janie saw a terrible change come over the man who always seemed so young, as though he now considered that everything worthwhile was behind him and it was only a matter of waiting for the lid of the coffin to be screwed down.

But there were others who saw another much happier, more content Chevalier.

The truth lies somewhere between the two. Maurice did not throw off show business with that last speech at the Champs-

Élysées Theater. A love affair that was virtually a marriage couldn't be ended by mere words when the suitor still found his old flame so alluring. Chevalier was as much in love with his audience as he had ever been before. And the people who formed that audience adored him perhaps more than they ever had. Yet it was Maurice who sought the ending of the affair, who proposed, demanded, and put into practice what was in effect the divorce.

But he was the kind of divorcé who had to speak to his former wife every day and write her love letters as soon as he got up. The letters were the new books he was writing for his French publishers with assurances of lucrative editions in America, England, and almost every other country in which he had appeared. In his eighty-first year his writing, which had always been so important to him, had again turned into a new career.

Each morning he would sit up in his rug-covered bed and write new chapters of a book that would tell the story of the eightieth birthday tour and beyond. Using a solid-gold fountain pen—his love of luxury had not diminished—with a nib specially made for him so that the ink would flow particularly smoothly, he began work on a book that would be called *Môme à Cheveux Blancs* (*The Boy With White Hair*).

That title, too, was an oversimplification. He may sometimes have seemed young and vigorous but the Peter Pan he had been on stage had quite definitely grown up and grown old simultaneously. He was wonderfully happy when left to his writing and the work that went hand in hand with it—perhaps because it was, in a way, a branch of the business of entertaining and perhaps, too, because there was still a lot to be said for a job that didn't make him feel out of wind. But it also gave him opportunities to contemplate the past and what he had done in that past, and those who were privy to his feelings saw a different man entirely.

"Retirement is the most honourable thing I can do now," he said once the die had been cast.

Unfortunately, people mistook the intention behind his decision. They accepted that he had packed up completely and, for the most part, after a time left him alone. But that really wasn't what he had in mind at all. The Champs-Élysées concert had been his farewell to the live stage. But he still wanted to make regular appearances on TV and perhaps make a film or two. The trouble was that once the stories of his *au revoirs* had appeared in the newspapers, the meaningful film and TV offers came to a halt.

Instinctively, people held back. They wondered if he was no longer well enough to act. They certainly didn't want to embarrass him. If he had let it be known that what he wanted most of all was simply to host a new TV talk show in which he would use his charm and his memories to introduce other celebrities—an idea that Vals suggested and which Maurice liked—the offers would undoubtedly have come pouring in. But nobody believed that he was available anymore. The scripts and other ideas that did come his way were not the kind for which he was looking. He had gone too far, and it didn't make him any happier to realize it. Before long much of what many people had believed about him became true. He put on a front of a *joie de vivre* he didn't really feel, but the ones who were close to him—and occasionally others who were not so close—saw through it.

Extreme old age, in fact, was now fitting Maurice rather like an unfastened straitjacket. He was officially a free man, but somehow practicing that freedom was not worth the effort. It was then that Félix Paquet started to dominate Maurice's life, subtly at first but ever more insidiously.

Guests who were at La Louque at that time can testify to the whispered words of Maurice's general factotum as he showed them to their places around the luncheon table. If Maurice showed surprise at seeing people or misheard what one of his guests said, Paquet was likely to say in an aside: "Take no notice of the old boy. He really doesn't know what's happening anymore. It's such a shame!"

Janie Michels told me that she heard him say that once and reprimanded him. Paquet laughed. His place at La Louque was perfectly secure, and he had his own plans for the future. The significance of what he did wasn't always apparent at that time. "I can see now that he was trying to drive a wedge between Maurice and me without at first saying very much," Janie told me. Paquet did it in a number of different ways. He was afraid that Janie's son, Jojo, was a little too close to Maurice, and when

the boy came for tea he always managed to arrange for the butler, Pierre, to bring his own son along, too. "I didn't at the time
realize why," Janie said, "but later on it became clearer. He was
frightened that Jojo would be made Maurice's heir."

Paquet did his best to make sure that Janie couldn't attend
the luncheons and arranged them on dates when he knew she
would be working, either painting or presiding at exhibitions.

"Oh, how Maurice tried to persuade him not to hold the
luncheons," she recalled. "But Paquet always insisted. They made
him feel important. And Maurice was too weak to argue with
him."

Paquet couldn't persuade him, however, to be sweet-tempered
if he didn't feel like it. Denise Grey, who was about eight years
Maurice's junior and had been a top French music-hall comedi-
enne, told me that when she was invited to Marnes-la-Coquette
for one of the lunches, she found Maurice in a great Chevalier
depression. He told her: "Since leaving the stage, it is impossible
for me to face eight o'clock in the evening, the time when I feel
I should start performing. Even now, I am always ready for the
stage at that time. In my heart I'm always there."

To make things easier for himself at moments like that, he
tried to avoid talking about the theater. "He would discuss life
insurance or constipation, but never the theater," she recalled.

And he would look at her and say, "Denise, you are always so
cheerful, always smiling."

"Yes," she told him, "because I think life is marvellous."

He studied her: "Yes, because you have your family. . . ."

It was a theme to which he would return again and again at
times when he could think only about the past.

In one of their moments together, he told François Vals: "If I
lived my life all over again, I think I would have been more
careful about my women and simplify my problem with them.
With your wife and with your daughter, Brigitte, you are happier than I could ever possibly be."

Chevalier may have regretted that he had no family of his
own, but there was no doubt that at La Louque he had been
very much the father figure. His elder brother Paul had long ago
died, but even when he was alive, it was Maurice who liked to
consider himself father to the household—to François, Madeleine,

and Brigitte Vals; to Félix Paquet and his wife; and, of course, to Janie and her children. Naturally, he also liked to feel that he was the master of his house; he didn't merely live at La Louque, he ruled it.

Paquet was doing what he could to shatter that illusion once and for all. He was taking more and more charge of Chevalier's life. By the mid-1960s Maurice couldn't fight it, but the effect would show itself in his moods.

Those moods could change completely if, as he often did, he received a warm letter from an important person like President Pompidou. He was always cheered, too, when his writing seemed to be going particularly well. Then he could be something very close to his old lively self.

When the film *Funny Girl* opened at L'Opéra in Paris, Columbia Pictures asked Maurice if he would escort its star, Barbra Streisand. He did it beautifully, still as unable to resist the charms of an attractive woman as ever before, and he found her very attractive. As always, Maurice arrived at her hotel on the dot of the appointed hour, and the chauffeured Rolls-Royce supplied by Columbia had to drive twice around the block so as not to arrive too early.

At moments like that, he was the Chevalier the public knew—except, as he confided time and again, he was still feeling "lovesick." He liked the applause of the people who saw them arrive at the theater, but instinctively he still felt his place was on stage entertaining those people, not sitting alongside them. Yet he continued to go to the theater and to the cinema, and to pretend he was making new discoveries. Instead he was discovering that he was rather lost. His inferiority complex had become a "has-been complex," and he didn't like the new one any more than he had the old.

The Americans still wouldn't believe he meant what he said. To prove it one management offered him a ten-year contract—for "annual farewell tours"! He had to tell them that, in his book farewell meant just what it said, although it made him weep to think of it. The Comédie Française, France's premier theater, asked him to star in three galas in March 1969. It would be the first time that an entertainer like Chevalier had been granted the honour. He was deeply moved and was going to accept, until he thought it would reflect badly on his decision to stay retired and so hold him up to ridicule. Painfully he told the Comédie that, on reflection, he wouldn't be able to accept their invitation.

He was soon to be presented with the annual Nuit du Cinéma award for what was designated a "triumphant international career," and the Federation of French Engravers decided to honour the best-known man who had ever tried his hand at an engraving apprenticeship. They presented him with an award for being "*le meilleur artisan de la chanson Française.*" He liked that. Everybody, it seemed, was feting him. The watchmakers of Switzerland held a dinner for him at Gstaad and printed the menu on a fine linen napkin.

He was also told by one of the most august organizations in France that after all those years he should no longer be called Chevalier. He was being promoted—from "Chevalier" of the order of the Légion d'honneur to Officier of the Légion.

Lesser people wanted to pay him tribute too, sometimes merely by recognizing him and smiling as he strolled down the Champs-Élysées or through Saint-Germain-des-Prés. Once a woman buttonholed him in a theater and said: "I can't believe how much you look like Maurice Chevalier."

"*Oui, madame,*" he recalled answering her. "People tell me that all the time."

"I never saw two people look so much alike," the woman said, still very impressed and still rather puzzled.

At the end of the performance, he went over to her, apologized for teasing her, and added: "The fact is, I *am* Maurice Chevalier."

When in 1970 Charles de Gaulle died, Maurice was the first to subscribe to his memorial appeal. In its way, it was a gesture of thanks for the hand of friendship from a man who could have broken Chevalier's life with a single word—collaborator.

In the same year there was a very brief break in his retirement. He recorded the title song for Walt Disney's new cartoon feature, *The Aristocats.* The film was set in Paris, and Maurice was more than grateful that someone so important as Disney still associated his name with the city. It was to be the last film for which Disney took personal responsibility. Maurice may or may not have realized that it would also be the last work he himself would ever do for the cinema.

Just occasionally now he would drink a lunchtime glass of whisky or champagne. He rather liked it. But one glass would often make his head spin, and wisely he decided to give it up again. Now it *had* to be enough merely to sniff the aroma. In the same way, he wrote: "I don't sing anymore—I hum."

22.
Paris Was Never Easy

My whole career has been a piece of embroidery, with two or three stitches added in each performance. My ambition still is to be a little better every day. I want the end to be perfect.

—MAURICE CHEVALIER

Frédérique Hébrard told me that it was "necessary to have time with Maurice, not to grab at him." Now that he had a great deal of time on his hands, he appreciated people who would share theirs with him.

Maurice read a lot; he was a discerning reader and best of all liked those books containing a message with which he fundamentally agreed. His favourite writer was Montaigne. With a little fear that it might not be so, he liked to quote his statement:

"I want to end my days able to look into the mirror and say: 'All is well.'"

Chevalier hoped he would be able to claim that, but he worried that he couldn't be sure; yet it did seem that writing was giving him greater satisfaction than anything ever had apart from a show or a film.

He was helped by a woman whom he admired greatly. Thérèse de Saint-Phalle was an editor at Presses de la Cité and a successful novelist in her own right. She took care of Maurice's books, helping him to shape not only *Môme à Cheveux Blancs* (which became *I Remember It Well* in the United States and Britain), but another volume, in which he expressed himself on a variety of subjects, called *Les Pensées de Momo*. Momo was a childhood name that he had quite suddenly adopted once more. There were thoughts on his profession, like: "All my life, my sole ambition has been to earn my bread without begging from anyone." He certainly could be satisfied that the begging had always come from his audiences—and always for more. And he wrote:

"My greater success of these last years seems to prove that the majority of the audiences in the world stay faithful to laughter and heart-stoppers. Perhaps we should thank perverse and muddy competition which thus lets us balance it by offering the opposite."

And he said:

"A French artist must live in Paris and spend his holidays where his heart leads him."

There were also thoughts on love:

"I loved women and now I worship them."

"Tenderness is a delicious dish which won't give you indigestion."

And he had thoughts on vice:

"Vice can have such a pretty face, and virtue such a desolate look."

He looked at young people and the old:

"Certain young people are no longer young. Certain old people still aren't old."

But he wrote with great truth:

"Paris was never easy at any age."

It was Thérèse de Saint-Phalle who was largely responsible for this amazing new spurt in Chevalier's life. She persuaded him to start thinking seriously about making writing his new profession. He didn't realize at the time how much of a drug it was going to be; quite as powerful at times as the stage had ever been. In a way, it provided even more satisfaction. The boy "without instruction" had, with his white hair, finally convinced himself he could succeed in a career so totally different from standing on stage with a straw hat and cane. Thérèse was sure of that before he was.

Before she or anyone had realized that his determination not to appear before a live audience again was total, she asked him why. "Because," he told her, "now I risk an accident and I love my people too much to risk anything. That is why I put my faith now in my books."

And he wrote them as an act of faith, putting into the volumes the same determination for perfection he had previously reserved for his stage activities. Thérèse would go to see him to discuss his work. He would show her the pages he had written, and she would tell him either how good they were or the changes that she thought were necessary.

She usually went to La Louque by taxi, and on one visit told her driver, a young Vietnamese: "Today we are going to see Maurice Chevalier." The driver smiled. "I've been over here for just three months," he told her, "and in Vietnam we know just two Frenchmen, General de Gaulle and Maurice Chevalier." When the car drew up at La Louque, she asked the driver not to return to Paris straightaway. "Wait," she instructed, "wait five minutes."

While he waited, Maurice came out of the house, tapped on the window of the cab, and shook hands with the driver. It was probably one of the best moments in the man's life. Maurice was excited by it, too. He still loved to know he was admired by people so far from Paris.

He showed his appreciation to Thérèse by once more refuting all those stories about his parsimonious behaviour. He bought her presents—a gold pen, a valuable lighter, and, for a joke, a miniature hatstand bearing half a dozen tiny hats of real straw.

For Thérèse, too, he broke the rule he had established soon after retiring—never going out to private dinners or receptions. "If you want to go far and long, you must spare yourself," he told her.

But when she gave a cocktail party for about 250 people, Maurice came. And he did more than just socialize and make polite conversation. "He did a damn good Charleston, too," she told me. "He was fantastic and everybody was looking at him."

His friendship with Thérèse was one of those relationships that Maurice still needed with women. He still required the comfort of feminine company, even without a sexual connection. As he told a radio interviewer in 1969: "A man needs feminine tenderness. Without it, life is very dry." And yet he was also a friend of Thérèse's husband.

There were, of course, always two kinds of friendships for him, the private and the public, and there was none that he paraded more openly than those with the big American entertainers. He still put those show-biz giants on top of the list of the people he admired most. When a party was given for Duke Ellington's seventieth birthday at the Alcazar Music Hall in the Latin Quarter (where he himself had appeared so often), it was Maurice who was the star attraction. He escorted the Duchess of Windsor, which was a tribute in itself. Ellington had particularly asked Maurice to present him with the greetings of Paris. He did more than that. He broke his retirement and momentarily danced on the stage. Then he presented the jazzman with a straw hat.

"Fancy me," said the Duke, "wearing your straw hat when no other artist can fill your shoes."

Maurice still liked being with people he loved and cared about, but hated more and more the thought that others might be using him. "Those people are eating me alive," he often told Janie.

Meanwhile, the love he showed for Janie herself appeared to be as strong as ever. She saw the frustrations he felt when he was not working, but for a time each seemed to find comfort in the other's company. Maurice would still take Jojo for his haircut and they would still play games together. Most evenings Maurice and Janie would have dinner together, discussing the day they had had and the people each had met, although as retirement began to take its toll, more and more often Maurice would decide to go to bed early. He also got up late the following morning, although he continued to write in bed.

Maurice enjoyed going to the races, looking as chic as ever in a new checked coat from Hawes and Curtis and in a smart hat.

One of his best friends now was Yves Saint-Martin, France's crack jockey and thirteen times winner of the Golden Whip Award. But one day at the racecourse, Maurice developed a bad headache. A woman he often met at the track noticed. She was the wife of a leading trainer, charming and with the sort of soft beauty that Maurice admired so much. He found it very easy to talk to her, frequently enjoying her company a great deal more than the racing. When on this occasion she saw he was not feeling well, she asked if he had any aspirin. He said he didn't, so he really ought to leave. Maurice kissed the woman on both cheeks and asked the ever-faithful Paquet to drive him home.

Within a few minutes of Maurice's returning to La Louque, his friend's chauffeur drove up to the house.

"Madame has asked me to deliver these aspirins to Monsieur Chevalier," he said and left.

Paquet laughed when he gave the tablets to Maurice.

"That stupid woman," he said.

Janie was with them and told me how upset she was that the charming gesture was dismissed so out of hand by Paquet. That night the friend telephoned La Louque to find out how Maurice felt. She asked to be put through to him. Paquet answered as Maurice stood by his side.

"Monsieur Chevalier is not here," he told her, while Maurice—who until then had delighted in talking to this bubbling, attractive woman—said nothing.

Janie was amazed.

"Maurice," she said. "I can't understand it. You always were so nice to her and she is always so nice to you." She expected him to say: "Félix, what's gotten into you? Give me my phone." He didn't; instead, he said nothing, looking vaguely into space.

The same kind of incident was repeated again and again. Men and women who had been among the closest of Maurice's friends were without any warning informed by Paquet that he was not there to talk to them. Mme. Albert Williemetz, whose husband had written "Valentine," was quite arbitrarily rebuffed. Before long these close friends realized that for them Maurice would never be in.

Paquet had apparently come to the conclusion that Maurice's time on earth was limited, and he wanted to be sure that he

himself would benefit by his employer's passing. La Louque and
the Chevalier fortune were within his grasp. He had very definite
ideas about how he was going to capture them. First, however,
the target must be to remove the other influences that were
obstructing his path. Maurice's nephew and his children would
surely get an important share of the Chevalier wealth. And there
was always the irritating presence of Janie and her family. What
if Maurice still wanted to make Jojo his heir? Paquet decided he
had to act now.

The year 1971 was ushered in with a wonderfully warm New
Year's party at La Louque. Maurice was as sparkling as the
champagne he served but didn't sip. He and Janie were quite
clearly sharing their old love for each other as completely as they
ever had. But Paquet knew how to change all that—although he
allowed the party to go on as planned.

During the evening, Maurice turned to Janie and said: "I've
told everybody about your marvellous exhibition. I'm so proud
of you." She had just exhibited her work at a leading Paris gallery on the avenue Matignon and it had been a tremendous
success.

A couple of days later, Maurice took Jojo as usual to have his
haircut.

On January 6 Janie rang him at La Louque. He answered the
phone immediately. "Janie," he said, "I'm not well. I have a sore
throat. I don't think you ought to come around today."

"Maurice," she replied, "that's a pity because you're going off
to Belgium and then to England soon, and I'm travelling, too.
So I won't be able to see you." Maurice seemed distant—just as
he had the day that the lady rang about the aspirin. He didn't
apologize or offer the sort of loving remark that she had been
accustomed to.

Instead, he told her: "I have to go now. I'm going to see the
doctor."

Janie rang the next day. This time Paquet answered the telephone. "I can't put you through," he said. "You see, Maurice has
a sore throat and doesn't want to speak."

"Is it that bad?" she asked, anxious about any deterioration
in Maurice's health.

"No," Paquet replied. "It's not bad. But he wants to rest." She told him she would ring again the next day, which she did.

This time Paquet told her: "Maurice asked me to say hello. He is a little better. Quite all right."

But he wouldn't come to the phone himself. Finally, Janie went round to La Louque. Maurice was not around. She went up to his room and found it locked. When he heard Janie being shown into the house, Paquet had locked Maurice's study and his bedroom, too.

It happened again and again to Janie and to other people, although until now no one has talked about this strange, sad development in the Maurice Chevalier story. All were told by Paquet: "Don't come, because Monsieur Chevalier is unwell and can't see anyone."

Janie never saw Maurice again. A short while after that final telephone call, she met Paquet. Naturally, she asked about the health of the man she still regarded as her loved one.

"Maurice has become so nervous," he told her. "It is impossible to live with him."

"Félix," she countered, "how could you say that? Maurice is always so nice with all of us."

"Yes," he replied, "so nice, but he is nervous and difficult to live with."

Paquet believed he had discovered how best to control Chevalier's final destiny. And he set about doing it in the way that had always worked before. He found Maurice women. "Put them into his bed" is how Janie described it to me. "Although he was no longer capable of making love to a woman; he was now so feeble." Certainly, Paquet introduced him to a number of women through whom he believed he could manipulate the strings to Maurice's fortune.

Maurice liked none of the women Paquet chose. Some were too intellectual for his tastes—he worried about their being better read than he was himself. On the other hand, others didn't come near to matching his ideas of beauty, charm, or intelligence.

For all Paquet's efforts, Maurice still required female company—even if he had known what had been done to Janie, which is doubtful.

Once, he asked Thérèse de Saint-Phalle: "Can't you find me somebody?" He emphasized that all he wanted was a woman's touch, and repeated to her that he hadn't had sex since he was sixty-one. But the right "touch" wasn't immediately forthcoming, and for a time he had to devote all his attention to his writing.

He brought out his book, *I Remember It Well*, and it was a tremendous success. Once more he was riding as high as if he had just left an audience at the Casino de Paris or the Waldorf-Astoria. Suddenly, the old man had regained a vestige of his youth. The book was translated into Dutch, and at a VIP dinner given by his publishers in Amsterdam, Maurice was feted as Chevalier the writer, a man who responded every bit as enthusiastically as Chevalier the entertainer. When he made his speech to his hosts and the other guests at the dinner, he was performing again. Only the straw hat was missing. The gestures and the pouting bottom lip were there as if he were singing "Valentine." He was once more intoxicated by an audience and he enjoyed the feeling.

Thérèse took him to the American Booksellers Association convention in Washington, D.C., the biggest event of the American publishing year, when publishers announced their new products to the bookselling trade. He was undoubtedly the star attraction. *I Remember It Well*, otherwise not a very exciting book nor anything like the best he wrote, would not be forgotten for a long time.

Inevitably people asked him yet again about retirement and he gave the same answers, which somehow still failed to completely convince his hearers.

"There is nothing so sad as a performer going on and on and repeating himself," he said. "If he is hungry, I understand that. I feel I am on velvet now because I was always for life, not for death. I am always hunting for something to give you a good evening. Sometimes, I would feel my age before entering the stage, but when I got through I'd feel thirty years younger. You receive what you give very often."

He was asked his views on contemporary life, particularly about the women's lib movement "I'm not against it," he said. "But a woman to be better than a good man? It's not natural."

After returning from Washington, Maurice was signing books all over France and telling Thérèse—whom he called *Marraine* (Godmother)—in a series of warm, charming notes (which to anyone not privy to their relationship, looked very much like love letters) how this activity had given him new life.

In one he wrote:

My darling Thérèse,

I've just tried—with no success—to join you at your country home—I know that you're there but I want to tell you that starting to work myself on *Momo*, I took stock of the talent and affection that you put into it. And that touched me in a warm spot. You've put me *en page* corrected, made better, in a way that reminds me of the great producers, making everything better by their presentation, a work in which they believe. This cooperation for my next book and more will fix us, one with the other . . . Can I say, without going too far, that I admire and love you?

MAURICE

And then after the "Charleston" party he wrote:

Dear Thérèse,

The other day you were the princess of the world's modern women, with a gaiety, a liveliness . . . and a memory that confirmed a super performance. Your guests—I'd like to have a list of them, because I'd like to put down on paper a timid assessment of this Nouveau Monde representing the most solid of talents. What a reunion! Several came up to me, several kind people whom I liked. I had to leave—*à l'anglaise* —without thanking your husband, who was very friendly, attentive to my comfort. Please excuse me—dear Thérèse. In a few days, very quickly, I'll ask for an appointment to talk about a possible signing session at Deauville on Saturday 9th or Sunday 10th August next.

Lovingly, your admirer,
MAURICE

Sometimes he used the English word "love" to sign his letters, which were always warm and contained an affection that was peculiarly his.

At the autograph sessions, he signed thousands of the books and in each one there was an entirely different message. Waiting in the line at one of these sessions at the Galleries Lafayette was an attractive, statuesque blonde. When the time came to put her book in front of Maurice, she looked at him in a way he found irresistible. Her beautiful, feminine face was enchanting. Even now he could still be affected by that sort of beauty. She was herself, however, proof that Maurice also still had an effect on women.

"Do you not remember me?" she asked softly, and he had to admit that he did not.

"My name is Odette Mélier." The name still didn't ring a bell. "I was with you at the Folies-Bergère twenty years ago," she said. Then he did remember.

He asked her to have dinner with him. He seemed spellbound by this woman of forty. She told him she was a widow and had a handicapped daughter. He asked to meet the girl and when he did was like a kind, old uncle towards her.

Within a few days, Odette had moved into La Louque with him.

Perhaps Odette would be the puppet Paquet could manipulate to his way of thinking to bring him nearer to the fortune. If he had ever sought a surrogate before, he believed he had found her now. He kept hoping, although as far as anyone could tell Maurice seemed to have found a new love. What was more, Maurice found ways of helping her daughter.

Maurice's old and trusted friends—Janie among them—were anything but happy about the way events were turning out. They loved Maurice too much to readily accept allowing him to withdraw from their lives.

Paquet may have thought that relationship would be useful to him. He still refused to allow many of Maurice's old friends into the house, although he encouraged those who he thought might be useful.

Members of the staff started telling stories around the village about their master becoming irritable and depressed; but when he did see people he liked, he tried not to show his ill humour. None of the friends, however, ever saw Odette. "She was never at lunch and was never discussed," Thérèse de Saint-Phalle told me.

Was he ashamed of her, and if not of her, for she was a charming, attractive woman, then perhaps of his need for her? Maurice, who had never been a particularly religious man, was now regularly meeting Père Carré, a brilliant priest and member of the Académie Française, who for years had been friendly with a number of people in show business.

Père Carré would hear Maurice's confession. The friends who knew speculated on how much his relationship with Odette would come out in the confessional booth, for it was about the same time Maurice met her that he started having his sessions with the priest.

Maurice's view on religion was summed up in one of his statements in *Les Pensées de Momo*:

"I believe in God, in simplifying what troubles me in the stories of what some men did. I understood on my mother's death that the soul, being loved, would remain living around you.

"I try to be less bad, to resist my low temptations, to recognize my limitations. I know that work is the most just and most loyal of my friends. I know that it helps one to live with oneself. I know that there is nothing untried when one falls to pieces, without finding in one the courage to try, to try again."

He would never go to Mass on Sundays. "The formality and the theatricality of the services had no appeal to him whatsoever," said François Vals. But like many people of his age, he began to question his attitude towards God. Now he would go quite regularly to the village church on a midweek afternoon and say his own prayers quietly and undisturbed if not always unrecognized.

Nobody ever saw Odette with him. She continued to mystify the people who knew she was in the house with him. His, or Paquet's, search for privacy didn't necessarily make him a recluse, but it seemed to cut him off from what had previously been his society. No one now would expect to see him taking tea in the village or organizing a party for the other villagers. His daily exercise was an hour's silent walking around the grounds of La Louque, always stopping before his mother's plaque and saying a silent prayer, he believed, with her.

He was very conscious of the changes in his life, and he kept referring to them without being sure what exactly it was that was happening.

In a letter to Rouben Mamoulian he wrote:

> Now I think life must change. I shouldn't run anymore. Just walk towards . . . what? TV . . . big screen . . . philosophy . . . reading . . . writing . . . admiring and loving Rouben Mamoulian.
>
> Your Maurice

And then in another note he indicated that the alterations to his existence had already happened.

"My life is changing, but I keep remembering the great moments. Rouben is one of them."

Sometimes he now felt that the greatest moments of all were when he could for a time forget his "complex of inferiority" and feel comfortable with members of the Académie Française. He had come to know a great many academicians through Père Carré. He greatly admired Marcel Pagnol, from whom he tried to learn a lot about life and philosophy. There were others, too, including one who said to him: "You know, Maurice, you ought to become a member of the Académie." He laughed at the notion of joining the celebrated forty to whom membership of the most exalted society in France was limited. Above all others he would have cherished that honour, but it never came.

In the spring of 1971 he came to London to launch *I Remember It Well*, which went immediately, if briefly, onto the best-seller lists. It was then that this biography was really born—at a meeting in the Savoy Hotel. I didn't know it at the time, but he was feeling quite ill. The strain of signing books at Selfridge's and other London shops was telling, and he had a chronic digestion problem. He told me: "I have started again. The artist is finished and the author is born. It is a new way to communicate with my audience." But it no longer meant the same to him.

He started work on another book, *Maurice Chevalier's Paris*, writing the text for a multicoloured guide to his native city. It gave him little satisfaction. At home, his moods got bleaker. He didn't think he had the love that he craved. So what was left?

Finally, in the late spring when he felt in a blacker mood than he had for years, Maurice answered that question for himself and decided that really there was nothing. He could no longer wait to die and to join the one person whom he believed had understood him, his mother. If he couldn't go with dignity in his sleep, the desire he now had above all others, he had to take matters into his own hands.

Early one morning he deliberately sat down and wrote a series of letters—to Odette, to Janie Michels, and to François Vals. There was another note to Paquet. He took out a bottle of sleeping tablets and washed them down with a glass of water from his bathroom. Then he took out his razor and, after getting back into bed, with a swift stroke slashed at his wrist . . .

There is no doubt that Maurice, riddled with misery and possibly with guilt, too, over what had happened in the last few months, wanted to die. But his action lacked the precision of Chevalier onstage. For once in his life his timing was wrong.

He was still alive when Pierre, the butler, knocked at his bedroom door before he brought in his early morning cup of coffee and found him unconscious in bed, the sheets drenched in blood. Pierre hastily bound the gushing wrist and called Paquet, who drove Maurice to the American Hospital.

He woke up dazed a short time later, his stomach pumped free of the poison, his arm bandaged.

The La Louque gardener told the story to Jojo, who with his mother rushed to the hospital. But Paquet had left word that Maurice did not want to see anyone. Janie penned a note, which she and her son signed: "Dear Maurice. We are here if you need us. Just tell us, please." But they heard nothing.

François Vals later told Janie that Maurice never received the letter.

A brief announcement was made to the press that M. Chevalier had entered the hospital for a checkup and would soon be released. Until now, the true reason has never been revealed. The letters he wrote were found by Paquet, who immediately took charge of them all. He was the only one who knew what they contained.

Twice before, Maurice had contemplated suicide, but this was the only time he had actually attempted it. A week later, he returned home, more morose than ever. Soon after his return, Paquet confronted Maurice with the letters he had written and used them to try to blackmail him. In his hand was a new will which he said he expected Maurice to sign. It would make Paquet his sole heir. If Maurice didn't—and Paquet would be bringing a lawyer with him to finalize matters—Paquet would publish the letters. He knew the disgrace this would bring on the Chevalier name would be too much for Maurice to bear. Maurice told Vals that he promised to do so, but begged to be left to sleep.

It was a fatal mistake on Paquet's part. A few weeks later, a lawyer did call at La Louque with a new will. It was not the testament he had hoped for. The new document made Odette the beneficiary of the house and most of his fortune. Paquet, who had anticipated sharing the proceeds, was to be left a comparatively small allowance, similar to the amount to go to François Vals. He had by then, however, decided not to repeat the blackmail. Vals and too many other people had been told of his threats.

To this day, Janie, who together with her children and Maurice's nephew had been the main beneficiaries of his previous will and were now totally excluded cannot understand what took place.

It is certain that Maurice was desperately unhappy. What remained for him now was mere existence. He saw only a few people—Paquet inspected the ones he did meet—did not answer telephone calls, did not reply to letters.

Then early in December 1971, he was taken ill. His doctor suggested he ought to go back to the American Hospital. Before he went, he called Vals to his bedside and pointed to a drawer in his bedroom. "You will find there a list," he told him. "Please get it." It was a collection of names—the people to whom Maurice wanted to send Christmas presents, including every member of his staff at La Louque. He asked François to write a number of envelopes and instructed him on exactly how much should be put into each.

After that, there were no more messages. The next time Vals saw him, Maurice was in a coma. The doctors had diagnosed kidney failure. His hospital room was sealed from everybody. No members of the family were allowed near him—because, it was said, Maurice wanted them to remember the man he once was.

For a time he seemed to recover his strength. Encouraging bulletins were issued by the hospital emphasizing his "good general condition," but then, on the first day of 1972, a searing pain ripped through his chest.

As Père Carré sat with him, holding his hand, giving him absolution, and offering promises of a new world, Maurice Chevalier died from a heart attack at the age of eighty-three. The show was finally over.

Le Roi

He's *le grand sympathique.*

—JEAN COCTEAU

Two hours after he died, Maurice's body was taken from the hospital to La Louque, but, obeying his own strict instructions, it was not put on view. The gates of the house were locked to even his closest friends.

Maurice's nephew, René Chevalier, told the hundreds of newsmen who flocked to Marnes-la-Coquette from all over the world: "He had always expressed the wish to go out discreetly and with dignity."

President Pompidou spoke for his countrymen: "The death of Maurice Chevalier," he said, "will have an emotional impact on everyone. His success with the French and international public went beyond the simple talent of singer or actor . . . the popular tenderness which will accompany him to the tomb will be even more touching than his triumphs in the theater."

At the 200-seat village church, built in 1861 by the Empress Eugènie, Père Carré and Père Louis le Tirant, the parish priest, conducted the service before the oak casket. Maurice's body had been dressed by the undertakers in a black tuxedo bearing the ribbons of the Croix de guerre and Légion d'honneur, and with straw hat placed in his hands.

Père le Tirant intoned:

"Maurice, our brother, we say *adieu* until the happy day when we see you again."

At that point the casket, with a bouquet of white and violet orchids on it, was carried out into the square, and Maurice Chevalier was laid to rest next to the grave of his mother—just 300 yards away from the other La Louque.

Princess Grace of Monaco headed the distinguished mourners —among whom were the French Minister of Culture, Jacques Duhamel, the old champ, Georges Carpentier, actors Michel Simon and Louis de Funes, and Maurice's dear friend, Marcel Pagnol.

These were the people the cameras concentrated upon. Most missed the ones who at some time had been the most important in his life, those who were weeping because a void, the extent of which only they themselves knew, had come to their lives: Odette, about whom very few knew anything, and Janie and her children, people whose privacy had been amazingly respected. Out of the past came other woman—like the still beautiful Nita Rayer and tiny Yvonne Vallée, mourning the man she had loved and married at the height of an earlier crisis.

Maurice had said just a few weeks earlier:

"Every fortnight, someone you know dies. Someone you loved. Sometimes when I see films, seven or eight of them have gone. . . .

"Let them come to my deathbed with their cameras. I'll try to say 'Good-bye, thank you, ladies and gentlemen.' When that comes, I hope I still have time to smile, saying, 'but I was waiting for you, madame, shall we go?'"

He left a fortune estimated at about $14 million, or 100 million francs.

Apart from the bequests to Odette and Paquet and François Vals, Maurice made generous provision to the Ris Orangis and other charities. A week or so after the will was published, Janie Michels had a visit from the lawyer who had witnessed Maurice's final will.

"You were in the previous will, madame," he told her.

"I told him I would rather have not heard about that," she recalled for me. "Then he said we would have to leave our house." The home which Maurice had given to her on the La Louque estate was now part of Odette Melier's property and she saw no reason to allow Janie to keep it.

La Louque kept its name, but the rue du Reservoir, in which it is situated, was named avenue Maurice Chevalier. The house at number 7, avenue Maurice Chevalier in what became known as Village Maurice Chevalier, was given over to La Société des Auteurs et Compositeurs de la Musique (the French version of ASCAP) as a rest home.

A year or so after Maurice's death, Félix Paquet was himself dead—after a fall from an upstairs window at his home. The verdict at the time was suicide, although there are those who have expressed doubts and think that he had enemies who might have their reasons for wanting him dead.

"I believe that was the most likely cause," Janie told me. "He was definitely not the kind to commit suicide."

Janie is today still highly successful, painting her portraits and pictures of horses at her studio near Deauville. Odette Melier lives quietly at La Louque to this day.

François Vals—who told me he couldn't possibly work for another man after being Chevalier's assistant for so long—is today an eminent hotelier and restaurateur in the south of France and has a stable of racehorses. Nita Rayer lives in Paris. Yvonne Vallée was last heard of living quietly on the Riviera.

The death of Maurice Chevalier was noted in sadness throughout the world. *The Times* commented in a three-column obituary:

"Now Maurice Chevalier is dead and Paris has lost another part of its history and its legend. He, too, represented the warmth and the gaiety of shabby little back streets and the heart and soul of a great city. Age meant nothing to him. [That was never true, but part of his success was that he made people think it was.] He was the same personality in youth as he was as a veteran actor. His of its history and its legend. He, too, represented the warmth and the gaiety of shabby little back streets and the heart and soul of a great city. Age meant nothing to him. [That was never true, but part of his success was that he made people think it was.] He was the same personality in youth as he was as a veteran actor. His popularity did not depend on his voice or his style or his charm. It had nothing to do with sex appeal."

Le Monde took a whole page to survey his career, and, quite extraordinarily for a paper that is proud of never using illustrations, featured a caricature silhouette of a straw-hatted entertainer.

Maurice knew his greatness. When a critic wrote that he was a simple but not a humble man, he said: "And why should I be humble? I ask you. Hasn't someone a right to be proud of his work? Doesn't the shoemaker who's made a good shoe, the carpenter who's made good furniture, the goldsmith who's fiddled over jewellery, don't they have a look which expresses their professional pride? Now that I can see the end of the road, I feel the legitimate pride in having earned my grub as an honest French workman."

He told me he was *trying* not to regret no longer being young, "because I've understood what I can still get from life, and what I must not get anymore from my life.

"I believe in bringing to the people the encouragement of living and I think I am lasting so long in the interest of people through something that comes of my personality and out of my work, which is just to be a sort of sunshine person."

And if he didn't always feel very sunny, the showman inside him never let his audiences know it. As the *Chicago Tribune* said on his death: "When Maurice Chevalier died at the age of eighty-three on Saturday, the world lost a little of its magic."

He once said: "I know that when you reach seventy, you have to have your travelling bag ready."

But he couldn't say, as Montaigne had written, that as he looked in the mirror, all was well. It wasn't. Chevalier died without that blessing.

The *Washington Post* wrote: "Artistically, you could not rate him a *grand cru* among the great wines. He was, rather, an ageless aperitif—light, zestful, enduring in relatively small doses and capable of giving all but the most insensate an appetite for everything else French . . . With that carefully cultivated broken accent, it was almost as if it had been bottled for export . . . he *was* France."

He was more than that. He was the spirit of an age when entertainers felt they had a duty to excite, to thrill, to give to their audiences. He gave it with a pouting lip, an inimitable chuckle, and a tilted straw hat. When a new millennium dawns, his memory will continue to conjure that image. And someone will say: "Ah, yes . . . I remember him well."